QUEER TERROR

NEW DIRECTIONS IN CRITICAL THEORY

NEW DIRECTIONS IN CRITICAL THEORY

Amy Allen, General Editor

New Directions in Critical Theory presents outstanding classic and contemporary texts in the tradition of critical social theory, broadly construed. The series aims to renew and advance the program of critical social theory, with a particular focus on theorizing contemporary struggles around gender, race, sexuality, class, and globalization and their complex interconnections.

For a complete list see page 243.

QUEER TERROR

LIFE, DEATH, AND DESIRE IN THE SETTLER COLONY

C. HEIKE SCHOTTEN

Columbia University Press
New York

Columbia University Press
Publishers Since 1893
New York   Chichester, West Sussex
cup.columbia.edu

Library of Congress Cataloging-in-Publication Data
Names: Schotten, C. Heike, author.
Title: Queer terror : life, death, and desire in the U.S. settler colony /
    C. Heike Schotten.
Description: New York : Columbia University Press, [2018] | Series: New directions
    in critical theory | Includes bibliographical references and index.
Identifiers: LCCN 2018007538 | ISBN 9780231187466 (cloth : alk. paper) |
    ISBN 9780231187473 (pbk. : alk. paper)
Subjects: LCSH: Biopolitics—Philosophy. | War on Terrorism, 2001–2009. |
    Fear—United States. | Marginality, Social—United States.
Classification: LCC JA80 .S365 2018 | DDC 320.01—dc23
LC record available at https://lccn.loc.gov/2018007538

Columbia University Press books are printed on permanent and durable
    acid-free paper.
Printed in the United States of America

Cover image: © MAYSUN
Cover design: Lisa Hamm

Early one morning, when we prayed together for the first time, they threatened to shoot us. But we kept on praying. If they wanted to shoot us, we thought, let them shoot. They didn't. They just yelled and made threats. Then a commander or some high-ranking officer came and spoke to us. He said we would be allowed to pray at the appointed times. Not because he wanted to do us any favors, but because he realized that we would rather die than not say our prayers. And they didn't want us to die because they still needed to interrogate us.

—Murat Kurnaz, *Five Years of My Life: An Innocent Man in Guantánamo*, released without charge in 2006

"You know who you are?" he asked me.

"Yes, Sir!"

"You are a terrorist!"

"Yes, Sir!"

"So let's do some math: if you killed five thousand people by your association with al Qaeda, we should kill you five thousand times."

—Mohamedou Ould Slahi, *Guantanamo Diary*, released without charge in 2016

CONTENTS

ACKNOWLEDGMENTS

This book took a long time to write, much longer than I expected, and it proved even harder to finish than it was to begin. Throughout, I was lucky to have had extraordinary intellectual, political, and personal companionship, all of which supported, sustained, and held me.

At the outset, I learned much from the students with whom I first studied this material, in their unwitting if inevitable role as guinea pigs for their professor's own research projects. To this day I am grateful for the observations, insights, essays, and critical analyses of Daniel Finn, Eric Jonas, Peter Jubinsky, Stasha Lampert, Carolyn Terranova, and Penelope Zogheib. Those classes were formative teaching and learning experiences for me, and I have to say: you all just have no idea how brilliant you are.

Later on, a number of very thoughtful and intelligent people read, heard, or talked me through various parts of the manuscript at different stages of its development. All of them had excellent questions, comments, suggestions, and even (on occasion) a well-deserved reprimand or two: Alia Al-Saji, Joe Brown, Tommy Cosgrove, Leila Brannstrom, Kevin Bruyneel, Sam Chambers, Jonathan Cutler, Tommy Davis, Lee Edelman, Daniel Finn, Jude Glaubman, Andrés Henao Castro, Cressida Heyes, Lynn Huffer, Colleen Jankovic, Eric Jonas, J. Kēhaulani Kauanui, Aaron Lecklider, Jason Lydon, Haneen Maikey, Vijay Prashad, Peter Spiegler, Lisa Stampnitzky, Chloë Taylor, and Shannon Winnubst. It should go without saying that none of these lovely people should be held responsible for the claims, arguments, or viewpoints expressed in this book, all of which are very much my own.

A few stalwart comrades read and commented on the entire manuscript: Simon Glezos, my brave first reader; Leila Farsakh, whose relational devotion and encyclopedic knowledge both continue to astonish me; and Gil Anidjar, who supported this project from the beginning and also helpfully figured out what its title should be. And I am enduringly grateful to Colleen Jankovic for constructing the book's index.

If my first book was dedicated to my families of origin (both natal and intellectual), this book is dedicated to my families of choice: to Agatha, Megan, and Brandon, who chose and have been with me for the long haul; and to Leila, Arjun, Jude, Sean (Klaus), and Bhavin, whom I chose and who chose me in this later, Boston chapter of my life. If I am simultaneously always seeking and trying to understand the meaning of unconditional love, I find that these are the people in my life who have best supplied it and, in so doing, taught me the most about it. I am so marvelously, overwhelmingly grateful for each of them.

Finally, and perhaps most of all, this book is for Sarah Dunbar. She of course knows every reason why.

INTRODUCTION

We value life; the terrorists ruthlessly destroy it.
—President George W. Bush, November 8, 2001[1]

Judgments, judgments of value, concerning life, for it or against it, can, in the end, never be true: they have value only as symptoms, they are worthy of consideration only as symptoms; in themselves such judgments are stupidities.
—Friedrich Nietzsche[2]

Critique doesn't have to be the premise of a deduction that concludes, "this, then, is what needs to be done." It should be an instrument for those who fight, those who resist and refuse what is. Its use should be in processes of conflict and confrontation, essays in refusal. It doesn't have to lay down the law for the law. It isn't a stage in programming. It is a challenge directed to what is.
—Michel Foucault[3]

Although the bleak days of the George W. Bush era are by now well behind us, the War on Terror he notoriously inaugurated nevertheless continues apace. It survived the two consecutive terms of his immediate presidential successor, who, despite inaugural promises to close the prison at Guantánamo Bay, actually expanded the agenda and reach of Bush's signature war through, among other things, open and hidden drone wars, extrajudicial assassinations of US citizens, elaborate FBI entrapments of Arab and Muslim people in so-called terror-ism plots, the unprecedented expansion of the surveillance of journalists, everyday citizens, and, in particular, Arab and Muslim communities, and vicious crackdowns on military and security system whistle-blowers (while simultaneously sheltering the CIA and its former directors from punish-ment for similar crimes as well as for ongoing torture at prisons and "black sites" around the world). The seeming nonpolicy of President Donald Trump appears to be no less malevolent on this front, as exemplified by, for example, his nakedly Islamophobic refugee/Muslim bans, indiscriminate bombings of Syria and Afghanistan, and forthright commitment to US exceptionalism. Beyond the quagmire of US presidential policy, however, the War on Terror also endures in the copious aftermath of Bush's other signature war, the Iraq invasion in 2003, an aftermath frequently abbrevi-ated by "terrorism"-obsessed Western media into the short-form "ISIS," but whose reach and complexity far exceed this crude discourse and continue to wreak untold havoc on the everyday lives of millions of people through-out West Asia. This suggests, among other things, that the War on Terror, the Islamophobic security culture it has engendered, and the distinctive discourse of "terrorism" that underpins and anchors it are noteworthy fea-tures of recent decades that demarcate not any particular conflict so much as a distinct political era, one with no clear end in sight. As with the deten-tion of "enemy combatants" at the still-operational Guantánamo Bay "gulag,"[4] the historical and cultural moment of the War on Terror has become, for all practical purposes, indefinite.

Queer Terror takes its impetus from the seeming endlessness and gra-tuitous vileness of the War on Terror to argue that the "terrorism" that serves as its ostensible justification has little to do with the material reali-ties of either political violence or the actual events of September 11, 2001. Rather, the War on Terror and the "terrorism" that is its pretext owe their political and cultural recalcitrance to a civilizationalist moralism of life and death that underpins, motivates, and defines the US imperial project, a moralism that has been in place since the settler establishment of the nation and in fact emerges from it. The purpose of this moralism is, ulti-mately, to sanctify both settlement and empire as noble and worthy endeav-ors, while vilifying any resistance to them as nihilism or evil. The War on Terror, then, does not actually pivot around or emerge from the events of 9/11, however concretized that origin story may have become; nor is its culprit, "terrorism," best understood as a problem of political violence. Rather, "terrorism"—whether considered as a political category, cultural discourse, or defining contour of US culture and politics after 9/11—is an ideological determination used moralizingly to insulate US settler-empire from critique, render its victims deserving of its abuses, and delegitimize any resistance to it as unthinkable and perverse.

Queer Terror offers an anatomy of this moralism, provided simultaneously in service to a rethinking of biopolitics, on the one hand, and critical resistance to US settler-empire, on the other. This is a necessary intervention insofar as biopolitics, itself a privileged site for theorizing the War on Terror and an obvious place to turn for any critical analysis of "life" and "death," by and large neglects the widespread moralization of these categories that otherwise pervades US imperial culture and is particularly acute when it comes to "terrorism." This oversight is due to the seemingly self-evident, perhaps even tautological construal of life or "bare life" within biopolitical theory as primarily a biological phenomenon. A central aim of *Queer Terror*, however, is to extract biopolitics and biopolitical analysis from the exclusive domain of biology, since life "itself" is never reducible to biology alone. Rather, *Queer Terror* will argue that life "itself" is as much an ideological as biological determination, the result of a wholly political imperative that constitutes "life" (and "death") as such. "Life" and "death," in other words, are not prepolitical givens (whether biological or otherwise) that are only retroactively politicized (however properly or improperly). Rather, they are political categories through and through, ideological from the outset. As such, they are symptomatic of larger power structures that must themselves be interrogated if critique is to have any political purchase.

Queer Terror argues that these larger power structures are, on the one hand, a modern European sovereignty that must be recognized as fundamentally settler colonial and, on the other, a reactionary privileging of settler life as the highest value and the basis of rationality in an otherwise nihilist and "savage" world. These underlying and mutually imbricated structures of power—settler colonialism and civilizationalist moralism—suggest the first of *Queer Terror's* interdisciplinary interventions, which is to link biopolitical studies of US empire and the War on Terror with inquiry in the fields of native studies and settler colonial studies. Native studies scholars have repeatedly emphasized that US empire and the War on Terror are intimately connected to settler colonialism. In a crucial interrogation, for example, Andrea Smith and J. Kēhaulani Kauanui ask:

> What happens to studies of American empire if we focus on empire from the context of the United States as a settler colonial country? Many American studies keynote speakers at the past several ASA [American Studies Association] conferences have critiqued the seeming erosion of civil liberties and democracy under the Bush regime. How is this critique affected if we understand the Bush regime not as the erosion of U.S. democracy but as its fulfillment? If we understand American democracy as predicated on the genocide of indigenous peoples? And finally, when we look toward building an alternative future, what if we do not presume that future forms of governance have to be based on nation-state models? How can we re-envision "nationalist" struggles that are beyond a heteronormative nation-state framework?[5]

Queer Terror attempts to concretize these links between biopolitics, US empire, and the settler colonial project that founded and continues daily to establish the United States, in order to generate a more satisfying and substantial critique of these interrelated phenomena. In addition, this critique is located specifically within the field of queer theory so as to analyze and resist, as Smith and Kauanui entreat, "the heteronormative nation-state framework." This suggests the second of *Queer Terror*'s interdisciplinary interventions, which is to link biopolitics, US empire, native studies, and settler colonial studies with queer theory, on the one hand, and canonical political theory, on the other. Using Lee Edelman's *No Future: Queer Theory and the Death Drive* as a point of departure to offer an unconventional reading of Thomas Hobbes's *Leviathan*, *Queer Terror* explains the biopolitics of settler sovereignty as operating primarily at the level of *desire*, not biology, which establishes the distinction between life and death via the institution of *temporality*, not (only) security. In other words, conquest brings a settler nation into being simultaneously as and through the constitution of life "itself" as future-oriented desire. *Queer Terror* holds that, just as the meaning, coherence, and legitimacy of modern settler sovereignty is established *materially* through violence, these are established *ideologically* through the futurist temporalization of desire.

This futurist temporalization of desire is, in fact, the "meaning of life" within settler sovereignty. Because of it, "life itself" is vested with a specifically moral content that goes unaccounted for when considered solely as a biological phenomenon. That moral content is the propriety of futurist desire, the possession of which marks one not simply as alive but also, simultaneously, as *valuable* life, as life worthy of the name and therefore worthy of security and protection. The name for the *im*properly desirous, the name of all those who refuse or fail the futurist temporalization of desire and its imposition of settler sovereignty, is "death." "Death" here designates not biological death but rather a hostile antagonism to life "itself" that threatens the disarticulation and destruction of the living through its mere existence and (thus dissident) perseverance. This "death" implies natives' externality to the rationality and goodness of settler sovereignty, their endurance as a continuing threat to that settler sovereignty, and, perhaps unsurprisingly, also names and justifies native elimination by that settler sovereignty. The biopolitics of (proper) desire, in other words, is simultaneously a necropolitics of (improper) desire. In short, sovereignty constitutes the full "value of life" in this scenario, and it does so through the moralization of ideological notions of life and death as determinations of absolute, irrefutable value and worth, thereby rationalizing—in an extrapolitical display of sanctimony and self-righteousness—genocide and dispossession.

Of course, if queer theory has taught us anything, it is that "proper desire" is a contradiction in terms, an impossible-to-achieve coercive ideal and inevitably political determination that queers the "improperly desirous" as anathema to the social order. For Lee Edelman, this is how reproductive futurism works. In *Queer Terror*, this is how moralism works, specified as the futurist, settler colonial operation of European sovereignty. That Thomas Hobbes's *Leviathan* is a blueprint for this moralized settler colonial sovereignty is elided in the canonization of this text as part of the broader history of liberalism, just as its highly rational theorization of sovereignty would seem to many political theorists to have nothing to do with sex/uality. However, a major methodological commitment of *Queer Terror* is to demonstrate the usefulness of a historicized queer theory not only for biopolitics, but also for political theory, traditionally understood. The widespread view in political theory that sex/uality is not political actually mirrors the relative absence of political-theoretic inquiry within queer theory, suggesting that neither field finds its concerns to overlap much, if at all, with the other. However, a relatively conventional definition of both political theory and queer theory is required to maintain these twin aporias, a conventionalism rooted in liberal presuppositions regarding the privacy of sex/uality and the publicity of power, with the latter limited to the state and its institutions. If, however, the problem of "life itself" cannot be separated from the problem of desire, and the problem of desire entails reckoning with fundamentally political matters such as sovereignty, temporality, and (settler) colonialism, then it is clear that political theory and queer theory cannot be disentangled from each other, and that to pursue one is and requires pursuit of the other.

Finally, *Queer Terror* offers these interdisciplinary interventions from an avowedly left perspective, as a critique of US empire as much as the canon of political theory that erases or colludes with it. In this sense, it is inspired by the antiracist, anti-imperial, radical critical queer theory unfolding under the rubric of "queer necropolitics."[6] Drawing on Achille Mbembe's influential formulation of "necropolitics" and/as the postcolonial critique of Giorgio Agamben and Michel Foucault,[7] queer necropolitics thinkers use radical and liberatory critical theory to analyze the ways that queerness functions as a lever of classed, racialized, and nationalized exclusion, with the result that some populations, whether "queer" or "queered," become either dead or disposable, either killable or eligible for targeted killing.[8] *Queer Terror* relies on a canonical archive, by contrast, not only in its reliance on Hobbes but also in foregrounding the work of Edelman, a queer theorist whose early work was crucial in establishing the field itself[9] and whose current work is considered definitive of an entire line of inquiry within queer theory, "the antisocial thesis."[10] I do this not to further entrench the power of already-established work, but rather to read this work as a valuable storehouse of information regarding the power formations both I and queer necropolitics thinkers seek to undermine and critique. Not only does *Queer Terror* suggest that the "life" of settler colonial sovereignty is best understood through the frame of desire (albeit divorced from the encumbrances of any particular psychoanalytic theory). But, via closer examination of a canonical text of settler colonial sovereignty, it also helpfully specifies the "death" of bio/necropolitics, which has been alternatively theorized not simply as biological death, of course, but also as social death,[11] slow death,[12] and overkill.[13] The editors of *Queer Necropolitics* characterize each of these as forms of "living death,"[14] suggesting in their introduction that part of the usefulness of "queer necropolitics" is "its ability to capture seemingly unrelated phenomena simultaneously, and to bring back into a shared plane of intelligibility struggles that we are often told are mutually exclusive,"[15] for example, "the 'welfare queen,' the 'monster-terrorist fag,' the 'black rioter,' and the 'hateful Muslim youth' as well as "the 'queer lover.' "[16] Useful and important as this collaborative theorizing indeed is, *Queer Terror* seeks also to clarify the specific *differences* among these forms of abjection—or, in other words, among these different types of "death." This specification is undertaken not in order to isolate movements from one another, but rather to clarify the stakes and contours of specific struggles so as to better tailor our resistances (when necessary) and to constitute truly genuine, shared grounds for struggle (when possible).

Specifying the kind of "death" inaugurated by settler colonial biopolitics also has the additional benefit of clarifying queer theory's distinct contribution to left politics, a question that is too often ignored, taken for granted, or dismissed as irrelevant and uninteresting, but that is a central motivation of this book to explain. If "life," in the settler sovereign scheme, is moralized as proper desire, and that propriety is what must be cherished and preserved and defended against "death" at all costs, then queer theory, or queerness, as both advocate and exemplar of *im*proper desire, is simultaneously a principled position of antimoralism and an unapologetic advocacy of "death." Queer theory's contribution, in other words, to both the biopolitical theory of settler colonialism and the project of left politics is its opposition to the punitive moralism that props up the one and castigates the other. Its contribution to a broader theory of liberation is its proposal of a world without morality, revelry in impropriety, and, indeed, a veritable celebration of "death." As this book will explore, such a view suggests important revisions to the revolutionary project that characterizes radical political thought; in particular, it suggests that the meaning of "death" and the meaning of "revolution" are one and the same.[17] This is simultaneously a contribution to the queer necropolitics project in its specification of the mechanism, medium, and character of the "life" and "death" that are so crucial to biopolitical theory, as well as a contribution to queer theory insofar as it lays out, in explicit detail, the meaning and content of queerness as dissidence or radical politics and argues for a rejuvenation of this meaning and commitment, albeit in an entirely mortal (not moral) form.

Queer Terror brings together the fields of settler colonial studies, native studies, queer theory, and canonical political theory in order to effect a reconceptualization of biopolitics that can account for US empire's origins in settler colonialism as well as its ideological veiling of those origins via a punishing moralism of life and death that unfolds, in at least one prominent site, in the discourse of "terrorism." The three epigraphs appended to this introduction, taken from three disparate if nevertheless influential commentators on modernity and the conditions of modern power, outline its agenda and scope. First, *Queer Terror* attempts to unravel the largely unremarked moralization of life and death that underlies Bush's juxtaposition between "us" and "the terrorists," a moralization that pervades US imperial culture and is particularly acute when it comes to "terrorism." Second, *Queer Terror* examines this moralism from a critical Nietzschean perspective that repudiates morality as such and is acutely attuned to its consistent camouflaging of its own will to power as sanctimony and righteousness. Third, *Queer Terror* seeks to account for this unremarked moralism of life and death in the form of a critique of US settler-empire. *Queer Terror* is intended, as Foucault puts it here, as an essay in refusal, an instrument for those who fight, a challenge directed to the US war machine. Importantly, it is a critique deliberately located within the field of queer theory because of its radical dissidence that also goes to some lengths to specify queer theory's specific contribution to left politics and radical criticism. I do this both to concretize the meaning and content of liberation and, perhaps, to reinvigorate queer theory's commitment to liberatory politics. *Queer Terror* suggests that resistance to US empire, indigenous liberation, and queer theory alike are practices of Foucauldian criticism and/as refusal, and that they share the same overall goal of what we might, in another context, call the decolonization of desire. The tarnished name for this criticism and this goal in the current moment of US domination is "terrorism," and *Queer Terror* will therefore argue that, whether as identification or cause, it is "terrorism" that demands our utmost, critical solidarity.

OUTLINE OF THE ARGUMENT

Chapter 1 examines the widespread academic uptake of Agamben's *Homo Sacer: Sovereign Power and Bare Life* to theorize and critique the War on Terror. This is both a specific argument about Agamben and a larger reckoning with the field of biopolitics, which has come to take Agamben's work as foundational. Whether it is Agamben or biopolitics, however, the towering influence of Hannah Arendt on both has been neglected, much to the detriment of the field. Agamben's critique of sovereignty relies on a striated understanding of "life" that he actually takes directly from Arendt: "bare life" in the form of *zoē*, on the one hand, and proper or political life, in the form of *bios*, on the other. Careful examination of Arendt, however, reveals not simply a profoundly racist and civilizationalist (not to mention misogynist and classist) denigration of *zoē* but, more broadly, an essentialist understanding of "bare life" as inherently abject, as that which must be fled or transcended if human freedom is to be realized. By adopting these same premises, Agamben imports their essentialist and hierarchical evaluative implications into his own work. Thus his analysis effectively duplicates Arendt's civilizationalist principle, whereby some (forms of) lives are higher, better, or more valuable than others, a principle that Arendt is clear is natural to human existence and constitutive of it. More importantly, it means that the field of biopolitics is itself indebted to these claims insofar as it draws on Agamben for any analysis of US empire.

Consequently, I argue that both Agamben and Arendt must be abandoned if biopolitics is to be adequate to the analysis and critique of US empire. Recalling Smith's and Kauanui's set of critical questions, in chapter 2 I propose a twofold resituation of biopolitics and biopolitical analysis: first, I suggest that the focus on "life" as biology be replaced by a focus on "life" as desire; second, I suggest that the focus on *racism* in biopolitical analysis be augmented by a focus on *sovereignty*. I demonstrate the relevance, importance, and usefulness of these suggestions by offering a rereading of Thomas Hobbes, that classic thinker of European sovereignty, on the basis of an appropriation of Lee Edelman's *No Future: Queer Theory and the Death Drive*. Using Edelman to read Hobbes foregrounds the role of (a decisively nonpsychoanalytic notion of) desire in constituting the category of life, thereby specifying and concretizing the link between queer theory and political theory. More profoundly, however, it suggests that the futurism Edelman outlines in *No Future* is a signal determinant of modern European sovereignty, indeed of modernity itself. The problem with sovereignty, then, is not its exceptionalizing of "bare life," as Agamben suggests, but rather its ideological construal of "life" as the highest value via a futurist temporalization of desire that, in Edelman's language, "queers" all those who think or act otherwise. In this sense, biopolitics is always already necropolitics, since the sovereign's seemingly self-evident insistence on the "value of life" is, in fact, a settler insistence on the value of settler lives at the expense, transfer, removal, and destruction of native peoples, who are not actually alive at all in this schema but rather emissaries and instantiations of "death," mortal threats to settler sovereignty that portend its destruction and the disarticulation of its claims to legitimacy.

This moralizing "value of life" discourse is flexible—it applies to the contemporary War on Terror as much as to the formation of US settler sovereignty. But this is no accident, since the War on Terror is a contemporary manifestation of the United States' unresolved settler status, whereby refusal to recognize native existence is simultaneous with its refusal to acknowledge the conquest that founded its own sovereignty. In other words, today's emissaries of death to the social order are so-called terrorists, not native peoples, who, in the confused logic of US settler colonialism, no longer exist, never existed in the first place, and are simultaneously no different from any other "minority" racial group capable of assimilation into the multicultural American dream. The obviously contradictory character of these fantastical ideological operations is muted or sidestepped by the frenzied obsession with "terrorism" as the latest and greatest threat to America, American freedoms, and the American way of life. But that, I will argue, is precisely its purpose and one of its most important functions. The undeniable significance and importance of the so-called value of life itself that anchors terrorism discourse, in other words, are its function as an essentially settler colonial value turned outward and used to serve imperial expansionist purposes.

If queer theory is relevant to theorizing modern biopolitical sovereignty, it is likewise essential to formulating a resistant, liberatory politics that opposes it. Chapters 3 and 4 thus substantiate the claim that queer theory is a specifically left project of radical dissidence—both in general, as a field, and specifically, with regard to *No Future* in particular. With respect to the field, I offer a rereading of Foucauldian genealogy as the basis for the kind of dissident and liberatory form of critique that "queer" was considered to herald in the heyday of that field's founding in the early 1990s. With regard to Edelman specifically, I suggest that he continues this radical tradition of liberatory queer dissidence by reading *No Future* as a manifesto. Putting these two unlikely readings together, of Foucault on the one hand and

Edelman on the other, I suggest that queer theory's specific contribution to radical/left politics is its antimoralism, whether that moralism takes the form of bourgeois repronormativity, as Edelman contends, or modernity's biopolitical civilizationalism, as I suggest. In short, however, insofar as "the value of life" is the moralization of an ideologically determined category that recognizes only itself as possible, thinkable, tolerable, and worthy of protection, queer theory is fundamentally antimoral, anti-"life," and, indeed, a representative and champion of "death."

Finally, in the last chapter, I discuss the adoption and adaptation of the "value of life" framework for the War on Terror and "terrorism" discourse. If, as suggested in chapter 2, the War on Terror is a continuation of the settler conquest that established the United States, then "terrorism" becomes legible not as an ostensibly objective classification of a specific type of political violence, but rather as the ideological name for any resistance to colonization or refusal to acknowledge its goodness, rightness, morality, or legitimacy. From the futurist perspective of the settler state, of course, the "terrorist" is the unthinkable assassin, the defender of death, the annihilator of civilization, freedom, and democracy. From the point of view of an antimoral, liberatory queer theory, however, the "terrorist" as emissary of "death" is a figure of radical resistance whose commitment to decolonization—not implication in any sort of violence, however real or imagined—renders them a mortal threat to the settler social order. This is true not only at the rhetorical and ideological level but also, as I will additionally show, historically, through an examination of the international development of "terrorism" as a specific category of political violence in the latter half of the twentieth century. The upshot of this analysis, however, is that when it comes to the question of dissent and dissident praxis, the only proper response to George W. Bush's famous dictum that "Either you are with us, or you are with the terrorists" is affirmation of solidarity with the "terrorists," who portend the death and destruction of "life" as "we" know it in the hegemonic form otherwise known as "civilization"— that is, empire, settler colonialism, and the American way.

■ ■ ■

Substantiating the claims made in *Queer Terror* will require challenging established consensuses in queer theory, political theory, and radical and critical theory, and thus entails the traversal of exceedingly important, if difficult and fraught, terrain. I therefore request the reader's patience with this endeavor and the presumption of goodwill, integrity, and emancipatory commitment on the part of its author. The claims made here are rooted in my own deep commitment to liberatory politics, my earnest attempts to understand just what, exactly, liberation might consist of or look like, and the very beginnings of what I presume will be a lifelong project of thinking about decolonization. In addition, these arguments are undeniably rooted in my own experience and positioning as someone trained, for better or for worse, in the canonical history of European political thought. As such, my political commitments and academic training are somewhat at odds with each other; this book can therefore also be read as an autobiographical attempt to reconcile two seemingly disparate yet deeply entrenched pieces of my character and subjective experience. As a student of Nietzsche, however (yet another academic hat that I wear, albeit increasingly infrequently), I am quite aware of the fact that my work, like all philosophy, is "the personal confession of its author and a kind of involuntary and unconscious memoir."[18] This fact is not a failing of theory but rather an inevitability of its production. Acknowledging as much does not dilute the force of its argument so much as give it greater depth, texture, and meaning regarding both its stakes and its origins. I offer this book, then, as part of a larger, liberatory project I imagine as the decolonization of desire, a project to be brought about via a practice of queer terror. I bring to it what I can given my particular subjective experiences and intellectual training, and offer it as one contribution to a much larger conversation about decolonization that I am only beginning to broach, a conversation I expect to (continue to) learn much more from than to which I can possibly contribute. More than "taking sides" in any particular academic or field-specific dispute, then, I hope that this book will be read as making some contribution, however modest, to the thinking through and enactment of liberation for all people(s). This would be the real meaning and best measure of its success.

QUEER
TERROR

1

THE BIOPOLITICS OF EMPIRE

Slavery and "the Muslim"

The life of a slave testified daily to the fact that "life is slavery."

—Hannah Arendt[1]

As the people that refuses to be integrated into the national political body, . . . the Jews are the representatives par excellence and almost the living symbol of the people and of the bare life that modernity necessarily creates within itself, but whose presence it can no longer tolerate in any way.

—Giorgio Agamben[2]

The lesson of Auschwitz remains at the center of post-9/11 discussions in American society.

—Mahmood Mamdani[3]

Giorgio Agamben's *Homo Sacer: Sovereign Power and Bare Life* was nothing short of an event in the US academy.[4] Due, in part, to its coincidental arrival with the George W. Bush era, the swift ascension of this text owed much to its seemingly uncanny ability to anticipate Bush's then-unprecedented expansion of presidential power and explain so many of his administration's bloody crimes and outlandish lies. Bolstered by the publication in 2005 of *State of Exception*, which discusses both the USA Patriot Act and the prison at Guantánamo Bay, Agamben's rendition of the "state of exception" appeared to make sense of the otherwise seemingly senseless horror chambers of Abu Ghraib,

Guantánamo, and CIA "black sites" around the globe, explaining them via recourse to a biopolitical sovereign decisionism that seemed amply illustrated by Bush's outrageous new doctrines, all of which were components of this "War on Terror": preemptive warfare, indefinite detention, extraordinary rendition, warrantless wiretapping, and authorized torture of "enemy combatants." The widespread sampling, application, and outright adoption of this text's central thesis, particularly in cultural studies and dissident feminist and political theory seeking to analyze the development of the "War on Terror" after 9/11, is a conspicuous feature of scholarship in the late 2000s. Many even took Agamben at his word that, as he put it, today "we are all virtually *homines sacri.*"[5]

The widespread uptake of this text is even more noteworthy given that it staked its oppositional posture on the resurrection of a familiar if then rather unfashionable term of our political vocabularies—*sovereignty*—and reinvigorated critical positions "against" it, positions of which we might, in less distressing times, have been more skeptical.[6] To take only one prominent example of this, Judith Butler revised Foucault's thesis regarding the demise of sovereignty based on her astonishment at Bush's complete suspension of law in the capture and imprisonment of "detainees" at Guantánamo Bay, who were to be tried by administrative, noncourt "military tribunals." Drawing explicitly on Agamben, Butler argued that one could only make sense of these outrageous abuses of power by seeing them as "a contemporary version of sovereignty, animated by an aggressive nostalgia that seeks to do away with the separation of powers." Attempting to reconcile this seeming reassertion of sovereignty with Foucault's characterization of modern power as governmentality, Butler wrote, "we have to consider the act of suspending the law as a performative one which brings a contemporary configuration of sovereignty into being or, more precisely, reanimates a spectral sovereignty within the field of governmentality."[7] In short, *Homo Sacer* was so influential that it seemed to call into question an entire line of Foucauldian research in history and political thought that had become a de facto point of departure in any number of academic fields.

However compelling *Homo Sacer* may have been in those fraught and distressing days of heightened US aggression (an aggression that, to be sure, has by no means abated), my argument in this chapter is that this text actually perpetuates the very War on Terror of which it was so widely taken to be critical. I make this claim not simply in order to "go back" and correct an error, however widespread it may have been. Rather, I pursue it given the importance of *Homo Sacer* to the ever-expanding field of biopolitics, itself a privileged site for critical theory of US empire and the War on Terror, neither of which shows signs of waning in the post-Obama era. Agamben opens *Homo Sacer* with his announcement that Foucault's thesis regarding biopolitics needs to be corrected, and the Agamben–Foucault dispute has become virtually canonized as one prominent genealogy of the field of biopolitics. Given this, if *Homo Sacer* is foundational to biopolitical theory, then its complicity with the War on Terror is of urgent political and theoretical importance to the field and must be reckoned with as such.

My suggestion is that Agamben's complicity with the War on Terror is due to his largely overlooked philosophical debt to Hannah Arendt, whose work must consequently be acknowledged as integral to the field of biopolitics and, therefore, any biopolitical analysis of US empire.[8] Agamben's bifurcated understanding of life in terms of *bios* and *zoē* is effectively a reiteration of Arendt's distinction between labor and action in *The Human Condition*, the difference being that Agamben situates biopolitics in the realm of sovereignty, which he characterizes as essentially arbitrary and oppressive, while Arendt situates biopolitics in the domain of embodiment, which she characterizes as fundamentally imprisoning. Both nevertheless rely on a tiered determination of life whose base or biological level signals a degraded stratum of existence. In Arendt's case, this biological life is ultimately the site of *slavery*, an unfortunate if inevitable fact of human life and the necessary price of political freedom. In Agamben's case, this bare or biological life is a strangely hypostasized figure of an abjected 1940s European Jewry, who achieve their utmost "sacredness" or instantiation of bare life when they become "Muslim," a specific type of degraded being in the Nazi death camps. Agamben's argument is potentially more liberatory than Arendt's insofar as he heroizes the domain of bare life she views as inherently abject, holding sovereignty to blame for its abjection rather than its innately imprisoning character as such. Whether it is praised or censured, however, the "bare life" of embodiment (in Arendt) or sovereign exceptionalism (in Agamben) remains tethered to an essentialist biologization of life that both thinkers seek to flee or leave behind. It is this bare or biological body that threatens the integrity of the political, which means that both thinkers are committed to the existence of some biological domain that is, by definition, *not* political. "Biopolitics" is thus a misleading moniker for the political theory of life being advanced by both Agamben and Arendt, since it is precisely life "itself" that each views as threatening, undermining, or contaminating politics.

This repudiation of life "itself" is more precisely stated as their normative commitment to the hierarchical valuation of some (forms of) life over others. In Arendt, this commitment takes the form of a racist civilizationalism that also embraces an unmitigated misogyny and hatred of the poor. In Agamben, it takes the form of a biopolitics that exceptionalizes European suffering and intra-European crime as its moral and political anchor in a form of Eurocentrism I call Holocaust Exceptionalism, itself a crucial if undertheorized ideological plank of the War on Terror. While Arendt's failings in these areas are by now well known (if only grudgingly acknowledged), less well established are the ways that Agamben's biopolitics, fundamentally indebted to Arendtian premises, perpetuates the War on Terror in the pious guise of grieving the irretrievable loss of the properly political and human life in the grotesque crimes of Auschwitz. Such failed premises demand a new articulation of biopolitics that is free of the hierarchical valuation of some life over others and, consequently, the degraded rejection of life "itself."

THE HUMAN CONDITION: SLAVERY

Agamben stages his widely cited *Homo Sacer: Sovereign Power and Bare Life* as, in part, a disagreement with Foucault. Citing the end of volume 1 of *The History of Sexuality*, Agamben notes that for Foucault, the "threshold of modernity" is reached when politics becomes *bio*politics—when power exercises control not simply over the bodies of living beings, but also, in fact, regulates, monitors, and manufactures the very life and life processes of those living beings.[9] Agamben agrees with Foucault that modern politics is biopolitics, but disagrees that biopolitics is distinctly modern. Instead, Agamben argues that biopolitics is as old as politics itself, because politics—at least in its Western version—is effectively a politics of sovereignty, and sovereignty, in Agamben's view, is inherently biopolitical.

Agamben attributes his disagreement with Foucault in part to what he sees as Foucault's surprising failure to engage Hannah Arendt, Foucault's near-contemporary and someone who, although having meditated extensively on modern biopolitics in *The Human Condition*, herself neglected to apply these same insights to her *The Origins of Totalitarianism*. What both thinkers neglect to account for, in Agamben's view, is not the emergence of biopolitics ("which is, in itself, absolutely ancient"),[10] but rather "the politicization of bare life as such," which Agamben names the truly "decisive moment of modernity."[11] According to this introductory setup, then, a reconciliation of these two thinkers' biopolitical theory in service to understanding the decisive moment of modernity is the task of *Homo Sacer*. Presenting himself as the third corner of this philosophical triangle, Agamben installs *Homo Sacer* as the place wherein Arendt's and Foucault's insights will be adequately fused so as to better diagnose our current moment, venturing that "The concept of 'bare life' or 'sacred life' is the focal lens through which we shall try to make their points of view converge."[12]

However compelling all this might sound, it is not exactly what Agamben accomplishes in *Homo Sacer*. Indeed, Foucault is not really even one of Agamben's primary interlocutors in this text (although many have taken him at his word about that). What's more true is that this introductory invocation of Foucault functions as a kind of stage setting for Agamben's own argument, which is more accurately described as an elaboration of Arendt's thesis in *The Human Condition* and, as he says, an application of it to "totalitarianism" and Nazism. While Agamben calls Foucault to task for overlooking Arendt, Arendt is faulted for not recognizing the importance of her own insights and relating them to one another. Thus, Agamben notes that Foucault's argument will have to be not only "corrected" but also "completed" insofar as it fails to recognize what Arendt already understood to be latent in the modern replacement of *bios* with *zoē* as its central political concern.[13]

The obviously disciplinary character of this reprimand is underremarked; I will return to its latent moralism at the end of this chapter. For now, it is sufficient to note that in *Homo Sacer*, Agamben essentially adopts Arendt's argument in *The Human Condition* regarding the twentieth century for an updated diagnosis of the twenty-first by recentering her biopolitical diagnosis of modern decadence around the Nazi death camps. His synopsis of her thesis there is, effectively, his own: "the transformation and decadence of the political realm in modern societies [are owed] to this very primacy of natural life over political action."[14] The difference is that

Agamben couches Arendt's understanding of life within the terms of sovereignty rather than embodiment (or, as she calls it, the human condition). As Agamben argues, in Western politics, "the inclusion of bare life in the political realm constitutes the original—if concealed—nucleus of *sovereign power*."[15] Echoing Carl Schmitt, Agamben asserts that "the exception" lies at the heart of sovereignty. Revising Schmitt, Agamben relates the exception to a specifically Arendtian reading of the Aristotelian distinction between life and the good life, or "bare life" ("*zoē*") and properly political life ("*bios*").

Agamben claims to cull the *zoē/bios* distinction from book 1 of Aristotle's *Politics*, wherein Aristotle says that the polis comes into being for the sake of life but remains in existence for the sake of living well, and commentators have mostly taken Agamben at his word on this.[16] Like Foucault, however, Aristotle is also largely immaterial to the argument of *Homo Sacer*, the citation from the *Politics* functioning as a device to introduce the *zoē/bios* distinction rather than as the philosophical basis of the argument.[17] Once again, Agamben instead follows Arendt in her reading of ancient Greek philosophy, sociology, and culture in *The Human Condition*, an interpretation that is related but not identical to Aristotle's view in the *Politics*.[18] Arendt occasionally references the *zoē/bios* divide explicitly;[19] more often, she speaks in terms of the distinction between private and public, household and city.[20] Referencing both Aristotle and Plato, Arendt says regarding the distinction between natural and political life: "In Plato and Aristotle, the distinction between spheres of household and political life was never doubted. Without mastering the necessities of life in the household, neither life nor the 'good life' is possible, but politics is never for the sake of life. As far as the members of the *polis* are concerned, household life exists for the sake of the 'good life' in the *polis*."[21] In this view, the meeting of biological needs is both necessary for life and yet necessary to leave behind in order to live a truly human life, the "good life" or living well (in Arendt's vocabulary, the life of action in the public sphere). In short, however, it is just as necessary to leave the domain of the household behind as it is to establish a domain of the household in the first place. The household is included within the frame of human life, albeit only by way of its exclusion from properly human life:

> Only in the household was one primarily concerned with one's own life and survival. Whoever entered the political realm had first to be ready

to risk his life, and too great a love for life obstructed freedom, was a sure sign of slavishness. . . . The "good life," as Aristotle called the life of the citizen, therefore was not merely better, more carefree or nobler than ordinary life, but of an altogether different quality. It was "good" to the extent that by having mastered the necessities of sheer life, by being freed from labor and work, and by overcoming the innate urge of all living creatures for their own survival, it was no longer bound to the biological life process.[22]

This is precisely the analysis on which Agamben bases the exceptional character of sovereignty. Agamben argues that bare life is always included within the polis, albeit only by means of an exclusion—it is the exception to politics that simultaneously sustains and facilitates it. He writes:

The peculiar phrase "born with regard to life, but existing essentially with regard to the good life" can be read not only as an implication of being born in being, but also as an inclusive exclusion (an *exceptio*) of *zoē* in the *polis*, almost as if politics were the place in which life had to transform itself into good life and in which what had to be politicized were always already bare life. In Western politics, bare life has the peculiar privilege of being that whose exclusion founds the city of men.[23]

Agamben does not offer any reason why *zoē* is exceptionalized; moreover, he never marks it as the realm of the household as such. He simply duplicates the Arendtian reading of the ancient Greeks and takes the necessity of *zoē's* inclusive exclusion for granted. It is this lack of explanation that leads readers to conclude that there is something essentialist or ahistorical about Agamben's notion of bare life, which of course there is.[24] But this aporia is not left open in Arendt, who is clear that *zoē* must be exceptionalized from politics because it is the natural place of both biological life and the activity of meeting its needs and, in her view, both this place and this activity are unfree. For Arendt, the domain of bodily need is the domain of necessity. Labor, as the activity that corresponds to and meets this necessity, is thus fundamentally dependent or unfree activity, chained as it is to the demands of the life process. Arendt counterposes this necessary labor to the domain of action, which takes place in the public realm and is characterized, in her view, not by labor and biological need, but by speech and collaboration among equals toward the end of establishing the new.[25]

Arendt thus makes clear that *zoē*'s domain is a necessary one, but that precisely because of its necessity it remains prepolitical and must be surpassed by the properly political.[26]

Arendt's association of labor with necessity, servitude, and unfreedom is a defining characteristic of *The Human Condition*, which is overstuffed with disparagements of laboring activity. To Arendt, labor is not simply slavish;[27] it is also boring,[28] repetitive,[29] painful,[30] burdensome,[31] menial,[32] futile,[33] incapable of speech,[34] oblivious to the external world,[35] unable to make or participate in a social world,[36] without beginning or end,[37] privatized and solitary,[38] automatic and "rhythmic" and so easily replaceable by machines,[39] socially "herdlike,"[40] and antipolitical.[41] It is imprisoned[42] and imprisoning.[43] It is trivial and routine. Its arduous travail leaves "no trace, no monument, no great work worthy of remembrance."[44] It has no higher or nobler purpose than mere survival: "The daily fight in which the human body is engaged to keep the world clean and prevent its decay bears little resemblance to heroic deeds; the endurance it needs to repair every day anew the waste of yesterday is not courage, and what makes the effort painful is not danger but its relentless repetition."[45] Far from the activity of the political realm, wherein participants audaciously risk themselves in collective enterprise to constitute the new, labor remains appropriately tucked away in the private household, imprisoned within its taxing, repetitive, and meaningless servitude to the maintenance and reproduction of biological life.

"The only possible advantage" of human labor that Arendt can see is its "ability to procure the necessities of life for more than one man or one family."[46] This "advantage" is what allows for the partitioning of labor onto some subset of human beings so that others might escape or transcend it. Put in starker terms, the realm of the household is not simply the realm of necessity, but that of slavery. A sociological and historical fact of Greek life, ancient slavery also reflects essential truths about human existence. As Arendt says, slavery is due to "the human condition itself."[47] The human condition she means here is embodiment, a facticity that must be transcended if the good life is to be possible. Ancient Greek slavery was therefore not "a device for cheap labor or an instrument of exploitation for profit," but rather "the attempt to exclude labor from the conditions of man's life."[48]

Arendt's thesis in *The Human Condition* is that modernity has ignored these truths and valorized labor, making it the center of political life. Her language for this is "the rise of society." Modernity is characterized by the emergence of a semipublic, politicized realm of "society" that attends to the economic and physical tasks of caring for and administering human life: "Society is the form in which the fact of mutual dependence for the sake of life and nothing else assumes public significance and where the activities connected with sheer survival are permitted to appear in public."[49] Displacing action, the only properly political activity, our politics now consists primarily of the prepolitical activity of "housekeeping."[50] The consequences of this transformation are the loss of an authentically political space and any notion of complete freedom:

> The danger here is obvious. Man cannot be free if he does not know that he is subject to necessity, because his freedom is always won in his never wholly successful attempts to liberate himself from necessity.[51]

> The rather uncomfortable truth of the matter is that the triumph the modern world has achieved over necessity is due to the emancipation of labor, that is, to the fact that the *animal laborans* was permitted to occupy the public realm; and yet, as long as the *animal laborans* remains in possession of it, there can be no true public realm, but only private activities displayed in the open.[52]

It is worth emphasizing that this is not simply Arendt's reading of the socioeconomics of ancient Greece. It is also her view regarding what is basically and essentially true of the human condition, and thus forms the basis for her clearly conservative diagnosis of modern decadence in *The Human Condition*.[53] Further evidence of this is its emergence in her work some fifteen years later, when she reiterates this claim in *On Revolution*. There she says forthrightly,

> All rulership has its original and its most legitimate source in man's wish to emancipate himself from life's necessity, and men achieved such liberation by means of violence, by forcing others to bear the burden of life for them. This was the core of slavery, and it is only with the rise of technology, and not the rise of modern political ideas as such, which has refuted the old and terrible truth that only violence and rule over others could make some men free.[54]

In *The Human Condition*, Arendt claims this situation is "unjust" yet "natural," awful but ineliminable from human life:

The price for the elimination of life's burden from the shoulders of all citizens was enormous and by no means consisted only in the violent injustice of forcing one part of humanity into the darkness of pain and necessity. Since this darkness is natural, inherent in the human condition—only the act of violence, when one group of men tries to rid itself of the shackles binding all of us to pain and necessity, is man-made—the price for absolute freedom from necessity is, in a sense, life itself, or rather the substitution of vicarious life for real life.[55]

For Arendt, in short, slavery is necessary for freedom. Put more precisely, the enslavement of some is necessary for the freedom of others. Indeed, it is not going too far to suggest that a foundational principle of Arendt's political theory is the "terrible truth" that the subordination of some is necessary so that others can be free. Although she correctly observes that slavery is an artificial mode of human social organization imposed only through violence and injustice, she does not therefore conclude from this premise that slavery is in any way problematic, nor does she take up the task of theorizing alternative forms of social and political organization that might avoid this formation. These recognitions instead *affirm her loyalty to slavery*, leading her to the conclusion that one of humankind's most distinctively violent and oppressive forms of social relationship[56] is ineliminable from human life if anyone (else) is to be truly free. Her outlandish aside regarding "the striking absence of serious slave rebellions in ancient and modern times"[57] and the summoning of this ostensible fact as evidence of slaves' animal-like activities and existence showcase not Arendt's ignorance exactly (although it does this too) so much as the depth of her conviction regarding the necessity—even legitimacy—of slavery for freedom, a conviction so powerful that she can omit the Haitian Revolution from her study of revolution in modernity and remain oblivious to the ubiquity of slave rebellions, which characterize, and are indeed concomitant with, the history of slavery itself.[58]

Arendt's commitment to slavery is inextricably tied to a set of civilizationalist investments that are perhaps uncomfortable to confront directly, given her flight from Nazi Germany[59] and noteworthy status as one of the only thinkers in the canon of European political thought to explicitly address the subjects of racism, colonialism, and empire.[60] Nevertheless, these investments are the consequences of her "philosophical" analysis of the human condition and the hierarchized reading of household and polis that she presents there and must be reckoned with as such. So, for example, in *The Origins of Totalitarianism*, Arendt examines a different concrete example of slavery beyond Ancient Greece. There, she considers that the reason for the Dutch enslavement of Southern African tribes on "the Dark Continent" is because Africans were so beholden to nature that they were incapable of world-making activity of their own. It was

> not at all the color of their skin but the fact that they behaved like a part of nature, that they treated nature as their undisputed master, that they had not created a human world, a human reality, and that therefore nature had remained, in all its majesty, the only overwhelming reality— compared to which they appeared to be phantoms, unreal and ghost-like. They were, as it were, "natural" human beings who lacked the specifically human character, the specifically human reality, so that when European men massacred them they somehow were not aware that they had committed murder.[61]

In other words, the tribes of Southern Africa were enslaved by the Dutch not because they were black (that is, not because they were slaves "by nature"), but because they were animalic in their relationship with the world. As pieces of nature themselves, they were both subject to necessity and content to dwell perennially within it, such that enslavement (and murder?) is almost an inevitable outcome of European contact as Arendt presents it here.[62] It is noteworthy that, in considering this particular episode of history, what Arendt condemns is neither massacre nor colonization nor the enslavement of colonized peoples, but rather the fact that, in this particular instance of slavery, the Dutch fell to the low level of savages in the laziness of their slaving, thereby forsaking their "Western" legacy:

> The Boers were the first European group to become completely alienated from the pride which Western man felt in living in a world created and fabricated by himself. They treated the natives as raw material and lived on them as one might live on the fruits of wild trees. Lazy and unproductive, they agreed to vegetate on essentially the same level as the black tribes had vegetated for thousands of years. The great horror which had seized European men at their first

confrontation with native life was stimulated by precisely this touch of inhumanity among human beings who apparently were as much a part of nature as wild animals. The Boers lived on their slaves exactly the way natives had lived on an unprepared and unchanged nature.[63]

Generalizing this analysis of the tribes of Southern Africa to all "savage" peoples, Arendt notes later: "the tragedy of savage tribes is that they inhabit an unchanged nature which they cannot master, yet upon whose abundance or frugality they depend for their livelihood, that they live and die without leaving any trace, without having contributed anything to a common world."[64] In considering the Dutch invasion of Southern Africa, then, Arendt reserves pity solely for the predicament of those she deems to reside *inappropriately* in the domain of nature, labor, servitude, and embodiment. For "savage tribes," this residency is natural. For the Dutch, it is a fall from grace, a devolution from civilization. Arendt does not challenge the notion that this domain is itself the site of abjection, nor does she question if and how power might be implicated in the production of this abjection. Rather, she simply equates nature with savagery and embodiment, finding only these depoliticized conditions to merit condemnation.

Perhaps unsurprisingly, there is significant overlap between Arendt's distaste for labor and "nature" in *The Human Condition* and her racist proclamations regarding "savage" and non-European people(s), particularly Africans,[65] who are by definition closer to nature and therefore prepolitical and unfree.[66] This is neither accidental nor assignable to her historical "context"; rather, it is the necessary consequence of her philosophical position, which is a hierarchical privileging of polis over household. Moreover, the purview of "nature," labor, and embodiment actually has quite a vast sweep in Arendt's work, a scope that expands even beyond predictable if no less hideous antiblack racism. So, for example, in *The Human Condition*, Arendt consistently marks the private realm as a place of "darkness,"[67] as the repository of what is "dark,"[68] or as the "darker ground which must remain hidden."[69] This calls up Christian-colonial tropes regarding the darkness of laborers (who work in the sun, unlike the light-skinned, who remain indoors) and the savage and infidel (prehistoric, darker "races" who reject the light of Christ's teaching). But, if it is not already obvious, it also invokes the female body as the site of shamefulness, sin, filth, and impure sexuality. In *Origins*, Arendt associates this darkness with the "givens" of nature itself as well as bodily existence and bodily "difference," her evasive terms for race and gender.[70] In *On Revolution*, this darkness is much more explicitly associated with the blackness of "Negro slavery"[71] in the colonial United States as well as, repeatedly, with poverty and poor people.[72] The distinction between private and public is therefore a distinction not simply between savage and civilized, slave and free, but also between black and not-black, female and male, poor and not poor. Coming back full circle to the distinction between polis and household, for Arendt, these two spheres correspond to a distinction between what should and should not be seen in public, a bizarre discourse that emerges only on the rare occasions when she mentions women explicitly.[73] Like slaves, women are associated with the body and its processes and must therefore—like the body itself—be shielded from public scrutiny. Arendt offers no explanation for why this should be so except to claim that this is how it has "always" been.[74]

The associations of women, labor, and servitude with embodiment and, therefore, the abject, are themes all too familiar to any student of the history of ideas in its Western canonical version.[75] That Arendt, too, traffics in this disgust is evident by her casual and largely unjustified advocacy of hiding anything to do with women, labor, and the body. Her conflation of all of these with prepolitical nature, backward savagery, and "darkness" resonates only too well with late-nineteenth- and early-twentieth-century theories of scientific racism, in which white women were deemed on a kind of parallel evolutionary track as "lower" races, who were both premodern and less humanly developed than their white male counterparts.[76] Admittedly, Arendt offers a "philosophical" justification for these hierarchies rather than an explicitly racialized one, arguing that

> Since the Greeks, we have known that highly developed political life breeds a deep-rooted suspicion of this private sphere, a deep resentment against the disturbing miracle contained in the fact that each of us is made as he is—single, unique, unchangeable. This whole sphere of the merely given, relegated to private life in civilized society, is a permanent threat to the public sphere, because the public sphere is as consistently based on the law of equality as the private sphere is based on the law of universal difference and differentiation.[77]

Yet Arendt does not explain why the realm of "the given" elicits "resentment," much less how and why "difference" is at odds with "equality." Moreover, although she avoids explicitly racialist (if not racist) logics, she reproduces civilizationalist ones, noting the importance of retaining the privacy of "the given" so as not to disturb the political equality of "civilized society." This is, in fact, the connection between the two. That is, there is a disavowed overlap in Arendt's thought between the domain of private labor and that of "darkness," women, savagery, and embodiment. Indeed, as she makes clear when discussing refugees rather than slaves, the "great danger" of being reduced solely to "natural givenness" or "mere differentiation" is that such people "begin to belong to the human race in much the same way as animals belong to a specific animal species." But this is the exact way she characterizes slaves and the condition of enslavement.[78]

In a kind of culmination, then, of this line of argument, in *On Revolution*, Arendt contends that the body itself is a kind of violence. Speaking of the Industrial Revolution, for example, she writes: "it had liberated them [the poor] from their masters only to put them under a stronger taskmaster, their daily needs and wants, the force, in other words, with which necessity drives and compels men and which is more compelling than violence."[79] This violence may be what links the (female) body with "savage tribes" and the abjection of poverty, since Arendt seems to see this collection of subservients—slaves and women, the "dark" and the poor—as representatives or instantiations of a kind of violent principle in political life. It is almost as if they themselves are a kind of violence.[80] This is perhaps why she suggests that violence is the appropriate mode of relation in the household's hidden and prepolitical heart of darkness:

> To be political, to live in a *polis*, means that everything was decided through words and persuasion and not through force and violence. In Greek self-understanding, to force people by violence, to command rather than persuade, were prepolitical ways to deal with people characteristic of life outside the *polis*, of home and family life, where the household head ruled with uncontested, despotic powers, or of life in the barbarian empires of Asia, whose despotism was frequently likened to the organization of the household.[81]

Confirming the racialized subtext of the "darkness" of the private sphere, here we see not only that violence toward women and slaves is both necessary and appropriate, but also that recognition and implementation of this fact are civilizational accomplishments. Arendt is clear that the vast majority of human beings do not and will not participate in the rarefied space of political action because of their "inequality,"[82] which is probably for the best since, as the Greeks well knew, large numbers of people involved in political life lead almost inevitably to "despotism"[83] such as that found in "Asia"[84] or "Persia."[85] The number of citizens allowed to participate in public life, then, must necessarily be limited, if tyranny is to be avoided and (Greek, that is, European) civilization upheld.[86] According to Arendt, the "ever-frustrated ambition" of all tyrants is to discourage the citizenry from participating in politics and to "transform the *agora* into an assemblage of shops like the bazaars of oriental despotism."[87] The Greeks knew better, however, than to be distracted from the public realm of action and did not treat one another with the violence with which they—properly and necessarily—treated their women and slaves. Unlike "Oriental" despots, the Greeks understood the distinctions between *polis* and *oikos* and conducted themselves accordingly. What makes Orientals oriental is the same as what them despotic; namely, their failure to distinguish between public and private, superior and inferior. Barbarian races rule over the public realm as if it were the domain of the household, namely, with violence. In failing to realize the proper *sphere* of despotism, Asian civilizations were themselves despotic. Hence only Greek civilization is properly civilized. Properly courageous and free Greek men do not treat *one another* with violence, for that would be barbaric. Violence is only appropriate with subordinates (and barbarians?), not equals.

There is real resistance in political theory to acknowledging the racism, misogyny, and hatred of the poor that comprise Arendt's fundamentally civilizationalist commitments.[88] My point here, however, is not simply to underscore the accuracy of these claims; it is also to demonstrate that they are inextricable (whether as cause or effect is unclear) from her seemingly more "philosophical" reflections about the human condition. Indeed, this inextricability raises the perennial chicken-and-egg question in political theory as to whether Arendt is committed to the expulsion of non-Europeans, women, and the poor from politics because of her philosophical hatred of the body, or whether she has a philosophical hatred of the body because she seeks to expel non-Europeans, women, and the poor from politics. This question, largely unanswerable from within the canon of political thought, cannot be satisfactorily disentangled in Arendt either.[89] However, it will be obscured entirely if we insist on the disconnect between her analysis of "the human condition" and her civilizationalist privileging of European male dominance as the meaning and content of human freedom.

By contrast, what is revealed by connecting Arendt's biopolitical premises with her civilizationalist, misogynist, racist, and classist investments is the fundamental core of her biopolitical philosophy, which is by definition antiliberatory or, as she might put it, a defense of the necessity of slavery. For, of course, there is no logical or normative force to her conclusion that labor, because it is necessary, is therefore repetitive, burdensome, unfree, or subhuman. One could accept the premise that certain kinds of labor are necessary to sustain human life, but argue that precisely because of their necessity, these labors—and those who perform them—are in fact the most important, dignified, and humanly valuable.[90] One could even go so far as to claim that the violent coercion that even Arendt agrees is required to maintain a subordinate laboring class is an injustice incompatible with freedom in any form, even the robust freedom of the elite few of the Greek polis. This would mean rereading the modern so-called emergence of the private sphere as the slaves' demand for inclusion in the domain of the human, an emancipatory demand to participate in the political life from which the vast majority of humanity is, on Arendt's Greek-inspired scheme, necessarily excluded. However, Arendt does not and cannot consider these readings of labor or "the rise of the social" because this sort of liberation is impossible in her view. Not simply distasteful or undesirable, but *impossible*. Human beings—either individually or as a species—cannot be freed from the constraints and necessity of the biological body; hence it is absurd to long for a day wherein the domain of the private or biological life (or those who toil there) might be "liberated." To Arendt, this emancipatory impulse is Marx's mistake and the failure of the French Revolution.[91] Instead, we must resign ourselves to the fact of slavery—servitude and violence in some form(s)—if anyone is ever to be free: "Because all human beings are subject to necessity, they are entitled to violence toward others; violence is the prepolitical act of liberating oneself from the necessity of life for the freedom of world."[92]

BARE LIFE: "THE MUSLIM"

It is thus natural and even necessary, on Arendt's telling, for a domain of life and sector of humanity to be (out)cast as exceptional, excluded from politics, abjected as the domain of necessity or bare life. It is only when that domain threatens to exceed its natural or necessary bounds—only, in other words, when it threatens to invade or encompass the lives and freedoms of the proper members of the political realm—that catastrophe looms. As with Agamben, who effectively follows her on this, the crisis of modernity is precisely that "the private" won't stay private anymore. Instead, all politics now concerns the domain of biological life, and those who had previously been able to escape this domain have been reduced to its level. For Arendt, this is the content of modern decadence. For Agamben, it is the meaning of the phrase *homo sacer*, which has come to define us all. Regardless of the form it takes, however, these interpretations of biopolitics entail a stratification of life whereby some versions of it are worth more than others and its base level can be neither eliminated nor transcended but only repudiated and expelled. This is why it is impossible to locate or derive an emancipatory politics from *Homo Sacer*—its Arendtian presuppositions render liberation an impossibility, its advocacy a form of political nihilism.[93]

It is rather too easy if nevertheless still important to point out that Arendt's and Agamben's shared horror at *zoē*, at "bare life" or the body or its needs and demands, much less the prospect that its presence might intrude upon and destroy the special sanctity that is "politics" or the "good life," is the Western tradition's by-now-familiar if astonishingly enduring hostility to women, children, foreigners, slaves, "savages," and "the insane," a hostility from which even members of these categories—as Arendt herself demonstrates—are by no means exempt. Indeed, this tangled thematic is so basic to canonical Western thought that it is impossible to know which came first—hatred of the body or hatred of women, children, foreigners, slaves, "savages," and "the insane." Agamben shares this distaste with Arendt but traffics in it less explicitly, assimilating her analysis of the necessary privacy of the household without explicitly endorsing it,[94] and offering resonantly Arendtian analyses of the categorial crisis posed by refugees (or "stateless persons"),[95] the Marxian hubris of believing that the "fundamental biopolitical fracture" (which Marx mistakenly calls "class conflict") might be overcome,[96] and the distinction between "the people" as citizenry vs. *le peuple* as plebs.[97] Far from a more abstract or ontological claim about the nature of Western politics, Agamben's annunciation of crisis in *Homo Sacer* is, in fact, the much more basic and quite familiar anxiety that the lives and bodies of Western Europe's "others" might intrude into the space of the political, thereby ruining it for those already there and making it possible to treat propertied white male citizens the same ways that the "others" who constitute the *zoē* of the polis have been treated for centuries.[98] Unsurprisingly, then, it is only now—when *zoē* and *bios* have entered into a "zone of indistinction" and the threat of being treated as mere life has expanded beyond the confines of those who more typically merit it—that the specters of crisis and "nihilism" loom so large for Agamben.[99]

While Agamben follows Arendt's reading of ancient Greece and even retains a version of her diagnosis of modernity as "a primacy of the private over the public,"[100] he does not simply take the polis as a normative standard and transpose its workings onto the failures and dysfunctions of contemporary politics. Rather, he argues that the logic implicit in the "rise of the social"—a logic Agamben instead believes is intrinsic to sovereignty—is eroding the otherwise crucial distinction between *bios* and *zoē* such that they have become indistinguishable from each other and the exceptional status of *zoē* has come to demarcate the domain of politics itself.[101] This gives rise to the phenomenon of "sacredness," a notion of *zoē* as human life that can be, in Agamben's now-famous formulation, "killed but not sacrificed."[102] The epitome of this sacredness is the resident of the Nazi death camp; Agamben argues that modernity's merger of *bios* and *zoē* finds its terrible and most gruesome culmination in the camps, which he says are "the materialization of the state of exception."[103] The crisis of modernity, then, is not so much the "rise of the social" as the "rise of the sacred," and Agamben warns that the unstoppable logic of sovereignty will transform everyone into *zoē*, too, if we don't put a stop to it.

That Agamben acknowledges the possibility of averting the spread of sacredness, however remote, suggests that Arendt's loathing of nature/embodiment surfaces elsewhere in his adoption of her tiered reading of life. Strangely, in the *Homo Sacer* series, Agamben appropriates and transforms Arendt's essentialized inferiority and servitude of labor into an essentialized superiority and exceptionalism of the Holocaust and, more specifically, Jewish people, whom he figures as quintessential victims of biopolitical sovereign decisionism. It is true that Agamben offers multiple examples of *zoē* throughout *Homo Sacer*, including not simply the residents of Nazi death camps but also the refugee or "stateless person," the *Versuchspersonen* (VPs) used for medical experimentation by Nazi doctors, and persons in a condition of "overcoma" (a stage of life beyond the cessation of vital functions). However, what becomes clear as he develops his analysis is that each of these is effectively the same figure for Agamben—the displaced and abjected Jew as object of Nazi violence.[104] Key to this figural collapse is yet another personage whom Agamben mentions only briefly in the conclusion to *Homo Sacer* but who receives extended scrutiny and analysis in the third volume of the *Homo Sacer* series, *Remnants of Auschwitz*. That personage is *der Muselmann*, or "the Muslim."[105] Though seemingly a departure from *Homo Sacer* in its narrower focus on "the Muslim," *Remnants of Auschwitz* in fact distills that text's argument, which can be obscured by its post-9/11 academic uptake as a critique of US empire and the various "states of exception" produced by it. While in *Homo Sacer* Agamben resists conflating "the Muslim" with pure *zoē*, instead claiming him[106] as a potential figure of resistance in the camps, by the time of *Remnants*, Agamben cites "the Muslim" as the figure of "the untestifiable, that to which no one has borne witness."[107] He will become "the absolute biopolitical substance" and, as such, the quintessential representation of *zoē* that must be rejected or refused if modern decadence is to be averted.[108] In short, "the Muslim" actually functions as the conduit through which Agamben examines the Holocaust and exalts an exceptionalized Jewish figure of victimization. The instrumentalization of "the Muslim" to exceptionalize Jewish people and/as Jewish victims both is the consequence of Agamben's adoption of Arendtian premises and works simultaneously to obscure and perpetuate the War on Terror.

Agamben explains the meaning and origin of the figure of *der Muselmann* as follows:

> The most likely explanation of the term can be found in the literal meaning of the Arabic word Muslim: the one who submits unconditionally to the will of God. It is this meaning that lies at the origin of the legends concerning Islam's supposed fatalism, legends which are found in European culture starting with the Middle Ages (this deprecatory sense of the term is present in European languages, particularly in Italian). But while

> the Muslim's resignation consists in the conviction that the will of Allah
> is at work every moment and in even the smallest events, the *Muselmann*
> of Auschwitz is instead defined by a loss of all will and consciousness.[109]

Agamben cites a number of sources in both *Homo Sacer* and *Remnants* in
coming to this conclusion, including survivor testimony, the writings of
Primo Levi, and the *Encyclopedia Judaica*.[110] Levi defines "the Muslim" as
"the most extreme figure of the camp inhabitant," "a being from whom
humiliation, horror, and fear had so taken away all consciousness and all
personality as to make him absolutely apathetic."[111] "Muslims" are described
in this text as "mummy-men, the living dead,"[112] "dull-witted and aim-
less," a person who "didn't defend himself,"[113] and "men of unconditional
fatalism."[114] Synonyms include donkeys, cretins, cripples, swimmers, cam-
els, tired sheikhs, trinkets, and—in the women's camp—*Muselweiber*.[115]
The anti-Arab and anti-Muslim references in this term are obvious enough
and, one would expect, highly significant for any analysis of the functioning of life and death in the camps and their consequences for contemporary, racialized (bio)politics.[116] Despite his nod to the "deprecatory" sense
of "Islam's supposed fatalism" in the term, however, Agamben simply
ignores its racism (all the more noteworthy given that it is used by and in
description of other racialized people in this context, Jews) and actually
relies upon and exploits it in order to derive the political theory he
advances in *Remnants*.[117] For example, Agamben writes about the "disfig-
ured face" of "the Muslim" as confronting other prisoners with his "'Oriental' agony,"[118] although, as Jill Jarvis notes, he "does not interrogate what
exactly is 'Oriental' about such agony, abjection, and lack of dignity."[119]
Agamben also associates "the Muslim" with "passivity" and pure receptiv-
ity;[120] however, "he offers no critical reflection on the European Orientalism at play in the construction of the 'muselman' by both camp inmates
and writers and historians of the Holocaust."[121] More significant than these
slights and oversights, however, is the overall thesis of the book, which
holds that "the Muslim" offers a "new paradigm" for understanding the
Nazi genocide as an "experiment beyond life and death in which the Jew is
transformed into a *Muselmann* and the human being into a non-human."[122]
According to this view, "the Muslim" demarcates the nonhuman and the
Jew the human. Indeed, Agamben notes repeatedly that "the Muslim"
calls into question the very existence of "man" and transforms the human

Jews of Auschwitz into nonhuman nonmen, or "Muslims."[123] Not only, then, is the human specifically male, but manhood is also specifically Jewish. While this gendering may seem simply to be Western philosophy's familiar if inessential conceit of conflating the male with the universal, its wholly necessary character is revealed when Agamben argues that this experimental transformation of the Jew into "the Muslim," the human into the nonhuman, is accomplished via his confrontation with the face of the Gorgon, "that horrid female head covered with serpents whose gaze produced death."[124] Referencing Levi once again, Agamben uses the Gorgon as a metaphor for the unwitnessable horror of the Nazi death camps, and suggests that precisely what makes "Muslims" "Muslims" is the fact that they have gazed upon that which cannot properly be seen by men and survived. Unlike Odysseus, who withstood the sirens' song by chaining himself to the sails of his ship, "Muslims" behold the face of the Medusa not only without dying, but also *without resisting.* They thus survive, albeit in a distinctly nonhuman/nonmanly form that is a submission beyond any notion of dignity or respect. This loss of manhood/humanity is equated with failure to either resist the demonic feminine or be obliterated by its explicitness. Transformation of the human into the nonhuman, Jew into "Muslim," then, is effected by "the Muslim" having survived what no man can or ought to survive: gazing upon the horrible face of the castrating woman: "There is a point," Agamben writes, "at which human beings, while apparently remaining human beings, cease to be human. This point is the *Muselmann,* and the camp is his exemplary site."[125] The persistence of life in the face of this dissolution of dignity, of survival amid the loss of "dignity and decency beyond imagination,"[126] is the meaning of "the Muslim": "The *Muselmann* is a limit figure of a special kind, in which not only categories such as dignity and respect but even the very idea of an ethical limit lose their meaning."[127]

Agamben thus uncritically reproduces the "deprecatory" sense of Islam's fatalism and submission in his book's main thesis, furthering tropes and stereotypes about Muslim fatalism and passivity and, in particular, the associations of Muslim men with effeminacy, faggotry, and other forms of failed masculinity. All of these are clearly lodged in his usage of this term to describe not only specific inmates of Auschwitz, but also the grand experiment that he understands the death camps to have undertaken. For what Agamben finds to be definitive of "the Muslim" is his passivity, apathy, and sheer lack of cognitive or emotional response, qualities that are explicitly gendered and sexualized in what we can recognize as the War on Terror's distinct civilizationalist discourse of Muslim perversity and savagery.[128] That these same characteristics qualify actual Muslims for targeting by the contemporary War on Terror, however, goes unremarked by Agamben. Indeed, for all his talk about "Muslims," Muslim people rarely appear in his work—only once, in fact, that I can find.[129] In his *State of Exception*, published in 2005, Agamben writes of the detainees at the Guantánamo Bay prison:

> What is new about President Bush's order is that it radically erases any legal status of the individual, thus producing a legally unnamable and unclassifiable being. Not only do the Taliban captured in Afghanistan not enjoy the status of POWs as defined by the Geneva Convention, they do not even have the status of persons charged with a crime according to American laws. Neither prisoners nor persons accused, but simply "detainees," they are the object of a pure de facto rule, of a detention that is indefinite not only in the temporal sense but in its very nature as well, since it is entirely removed from the law and from judicial oversight. The *only* thing to which it could *possibly* be compared is the legal situation of the Jews in the Nazi *Lager* [camps], who, along with their citizenship, had lost every legal identity, but at least retained their identity as Jews.[130]

What makes the situation of Guantánamo prisoners disturbing to Agamben is the fact that it is analogous to the situation of Jews in the Nazi death camps, the "only" possible situation with which Guantánamo can be compared. Agamben is simply unable to conceive of any mode of political injustice that does not ultimately refer to Auschwitz or any victim of bio-political decisionism other than Jews in the Nazi period.[131] This double displacement of "Muslims" into Jews and Jews into the Jews of 1940s Europe obscures the facts of twenty-first century politics, wherein actual Muslim people are the targets of an explicitly racialized, moralized, civilizational War on Terror as well as the subjects of ongoing military occupation and warfare throughout West Asia, while the victims of and refugees from European anti-Semitism have become today's colonizers in the land of Palestine. What becomes clear in *Remnants* is that the only political event that ever really interested Agamben in the *Homo Sacer* series was the Nazi genocide of the Jews (abbreviated by his focus on and consequent fore-shortening of this event into, simply, "Auschwitz," "a metonym he employs and apparently finds unproblematic").[132] In the age of the War on Terror, however, "the Muslim" simply cannot stand in for the figure of the degraded Jew, if such a substitution was ever plausible to begin with. Today, "the Muslim"—scare quotes around which are now justified by the racialization of Arabs and all those who "look" Muslim into a single category of threat and terror[133]—is actual Muslims and Muslim people. Such an unlikely substitution also obscures the contemporary facts of Israeli colonization and apartheid—no longer the dispossessed of Europe, "the Jews" (if it even makes sense to speak this way) are no longer the abject victims Agamben would prefer to consider (and contain) them to be.[134] Agamben's racist reliance on *der Muselmann* in order to theorize and central-ize the Nazi Holocaust reveals the impossibility of escaping the conse-quences of Arendt's hierarchical biopolitical premises and demands the devaluation of the very life whose "bareness" is being valorized in his ostensible critique of biopolitical oppression. The Eurocentric, civiliza-tionalist, and racist commitments underpinning the contemporary War on Terror thus are not challenged in *Homo Sacer* so much as reproduced by it. This reproduction is due to the text's reliance on Arendtian biopo-litical premises that must be dislodged in order to adequately formulate a critical biopolitics of US empire.

HOLOCAUST EXCEPTIONALISM AND THE WAR ON TERROR

Some readers take Agamben at his word that the texts of *Homo Sacer* aim to deexceptionalize the exception, to show how utterly predictable, ordinary, and ubiquitous such "camps" have now become. On this view, Auschwitz is no more or less remarkable than any other camp; it is rather the culmina-tion of an existing logic that has since been replicated in other places such as Guantánamo Bay. Others suggest that Agamben's distinctive use of "par-adigm" accounts for his seemingly totalizing assertion that the camp, "now securely lodged within the city's interior, is the new biopolitical *nomos* of the planet."[135] Yet these paradigms also have specific referents that are effectively privileged via their paradigmatic status. For example, when it comes to the camp, the paradigm of Auschwitz functions simultaneously as both the rule and the exception. It is that against which all other "camps" or states of exception are measured, so it is the rule; yet it is the premier example of the camp that surpasses all others and against which they pale in comparison, so it is also the exception. Agamben himself notes the difficulty of distinguishing between "example" and "exception" more generally;[136] taking his own analysis one step further, Auschwitz functions not simply as an exception, but also as a kind of exception*ism*. That is, Auschwitz is not merely a deviation from the rule insofar as it also confirms the rule, as Agamben has it in his analysis of the example and the exception. Auschwitz is also a deviation from the rule of sovereign biopolitics insofar as it confirms this rule to the utmost, more than any other example possibly could. It is both unlike any other camp that has ever existed and, in some sense, higher or better or more perfect than any other camp. That Auschwitz—or the Nazi death camps in general—has this status in Agamben is indisputable:

> The [Nazi] camp is merely the place in which the most absolute *conditio inhumana* that has ever existed on earth was realized: this is what counts in the last analysis, for the victims as for those who come after.[137]

> Insofar as its inhabitants were stripped of every political status and wholly reduced to bare life, the camp was also the most absolute biopolitical space ever to have been realized, in which power confronts nothing but pure life, without any mediation.[138]

> In the camps, city and house became indistinguishable, and the possibility of differentiating between our biological body and our political body—between what is incommunicable and mute and what is communicable and sayable—was taken from us forever.[139]

There is, in other words, a kind of privileging of Auschwitz going on in Agamben's account, a privileging that serves to reinforce not simply the horror of Auschwitz, but also its unique and supreme horror such that it not only confirms the logic of Western biopolitics, but also confirms it better than any other historical example or incident possibly could. Thus he calls Auschwitz "the decisive lesson of the century,"[140] and declares, "The phenomenon of Auschwitz is unique (certainly in the past, and we can only hope for the future)."[141]

Yet, as a multitude of Agamben's critics have made clear, for most of the people(s) of the globe, the supposedly exceptional character of sovereignty is rather the rule. As Yehouda Shenhav and Stephen Morton each make clear, not only were colonialism and imperialism the veritable staging grounds of European sovereign exceptionalism, but, from the perspective of the colonized, the exceptional character of European sovereignty is, in fact, the rule.[142] In Achille Mbembe's words, the colony itself is "a formation of terror."[143] Sunera Thobani observes, "Agamben's identification of Auschwitz as the exemplary site for the state of exception ignores the historical antecedents of the Nazi camp, namely, the Indian reservation in the settler societies as well as the residential schools that sought to 'Kill the Indian, Save the Child'; the slave plantation and the Bantustan; and the native quarters and medinas in the colony."[144] Meanwhile, Alexander Weheliye points out that slaves are never considered to be *homo sacer* (whether by Agamben or anyone else), nor is the Middle Passage ever considered to be a "camp" or "state of exception," because black bodies are never considered human enough to be recognized as systematically dehumanized (an observation confirmed by Arendt's "philosophical" reflections on embodiment and duplicated in Western political theory's consistent exclusion of its own crimes from its theorizations of modernity writ large).[145] It would seem as though Agamben might recognize or have anticipated such criticisms, given the oppositional posture he takes toward the biopolitical sovereignty he diagnoses. He even quotes Walter Benjamin, an important interlocutor for him, as saying as much: "The tradition of the oppressed teaches us that the 'state of exception' in which we live is the rule."[146] Yet Benjamin's referent here remains Agamben's referent thirty years later; as Benjamin continues, "We must attain to a conception of history that is in keeping with this insight. Then we shall clearly realize that it is our task to bring about a real state of emergency, and this will improve our own position in the struggle against Fascism." In other words, the "tradition of the oppressed" Agamben uses Benjamin to reference remains a European tradition, and the referent for the oppressed remains the Jewish victims of Nazism. The "amazement" Benjamin suggests is untenable is the amazement Agamben still seeks to quash in *Homo Sacer*, namely, "the amazement that what we are experiencing is 'still' possible in the twentieth century."

Effaced is the fact that such amazement is premised on the complete disregard of similar such crimes having taken place outside the boundaries of Europe, crimes that are considered serious, definitive, and epoch-making only when visited upon other, retroactively Europeanized populations.[147]

Regardless of whether one is amazed that concentration camps were possible in twentieth-century Europe or whether, like Agamben, one is philosophically certain that those camps represent the culmination of a centuries-long legacy of biopolitical exceptionalism, in either case the culminating referent for sovereign decisionism remains Nazism and the premiere referent for the camp is Auschwitz, the fulcrum upon which these historical and philosophical analyses pivot. *Homo Sacer*'s hard reckoning with the dysfunctions of Western politics is therefore less a soul-searching of the Western canon than it is a reiteration of it in a particular version of Eurocentrism that I call Holocaust Exceptionalism, the view that the Holocaust was the most enormous or most efficient or most monstrous (or some other adjectival superlative) genocide ever to have taken place, and that its occurrence is a dire warning for humanity and an unmistakable turning point in modern political history.[148] Related but distinct claims include the assertion that the Holocaust is the very meaning or content of evil (the moral version) or history's best and most incontrovertible example of that which is universally wrong (the philosophical version).[149] Holocaust Exceptionalism demotes other historical injustices as insignificantly horrible by comparison, particularly the injustices that have undergirded and fortified the very Western sovereignty Agamben documents and claims to critique, for example, colonization, chattel slavery, and indigenous genocide and dispossession.[150] It therefore explains Agamben's oversight of not only colonialism in general, but also Germany's use of concentration camps for eugenics purposes outside of Europe, in the colonies,[151] as well as the specifically Italian history of colonialism and its own use of concentration camps in what is now Libya.[152] Indeed, it may even explain his otherwise bafflingly ahistorical repurposing of *der Muselmann* as the epitome of biopolitical bareness. As Jarvis makes clear, however, the use of a variation of "Muslim" to denominate particular Auschwitz prisoners did not emerge ex nihilo in the Nazi concentration camps. Rather,

> the use of the epithet "muselman" at Auschwitz coincided with its simultaneous function as a juridical category of exception experimented with

by the French in Algeria since at least its 1848 departmentalization—when the constitution of the French Second Republic annexed Algeria to France, carved it into three departments, and drew a juridical distinction between "les citoyens français" (bearers of full citizenship rights) and "les sujets français" (subject to military conscription, forced labor, and a disciplinary system that included concentration camps) in order to facilitate redistribution and exploitation of Algeria's immensely profitable arable land. The 1865 "Sénatus-consulte sur l'état des personnes et la naturalisation en Algérie" further classified "subjets français" as either "indigènes israëlites" or "indigènes musulmans" until 1946. The word "musulman" was never a transparent religious or cultural description in Algérie française, and it is not identical with "muslim," although it operates as its translation. During World War II, "musulman" was a *French* legal term still used to classify which bodies the French imperial nation-state would protect and which it could dispose.[153]

In other words, the use of "Muslim" as a term of both exceptionalism and exceptional derogation dates to the nineteenth-century French colonization of Algeria. Thus Agamben's inflation of the term and its importance forecloses "institutionalized French state terror against North Africans,"[154] which is a predictable effect of Holocaust Exceptionalism and, as Jarvis points out, is "symptomatic of broader problems in literary scholarship of recent decades, particularly in studies of trauma, testimony, and memory oriented primarily if not exclusively by examples drawn from the Holocaust archive, and more generally in scholarship that holds May 1945 as a decisive rupture in the history of modern state violence."[155]

Agamben exceptionalizes not simply Auschwitz, it is worth pointing out, but also Jews and (the)[156] Jewish people. As he writes, "The Jew living under Nazism is the privileged negative referent of the new biopolitical sovereignty and is, as such, a flagrant case of a *homo sacer* in the sense of a life that may be killed but not sacrificed."[157] The insistence that European Jews of the 1940s are the "privileged negative referent" of *homo sacer* makes clear where Agamben's primary theoretical and political interests lie, and explains his otherwise inexplicable nonchalance regarding the racist connotations and usage of the term *Muslim* as a determination of Auschwitz prisoners.[158] The fact is, Agamben is not really interested in "Muslims" unless they are Jews, and he is not really interested in Jews unless they are the abjected victims of twentieth-century European genocidal violence. Indeed, the entire odd lot of characters Agamben summons to illustrate his conception of *homo sacer*—the overcomatose, VPs, foreign travelers held in detention zones in airports or hotels,[159] "certain outskirts of our cities,"[160] and, if we do not put a stop to the machinations of modernity, "the entire population of the Third World"[161]—is ultimately of interest and significance to Agamben only if and insofar as they are analogues or substitutes for the Jews of Germany and Eastern Europe in the 1940s. The standard for each member of this motley crew remains the resident of Auschwitz, just as the idealized blueprint for the state of exception remains the Nazi death camp.

This myopic fixation on the Holocaust not only obscures the civilizational commitments of contemporary US empire that deliberately target Muslims as backward, savage, perverse, and "terrorist." It also reinscribes those imperial commitments by singling out the Holocaust and Jewish people for special examination and ongoing exceptionalism. In only noticing "the Muslim" if and when "the Muslim" is a Jew, and in remarking on the existence of that "Muslim" as the emergence of a new biopolitical substance of inhumanity in Auschwitz, Agamben has it both ways: he establishes the humanity of Jewish people through a victimology that elevates them to the status of modernity's exemplary biopolitical targets, and reinscribes the racialized, civilizational inhumanity of Muslims, albeit without attending to the actual facts of Muslims' de facto dehumanized status in the twenty-first century. "Muslims" are important to Agamben, then, only insofar as they are Jews, and only insofar as they support the inevitable and already-agreed-upon presupposition that the Jews are history's quintessential victims—and not, in fact, complicit, in ideological and state forms, with today's aggressors in a civilizational War on Terror. Agamben's commitment to the exceptional singularity of the Holocaust—as historical event, as biopolitical experiment, as ethical break—renders him oblivious to the racial and imperial politics of his own analysis, which invites the hackneyed justificatory narrative of Israel's creation—as the only and necessary refuge of a ceaselessly persecuted people—and effaces the horror of the catastrophes of history otherwise known as colonization, conquest, and chattel slavery, reifying Jewish people as history's perennial victims and exceptional sufferers and establishing Muslims as their new existential threat.[162] It is not a far step from here to see Agamben's affinity with the anti-Semitism of Zionists who can leave room for Jews and Jewish people only insofar as they remain committed to a nationalist project in Palestine in the guise of righteous victimhood.

In sum, although Agamben adopts Arendt's reading of the human condition for his understanding of bare life, unlike her he does not repudiate or condemn it. Rather, he rejects the sovereignty that, in his view, constitutes the bare life that is so abjected in modernity. In this he is slightly more progressive, acknowledging at least the possibility of transformation of modern biopolitics and an escape from the exceptional decisionism that constitutes bare life. But, through his strange valorization of a hypostasized 1940s European Jewry as the Nazis' exemplary victims and the Holocaust as paradigmatic biopolitical oppression, Agamben reproduces Arendt's tiered and necessarily hierarchical valuation of some life over others. Ironically, his Holocaust Exceptionalism produces the Jews as history's unique and most privileged victims, thereby obscuring the contemporary contours of imperial biopolitics that singles out not Jews but rather Muslims for targeting, surveillance, transfer, and death, an imperial biopolitics waged specifically and purposively by Israel alongside the United States in the ostensible name of freedom, democracy, and civilization.

Regardless of whether one condemns or celebrates bare life, then, this particular hierarchical determination of biopolitics commits one to the valuation of some lives over others, or some types of life over other types, because this hierarchical valuation is premised on a rejection of "bare life" or the body that inextricably overlaps with familiar, entrenched hierarchies of race, class, gender, and "civilization" that define canonical "Western" political thought. I think Agamben is right to suggest that sovereignty is a biopolitical regime, and I think he is also right that it is a biopolitical regime that we must ultimately reject and seek to overcome. However, relying on an Arendtian biopolitical analysis of the human condition will not allow for that rejection, since her analysis weds us to an apolitical understanding of life that requires the repudiation and denigration of its very existence and strands us in the mire of perpetual, "natural" enslavement. If we are to reject biopolitical sovereignty and the empire perpetuated in its name, the logic of bare life vs. proper life must be abandoned entirely, not to mention the Holocaust Exceptionalism that centers Jewish oppression in order to obfuscate the colonial violence that founded the settler and imperial states today perpetrating the War on Terror. Opposing US empire means grappling more carefully with the biopolitical sovereignty of which it consists, while simultaneously refusing the hierarchies and moralisms that attend any invocation of life "itself." It is to this task that I turn in the next chapter.

2

THE BIOPOLITICS OF SETTLEMENT

Temporality, Desire, and Civilization

Politics is a name for the temporalization of desire, for its translation into a narrative, for its teleological determination.

—Lee Edelman[1]

To have no desire is to be dead.

—Thomas Hobbes[2]

Even in its consolidation, the United States is haunted by the specters of its origins.

—Jodi Byrd[3]

In the grammar of Islamophobia, the future is tense.

—Moustafa Bayoumi[4]

N ative studies scholars and anticolonial critics alike have argued that contemporary US imperial formations remain bound to the European incursions in North America and the violences of genocide, dispossession, warfare, disease, transfer, and forced removal that characterized the emergence and establishment of the US nation-state. These scholars suggest that the study of contemporary empire must not only acknowledge the fact of this connection, but actively seek to excavate the historical, political, and cultural continuities between them in order to clarify the character of what Derek Gregory has called "the colonial present."[5] As Jodi Byrd explains, US empire was begun with "the birth of the

United States" and "its assumption of European colonialist agendas that sought to appropriate indigenous lands, knowledges, presences, and identities for its own use."[6] Perry Anderson points out that this is uniquely characteristic of the United States, whose "originating coordinates of empire were coeval with the nation."[7] As Moon-Kie Jung argues, the United States should be reconceived not as a nation-state but rather as an "empire-state," since "for the United States, the political community to which the state has been coupled has never been the nation," but rather hierarchically differentiated populations and unequal sovereignties. Specifically, when viewed from "the vantage point of the Native peoples of North America," it is clear that "the birth of the United States as a state was at once the birth of the United States as an empire-state."[8] Reading biopolitical sovereignty in and for the twenty-first century, then, requires taking into account not simply its imperial manifestations, which I have argued Agamben neglects, but also its colonial origins. Failing to do so risks producing an anti-imperial political analysis that covers over, colludes with, or consolidates settler colonialism.[9]

In this chapter, I offer an account of biopolitical sovereignty that avoids Arendt's and Agamben's hierarchical disaggregation and prioritization of (some forms of) life (over others) that also responds to this call from native studies scholars and anticolonial critics. However, I do so from within the terms of a different field altogether—that of queer theory—and from what I call a critical Nietzschean perspective. Using queer theory to interpret European sovereignty—in particular, using the work of Lee Edelman to reread that classic thinker of sovereignty, Thomas Hobbes—makes clear that sovereignty is biopolitical not because of an exceptionalist understanding of life, as Agamben has it, but rather because sovereignty is what constitutes life *as* life to begin with. In other words, life is not a "bare" biological phenomenon that is only subsequently and inappropriately politicized. Rather, it is political through and through, an ideological determination constituted via the apparatus of sovereignty. Further, life is constituted "in itself" as overloaded with civilizational value. A privileged object of value and rationality, "life" in sovereign biopolitics is what is impossible to refuse without being constituted as backward, irrational, unthinkable, and abominable. Thus this production of "life itself" entails the simultaneous production of "death," a wholesale negation of "life itself" that is figured as simultaneously hostile and absurd.

This reading of biopolitics is both an elaboration and a revision of Foucault's formulation of racism in *"Society Must Be Defended."*[10] As is well known, in this text Foucault argues that modern biopower, which nurtures (the) life (of some) while leaving others to die, can only become actively murderous when it becomes racist. So, for example, while massacres, wars, genocides, drone strikes, and targeted assassinations may appear to contradict the biopolitical project of fostering life, racism resolves this paradox by inserting a biological breach in the population: "What in fact is racism? It is primarily a way of introducing a break into the domain of life that is under power's control: the break between what must live and what must die."[11] Foucault argues that state racism "makes it possible to establish a relationship between my life and the death of the other that is not a military or warlike relationship of confrontation, but a biological type relationship."[12] Thus:

> the enemies who have to be done away with are not adversaries in the political sense of the term; they are threats, either external or internal, to the population and for the population. In the biopower system, in other words, killing or the imperative to kill is acceptable only if it results not in a victory over political adversaries, but in the elimination of the biological threat to and the improvement of the species or race. There is a direct connection between the two. In a normalizing society, race or racism is the precondition that makes killing acceptable.[13]

However, following Mark Rifkin's insight that a Foucauldian understanding of racism and biopolitics obscures and potentially naturalizes the settler state,[14] as well as a host of scholars who have noted Foucault's oversight of the history of European colonization in his excavations of modern power,[15] I want to resituate Foucauldian biopolitics more fully within this history in a way that does not occlude the fact of settlement. While Foucault suggests that the biological breach between what must live and what must die is the biopolitical operation of (specifically state) *racism* (his main referent for which is the Nazi genocide, the hazards of which I detailed in the previous chapter), I want to suggest instead that this biopolitical operation is the specifically *settler colonial* function of *sovereignty*, which produces the native as "savage" simultaneously as it brings the settler into being as "civilized." The assertion of a "caesura," in other words, is the operation of not racism but, rather, settler sovereignty. As I will elaborate later, sovereignty can institute the category and value of "life" only in and through the simultaneous positing of the deathly threat to that life, which must be ceaselessly warded off, repudiated, and destroyed. It is this establishment of "civilization," in other words, that brings into being the vile and absurd threat of "savagery," otherwise known as the existence and endurance of indigenous people(s). As Kevin Bruyneel notes, "Only after centuries of European-based conquest, colonization, and settlement in North America did terms like *Indian* or *indigenous* gain any meaning at all by setting the collective identity of people such as the Cherokee, Pequot, Mohawk, Chippewa, and hundreds of other tribes and nations into contrast with the emerging Eurocentric settler societies. . . . The words *Indian* and *American Indian*, like *Native American*, *aboriginal*, and *indigenous*, emerged as a product of a co-constitutive relationship with terms such as *colonizers, settler*, and *American*."[16]

This interpretation breaks with Foucault's thesis that biopolitics more or less surpasses older, sovereign configurations of power.[17] Moreover, it attends to the suggestion of many native studies scholars that closer attention be paid to the differences between racism and (settler) colonization.[18] Finally, using Edelman to elucidate Hobbes offers its own, specifically *queer* contribution to the literature on biopolitics and biopolitical theory. Reading Hobbes from a queer theory perspective foregrounds an oft-unremarked feature of *Leviathan*, namely, the life it champions is fundamentally a phenomenon of *desire*, not biology and its proper or improper politicization. Although Edelman relies upon Lacan to theorize desire, Hobbes is rarely given credit for having his own psychological theory, one that is by no means a depth psychology and obviously well predates the emergence of psychoanalysis. Nevertheless, when Hobbes defines the motion that is life as fundamentally a matter of desire, he thereby anchors sovereignty in desire, since sovereignty exists in his schema solely to secure the motion that is life.

Turning our attention from biology to desire, however, is not simply an innovation in biopolitical theory. It also allows the ideological and specifically *moralizing* elements of biopolitics and settler sovereignty to come into view. Unlike Nietzsche, who sees morality as the vengeful accomplishment of weak people who resentfully deploy it as and through punishment, Edelman instead argues that the moralization of life becomes possible via the transformation of human existence into a narrative of desire and its (dis)satisfaction. In my Nietzschean appropriation of Edelman and application of his work to biopolitical settler sovereignty, this means that the moralization of biopolitics and its civilizational investments are enabled by a particular story about desire that subjects human life to a futurist temporality, a logic that I will argue is a fundamentally settler colonial logic. What this chapter will show, then, is that at the heart of European sovereign biopolitics is an oppressive, heteronormative ordering of time that queers all those before, beyond, or outside its civilized progress narrative as specters of death, "savage" and immoral others who become valid targets of necropolitical elimination, and precisely in the sanctimonious name of preserving "life itself" and upholding its value.[19] Necropolitics is therefore not somehow at odds with the biopolitical order such that it requires racism to explain it, as Foucault argues. Rather, necropolitics is the very operation of biopolitics that establishes life, the value of life, and those whose lives are valuable (that is, "civilization"), through the vehicle of settler sovereignty and simultaneously *through* its demarcation of death, the nihilism and meaninglessness of death, and those whose lives amount to a deathly threat to all meaning and value (that is, "savagery").

This intervention suggests productive collaborations among settler colonial studies, critical indigenous studies, canonical political theory, and queer theory. Indeed, a motivation of this chapter is to show that these different fields of inquiry can together provide a robust and critical picture of the biopolitical machinations of settler colonial sovereignty. As I hope to show in chapter 5, this reading also elucidates the contemporary hypermoralization of the "value of life" in contemporary War on Terror discourse. If, as John Collins suggests, the global War on Terror is an outgrowth of the deep structures of colonialism that founded settler states,[20] then there is much to be gleaned from returning to their theoretical origins and interrogating them from a broader perspective that can account not simply for their historical injustices, but also for their foundational understanding of desire and its futurist narrativization that constitutes, on the one hand, "civilized" subjects of life and, on the other, irrational, immoral, queer(ed) "savages" who both represent and portend death to those civilized beings and their civilization itself.

THE FUTURE IS MODERN

In *No Future: Queer Theory and the Death Drive*, Lee Edelman argues that temporality itself is heteronormative, unfolding a linear, teleological progress narrative that demands self-sacrificial anticipation of an ideologically rosy future that, by definition, never arrives.[21] That future, symbolized by an iconographic Child, is innocent, infinitely valuable, and vested with redemptive potential. The future as Child is a future that never ends, a future that never grows up, a future in which life and survival—if not ours alone, then ours in the guise of the species and its future generations—will be preserved to infinity. The impossibility of such an achievement, of course, is by both definition and design. Yet futurism obscures this impossibility and secures its own smooth functioning, Edelman argues, via the production of queerness. "Queer" designates all those who reject the future or stand in the way of reproduction or refuse to compromise their present aims or defer gratification. Queerness, in short, is a threat to survival. Edelman argues that queers instantiate a "death drive" within the social, a nihilistic and perverse harbinger of the disintegration of all meaning and cohesion that haunt any, only ever tenuous, stable human formation. At the political level, he recommends an embrace of this death drive as *the* act of resistance. That such an embrace entails the destruction of the social as such in its annihilation of futurism is no objection in his view, since putting a stop to the futurist narrativization of desire will also bring an end to the sociopolitical machinations by which queerness is produced precisely *as* death, nihilism, and the destruction of sociality as such. A defense of queerness, Edelman's argument is also an embrace of death.

Setting aside both the Lacanian framework that grounds this analysis as well as the commonly received version of *No Future*, wherein reproductive futurism relegates homosexuals to the domain of the childless and perverse, I want to suggest instead that *No Future* be read as articulating the *ideology of survival* that underpins settler colonial civilizationalism. Rather than a psychoanalytic theory of white, bourgeois heteronormativity, I read *No Future* as a biopolitics of modern sovereignty that, when put into conversation with Thomas Hobbes (as I will do in the following sections), makes clear the specifically *settler* character of that sovereignty and the temporal logic of desire that explains settler colonies' transformation into expansionist security states. Challenging Edelman's presentation of both "futurism" and "politics" as unmarked, universal entities and situating them instead within the colonial history of European political thought make clear that the temporality he analyzes originates in a colonial project that is distinctively modern and vested with specifically settler anxieties about its own existence and future, anxieties that explain its transformation into securitized imperial expansionism.[22]

Crucial to this rereading of Edelman's work is distinguishing between what he calls "reproductive futurism" and what I see as the more general logic of futurism as such. While much attention has been paid to the reproductive futurism that dooms homosexuals and feminists to instantiating society's death drive in this text (although his mention of feminists is often overlooked), Edelman's theory of politics and the more generic logic of futurism he outlines have to date been underrecognized.[23] Yet *No Future* certainly offers a political theory insofar as it claims to delineate "the logic within which the political itself must be thought."[24] That logic is futurism, of which I suggest that *reproductive* futurism be understood merely as one particular type. Put simply, *futurism* synopsizes the "presupposition that the body politic must survive,"[25] the putatively apolitical article of faith in the necessary continuity of politics as such. *Reproductive futurism* is characterized more specifically by "a set of values widely thought of as extrapolitical: values that center on the family, to be sure, but that focus on the protection of children."[26] Futurism's hallmark telos is survival, while that of reproductive futurism is, as its name suggests, reproduction; hence its specific iconographic signifier, the Child. However, the Child is only one possible version of the future's symbolization; this iconography can take any number of forms insofar as the future itself can take any number of forms. Regardless, whether discussing the survival of the body politic in general (that is, futurism) or the future as characterized specifically by the Child (that is, reproductive futurism), Edelman importantly argues that their presuppositions are taken to be apolitical, which is precisely what makes them "so oppressively political."[27] For in either case, whether it is survival or children, the future is what cannot be opposed if political meaning and intelligibility are to be possible. To participate in politics at all, even in protest or dissent, means to "submit to the framing of political debate—and, indeed, of the political field—as defined by the terms of . . . reproductive futurism: terms that impose an ideological limit on political discourse as such."[28] The question of the future, in other words, is beyond debate, beyond any pro or con; the issue of futurity is wholly one-sided and definitely prolife (as Edelman puts it, futurism is the "party line" that "every party endorses").[29] Regardless of the form it takes, then—whether it is survival in general or children in particular—demarcations of the future circumscribe the contours of the political itself and determine what can and cannot be spoken there, what can and cannot be "reasonably" upheld or advocated as politically viable. It is the absolute limit of intelligibility, sociality, community, and belonging, and this whether we are discussing a politics of the Right or the Left.

Edelman's bold assertion that *"every political vision is a vision of futurity,"*[30] however, requires some qualification if it is to be fully appropriable for critical biopolitical theory. Suspicious reader John Brenkman helpfully provides the political theory references missing from *No Future*, noting that "modern critical social discourse, whether among the Enlightenment's *philosophes*, French revolutionaries, Marxists, social democrats, or contemporary socialists and democrats," engages in the kind of future-wagering Edelman describes as definitively political.[31] What goes unremarked in Brenkman's otherwise apt observation is its historical and geographical qualifications. That is, futurism is a decisively *modern* and *European* phenomenon that must be tethered to, among other things, colonization of the so-called New World, the rise of the nation-state, and the advent of capitalism. Futurism is less an ahistorical or universalized psychoanalytic theory of the subject and its (de)formation than it is a fundamental baseline of modern culture and the workings of modern, necessarily European and Eurocentric politics. Although, in *No Future*, Edelman appears to dismiss the necessity of historicizing his work,[32] he nevertheless seems to do so himself in another essay, "Against Survival," which clarifies and elaborates the argument of *No Future*. There he discusses something he calls "modernity's ideology of cultural survival,"[33] which sounds rather like the general logic of futurism I am interested in. In addition, in his contribution to a panel discussion of the antisocial thesis, he suggests that *No Future* "approaches negativity as society's constitutive antagonism, which sustains itself only on the promise of resolution in futurity's time to come, much as capitalism is able to sustain itself only by finding and exploiting new markets."[34] The analogizing of futurism to capitalism certainly suggests its status as a signal determinant of that historical and cultural formation known as "modernity." Moreover, although Edelman does not offer *No Future* as a reading of either modernity or biopolitics, he does make clear that its argument unfolds on at least two levels, only one of which is the seemingly more "straightforward" level of hetero-repronormativity and queered homosexuality. As he writes, in response to a question regarding what might come "after" queer theory,

> This compulsion to produce the "after" of sex through the naturalization of history expresses itself in two very different, though not unrelated, ways: first, in the privileging of reproduction as the after-event of sex—an after-event whose potential, implicit in the ideal, if not always in the reality, of heterogenital coupling, imbues straight sex with its meaning as the agent of historical continuity; second, in the conflation of meaning itself with those forms of historical knowing whose authority depends on the fetishistic prestige of origin, genealogy, telos. In each case the entry into history coincides with the entry into social narratives that work to domesticate the incoherence, at once affective and conceptual, that's designated by "sex."[35]

Here Edelman seems to suggest that reproductive futurism—and the Child and *sinthom*osexual who are its starring antagonists—is both analogous with and simultaneously a specification of a broader phenomenon called "meaning itself," which only becomes possible through a naturalized, progressive, narrative construal of history that "sex," now in quotation marks, troubles, because it is "the site of drives not predetermined by any fixed goal or end" and, therefore, the site "where the subject of social regulation might come undone and with it the seeming consistency of the social order itself."[36] This is the version of futurism I'm interested in appropriating. My contention is that this form of futurism unqualified is the generalized temporalization of desire that resolves the broader question of "meaning itself," and that this futurism is a specifically modern, European phenomenon. Indeed, in this same article, Edelman presents the Child as interchangeable with both "the absolutism of identity" and "the fixity of what is,"[37] making clear both the social/symbolic overlap of futurism with reproductive futurism and the nonnecessity of their coincidence or identification.[38]

If futurism can be read as the temporal logic of modern, European, and Eurocentric politics and political theory, then both the "queer" and the

"Child" of Edelman's model of reproductive futurism are placeholders as much as specifically defined references to, on the one hand, actual queer people and, on the other, "historical children."[39] *No Future* has garnered criticism for seeming anachronistically to overstate the threat of homosexuality to sociality; for example, Tavia Nyong'o has suggested that Edelman's reading of homophobia and heteronormativity is nostalgic for a political moment already past, when homosexuality really did pose an ominous and spectral threat to the social order.[40] However, when Edelman talks about "queers," he does not necessarily mean LGBTQ people; rather, he means "all [those] so stigmatized for failing to comply with heteronormative mandates."[41] He actually is quite clear about this, saying that there is "nothing intrinsic to the constitution of those identifying as lesbian, gay, bisexual, transgendered, transsexual, or queer" that "predisposes them to resist the appeal of futurity, to refuse the temptation to reproduce, or to place themselves outside or against the acculturating logic of the Symbolic."[42] Instead, Edelman argues, queerness "figures . . . the place of the social order's death drive."[43] Queerness is the *structural position*[44] endlessly generated by the futurist logic that is politics:

> Queerness could never constitute an authentic or substantive identity, but only a structural position determined by the imperative of figuration; for the gap, the noncoincidence, that the order of the signifier installs both informs and inhabits queerness as it inhabits reproductive futurism. But it does so with a difference. Where futurism always anticipates, in the image of an Imaginary past, a realization of meaning that will suture identity by closing that gap, queerness undoes the identities through which we experience ourselves as subjects, insisting on the Real of a jouissance that social reality and the futurism on which it relies have already foreclosed.[45]

In this account, the queer is the necessary counterpart to the Child and what most threatens it. This is both a descriptive claim ("The sacralization of the Child . . . necessitates the sacrifice of the queer")[46] and a normative one, for Edelman insists that "queerness *should* and *must* redefine such notions as 'civil order' through a rupturing of our foundational faith in the reproduction of futurity."[47] I will return to the normative component of this argument in chapters 4 and 5. For now, what's important to take away from this discussion is that queers are *structurally* opposed to the social order insofar as they refuse futurity's seduction and prevent its realization: "the queer dispossesses the social order of the ground on which it rests: a faith in the consistent reality of the social—and by extension, of the social subject; a faith that politics, whether of the left or of the right, implicitly affirms."[48] What's also clear is that, while the queer as homosexual and the Child as historical child may be concrete, daily exemplars of certain ubiquitous (if by no means exclusive) forms of white bourgeois heteronormativity, understood as a specific version of a more generalized futurist logic, the Child cannot simply be equated with reproduction, child-bearing, and child-rearing, just as the queer cannot simply be equated with the homosexual in Edelman's temporal sense. The queer and the Child, while having specific material referents in Edelman's particular reading of *reproductive* futurism, also hold structural places in the larger logic of *generic* futurism, and thus render this queer theory a political theory of modernity by which we can read the futurism of sovereign biopolitics. As will become clear in this chapter, the future of European biopolitical sovereignty is encapsulated by the notion of "civilization," while the figure of the queer is the "savage."

THE FUTURE IS BIOPOLITICAL

Using Hobbes to illustrate generic futurism makes clear that futurism is specifically a *biopolitics* since, in Hobbes, sovereign is he who makes life. This is not an Agambian biopolitics that declares, following Schmitt, that "Sovereign is he who decides on the exception."[49] On the contrary, in Hobbes, sovereign is he who produces life itself, both its existence and its content, and not its exceptionality from properly political life. Seeking a solution for (civil) war, in *Leviathan* Hobbes looks for a mechanism by which life—if not (only) of the individual, then at least of the commonwealth that unites all subjects into one enormous individual (as illustrated by the book's famous frontispiece)—may be preserved forever, an obviously futurist endeavor. More radically, however, Hobbes also suggests that the sovereign constitutes life *as* life to begin with, and that he does so by bringing the future into existence. Explaining and substantiating such an interpretation will require me to (re)turn to the already well-trodden ground of that all-too-familiar, foundational—some might even say primal—scene of modern political theory, the state of nature. More than simply a theoretical or interpretive exercise, however, such an examination sheds light on the very real settler contours of biopolitical sovereignty (and their consequent, material impact). Indeed, Robert Nichols has made clear that the state of nature narrative was crucial to the portrayal of indigenous peoples as "savage" and backward and therefore to their retroactive erasure and European denial of their claims to land and sovereignty. Such portrayals were effectively materialized, for example, in eighteenth- and nineteenth-century US Indian policy.[50] Such stories are by no means harmless, then, or mere philosophical devices, or inessential to the material workings of violence. They are part and parcel of conquest.

In that storied state of nature, then, which Hobbes defines as a situation where there is no security, no "power able to over-awe them all,"[51] there is, in Edelman's terms, *no future*. This is true in the most basic sense. As Hobbes observes, in the state of nature "there is no place for Industry; because the fruit thereof is uncertain: and consequently no Culture of the Earth."[52] Without any assurance that what we make will see the light of day, much less remain ours long enough to be used or consumed by us, there is clearly no incentive to produce anything. Nor does agriculture make any sense, requiring as it does a long-term investment of time and labor in tracts of land that themselves must be constantly guarded when not being cultivated. All this is seemingly self-evident, following as it does from Hobbes's assertion that the state of nature lacks any guarantee of security.

Yet the situation is in fact more dire than this, and Hobbes's argument more radical. While it is true that there is no agriculture, manufacture, or "commodious Building" in the state of nature (since large-scale social cooperation is impossible), Hobbes also relates the more complicated cultural and existential deprivations human beings face there, including "no Knowledge of the face of the Earth; no account of Time; no Arts; no Letters; no Society."[53] Perhaps unwittingly revealing his class background, Hobbes acknowledges the impossibility of cultural formations like art, literature, and geography—"society" in its bourgeois sense—in the state of nature. And yet, it is not simply the case that there is no Rembrandt in the state of nature; rather, there is no *imagery*. It is not simply that there are no maps in the state of nature; rather, there is no *representation*. It is not simply that there is no Shakespeare or Molière or Cervantes in the state of nature; rather, there is no *written word*. Put otherwise, it is not simply that material goods cannot exist where there is no sovereign because both the process and the product of labor are endangered. More primarily, the kinds of cognitive, affective, and symbolic processes upon which these rely are impossible. By guaranteeing security, the sovereign not only protects the production process by which a map is made and secures the physical map itself from theft or destruction. He also makes possible the conditions necessary for the activity of representation itself, which allows for the possibility of maps or paintings or literature in the first place. In short, without a sovereign, representational or imaginary activity is impossible.

Similarly, then, Hobbes acknowledges that there is no "accounting of Time" in the state of nature. The argument here, I think, is the same. It is not simply that there are no clocks or calendars in the state of nature (although there surely are none) but more primarily that, in the state of nature, human beings have no way of measuring or marking for themselves the passage of time. In Edelman's terms, they are unable to transform *time* into *temporality*. To produce a calendar, for instance, requires that one has observed a pattern of events with sufficient regularity such that they can be graphically mapped or represented and projected into the future. Similarly, to make a watch (Hobbes's specific example of inorganic life in the introduction and a significant fetish in this context), one has to have a sense of the passage of time—a notion of past, present, and (anticipated) future. According to Hobbes, without a sovereign, we not only lack machines or devices by which to measure time, but we are unable to make time comprehensible to ourselves, unable to render it into temporality or understand it as a feature of lived human existence. Of course, this makes sense given Hobbes's account of the state of nature as the lack of all security. When one is engaged in an unending struggle to secure one's present existence, not only is the future unimaginable (because so tenuous), but the past becomes effectively irrelevant. One's entire attention is devoted to securing the endurance of *now*, which is the only reality one is capable of knowing. However, this means that, in Hobbes's account, time is not a natural feature of human existence. Like art, literature, geography, and sociality, temporality is one political construct among many. Inhabitants of the state of nature abide in an enduring present that they are unaware of *as* an enduring present.[54]

Surprisingly, then, time is critical for Hobbes's understanding of war. Just before the paragraph from which I have been quoting, Hobbes offers a description—he does not call it a definition—of war and how it is to be recognized. Time is crucial to it:

> Hereby it is manifest, that during the time men live without a common Power to keep them all in awe, they are in that condition which is called Warre; and such a warre, as is of every man, against every man. For WARRE, consisteth not in Battell onely, or the act of fighting; but in a tract of time, wherein the will to contend by Battell is sufficiently known: and therefore the notion of *Time*, is to be considered in the nature of Warre; as it is in the nature of Weather. For as the nature of Foule weather, lyeth not in a showre or two of rain; but in an inclination thereto of many dayes together: So the nature of War, consisteth not in actuall fighting; but in the known disposition thereto, during all the time there is no assurance to the contrary. All other time is PEACE.[55]

Both poetic and apt, the analogy of war to bad weather captures the projective uncertainty that defines life in the state of nature and renders an "accounting of Time" there impossible. For of course it is impossible to determine with certainty the "inclination" of either another person or the weather. Just as cloudy weather does not necessarily forecast rain, so too do hostile neighbors not necessarily portend one's imminent, violent demise.[56] It is only when there is no guarantee otherwise that such conditions can amount to bad weather or war, respectively. Effectively, Hobbes is saying, unless the sun is incontestably shining, the weather is bad. Unless there is an indisputable reign of an all-powerful sovereign authority, there is war.[57]

This is a curious claim for Hobbes to make, however, given that he then goes on to assert that there is no accounting of time in the state of nature. War may, indeed, consist of a "tract of time," as he says, but there is no way such a tract could be parceled out, determined, or recognized by anyone actually inhabiting the state of nature, since this would require an ability to distinguish between before, now, and after. I think the resolution of this seeming contradiction lies in recognizing that Hobbes's assertion that war is constituted by a "tract of time" holds true only *after* war has come to a close. It is an observation possible only from a subsequent perspective of security and peace, a position wherein one has the comfort and leisure to reflect upon prior experiences and characterize them as being in relationship with other moments in time. Put differently, Hobbes's claims about the state of nature and what happens there are anachronistic. They are statements about *time* from the perspective of *temporality*.

Therefore, while the sovereign is crucial to bringing war to an end, what Hobbes's discussion of war makes clear is that the sovereign brings it to an end via the creation of *temporality*. Oddly enough, the sovereign guarantees our physical survival by instituting the passage of time—specifically, by securing (the possibility of) a future.[58] A significant consequence of this reading is that the sovereign effectively constitutes the very meaning and content of life itself. For, considered temporally, there is a way in which there is no distinction between life and death in the state of nature, insofar as there is no way to tell present from future. The state of nature's enduring present entails that "life" there is a kind of limbo-like existence, a suspension of living or perpetual near-death experience wherein we can never be certain of anything—even the one thing Hobbes deems a certainty in this text, self-preservation. Even more of a political theology than Schmitt imagined, Hobbes's sovereign is effectively the speaker of the sentence "Let there be life." This is perhaps why it is so important to institute the commonwealth in the first place—not simply to preserve life, as Hobbes explicitly suggests, but, more primarily, to definitively demarcate life *as* life in the first place and differentiate it from death. Sovereignty, in short, is *the* definitive biopolitical regime, not insofar as it facilitates the proper life of some by abandoning others to an exceptionalized or "bare" life, as Agamben suggests, but rather because it *constitutes* and *determines* life as such, thereby distinguishing it from what becomes only subsequently recognizable as death.

Using *No Future* to read sovereign biopolitics also has the added virtue of foregrounding the role of desire in this schema. For, by inaugurating temporality, the sovereign does more than simply guard our physical bodies; he also constitutes us as subjects. In his introduction to *Leviathan*, Hobbes defines life as "but a motion of limbs, the beginning whereof is in some principall part within."[59] It is on the basis of this admittedly spare definition that he argues that watches and engines are also alive, since "life" consists of no more or less than internally initiated motion. Yet, later on in the text, Hobbes offers much more than simply a physics of human motion, presenting an elaborate psychology in chapter 6 describing the internally initiated motion of human beings specifically in terms of affect and desire. However "thin" this psychology may be, it is not on the table at all with regard to watches and engines, suggesting that human "life" consists of something more or other than purely physical motion and thus that the problem of security cannot be solved within the physical domain alone. Security is also established via temporality, and its existence is performing more than simply a physical function. Indeed, the very fact that a future is necessary for survival at all suggests that "life" is more or other than a barely physiological category.

The importance of psychology to life and security is clear in Hobbes's account of the state of nature, which is characterized not simply by the ever-present threat of physical death, but also by a lack of hope, and thus the ever-present threat of an emotional stasis that, in the motionlessness it portends, effectively amounts to death in the Hobbesian scheme. Physically, of course, and as is well known, life in Hobbes's state of nature is a kind of unceasing, mortal iteration of King of the Hill. He describes the rise of warfare in it this way:

> If any two men desire the same thing, which nevertthelesse they cannot both enjoy, they become enemies; and in the way to their End, (which is principally their owne conservation, and sometimes their delectation only,) endeavour to destroy, or subdue one an other. And from hence it comes to passe, that where an Invader hath no more to feare, than an other mans single power; if one plant, sow, build, or possesse a convenient Seat, others may probably be expected to come prepared with forces united, to dispossesse, and deprive him, not only of the fruit of his labor, but also of his life, or liberty. And the Invader again is in the like danger of another.[60]

Humans' natural equality leads to competition, and the lack of security makes every other person a potential threat to one's own existence. Even if one did manage to secure some precious morsel—food, say, or a (relatively) safe resting spot—by triumphing over the "single power" of a competitor, one has to fear yet another "Invader" who might arrive on the scene, perhaps in alliance with others, to dispossess him and potentially also enslave or kill him. (As Hobbes notes near the end of the chapter, there is no property in the state of nature, "no *Mine* and *Thine* distinct";[61] rather, something is yours only if you can get it, and only for as long as you can hang onto it.) Victory in a single battle, then, is insufficient to secure oneself, for one will simply face bigger, more powerful enemies down the road. And this is as true for the succeeding "Invader" as it was for the initial victor— both face exactly the same dilemma.

Considered psychically, however, it turns out that life in the Hobbesian state of nature is similarly difficult to endure. Human relations there are governed by what he calls "diffidence of one another."[62] Diffidence is importantly different from fear, the emotion most often associated with Hobbes and his state of nature. But Hobbes does not actually claim either fear in general or fear of death in particular as a cause of war, nor does he claim that either characterizes the development of war in the state of nature. Rather, he says that death is the worst "inconvenience" of the state of nature and actually names fear as one of the three passions (along with desire and hope) that incline men to *peace*.[63] Hobbes instead blames war on diffidence, which is a subset or amplification of despair—he defines it as "Constant *Despayre*."[64] Both fear and despair require "opinion"—they are feelings coupled with beliefs about either our own capacity or the capacity of the object, and these beliefs are crucial to the affective experience. But diffidence emphasizes not the power of the object, as fear does, but rather the powerlessness of the subject.[65] Unlike the fear of death, which anticipates threat from outside, diffidence is a potentially immobilizing angst about the inadequacy of our own power. Moreover, Hobbes's qualification of diffidence as *constant* despair suggests that regular or typical despair is time-limited, a feeling that at some point comes to an end. Diffidence is thus the *enduring* belief that one is unable to get what one wants. The constant waiting, wanting, and seeking that is life in the state of nature, then, coupled with the prospect of a never-ending train of ever-stronger and more powerful invaders, causes one to succumb to uninterrupted hopelessness about the prospect of attaining anything at all. And while the experience of diffidence may not seem equivalent to the experience of death, the motionlessness it portends suggests that it is not simply physical violence that threatens death in the state of nature, but also psychological dis-ease.

To escape the insecurity and diffidence of the state of nature, one must not simply confront and topple competitors for desired objects like food or shelter. Momentary triumph in a game of King of the Hill is only that—momentary. Rather, one must actively seek to expand one's sphere of influence to include ever-greater reaches of power to the extent that one is dominating as many other people as possible—not just King of the Hill, but King of the Playground, the entire school, block, neighborhood, and so on. Hobbes writes, "And from this diffidence of one another, there is no way for any man to secure himself, so reasonable, as Anticipation; that is, by force, or wiles, to master the persons of all men he can, so long, till he see no other power great enough to endanger him: And this is no more than his own conservation requireth, and is generally allowed."[66] This preemptive prerogative to dominate is also the legitimacy of the sovereign power Hobbes articulates in *Leviathan*, for this is its exact function. By extending his sphere of influence over an entire body of people, the sovereign becomes perpetual King of the Hill, instituting a future for all by ensuring their defense and survival. No longer a temporary triumph, the sovereign brings the enduring present of the state of nature to a conclusion, putting an end to people's diffidence, alleviating their constant despair of their own power, and securing the indefinite future of sovereignty. The emergence of the commonwealth is indeed the emergence of temporality, then, and in simultaneously physical and psychological terms. The commonwealth allows one not simply to desire, but to believe it likely that you will attain the objects of your desire. It is the solution to competition and the deescalation of diffidence, an alleviation of the psychic anguish that is, in Hobbes's telling, inseparable from physical insecurity.

All this means that "life itself" in Hobbes exceeds mere biological subsistence. Life *as* life is not defined by a biopolitical substratum of minimal existence, akin to the neomort, the overcomatose, or the resident of a concentration camp. Rather, life is internally initiated motion, preservation of which requires the removal of obstacles that are simultaneously physical (that is, violence) and psychic (that is, despair) at once. The futurelessness of the state of nature means not simply that one will die, likely soon, likely at the hands of another. It also means that one can have no other aspiration for oneself other than death, likely soon, at the hands of another. The preservation of life therefore requires not just physical survival, but also some measure of peace of mind and a sense of our own perseverance into the future. Physical existence without hope is just as motionless as a hopeful if blocked or incapacitated body; close reading of Hobbes makes clear that one needs both in order to be alive in his schema. In this he underscores an Edelman-esque point: the "survival" of the subject requires not just freedom from violence, but also some psychological salve, some promise, however proximate or tentative, that our efforts are not simply in vain, hopeless, or without a future.[67] The commonwealth, in the figure of the sovereign, embodies this promise, and the more powerful he is, the more promising his guarantee. The commonwealth therefore wards off not only our imminent demise at the hands of others, but also the debilitating torment induced by the constant threat of this imminent demise. In his enactment of the biblical decree "Let there be life!" the sovereign brings into existence the desiring subjectivity of living beings, transforming the otherwise stuck and conflict-prone bits of matter that populate the state of nature into bodies in motion, living human subjects capable of imagining and desiring the future he makes possible for them.

THE FUTURE IS SETTLER COLONIAL

Despite my emphasis so far on life and survival, the production of "death" through the inauguration of temporality is just as important as the constitution of life. After all, if life only becomes recognizable *as* life retrospectively, the same can and must be true about death. Thus, while the sovereign is consistently presented as the beacon of peace in *Leviathan*, war and death are just as much his creations as are peace and life. This is one, merely formal way of substantiating the claim that biopolitics is simultaneously and necessarily a necropolitics. However, what is also evident in Hobbes (but notably absent in Edelman) is the important qualification of this bio/necropolitics as specifically *colonial*. Closer examination of the time/place that is the state of nature makes clear that Hobbes's championing of life is a celebration and protection only of the lives of those who are "civilized," a safeguarding that comes at the necessary expense, obliteration, transfer, removal, and dispossession of "savage" others. In other words, "life" in biopolitical sovereignty is specifically settler life, characterized as "civilization," while "death" demarcates "savagery," or all those who cannot or will not conform to this particular political formation, as its foremost threat. In other words, it is the specifically settler character of "life" that explains the simultaneity and coincidence of sovereignty's bio- and necropolitics.

Returning once more to that notorious state of nature, recall my claim that time cannot exist there. Hobbes might potentially be seen as acknowledging this fact insofar as he refers to the state of nature as not only a "time" but also a "condition," two terms he seems to use interchangeably throughout chapter 13. For example, in the first sentence of the paragraph about war, he writes that "during the *time* men live without a common Power to keep them all in awe, they are in that *condition* which is called Warre."[68] Later, entertaining objections to his arguments about the state of nature, he muses, "It may peradventure be thought, there was never such a *time*, nor *condition* of warre as this."[69] He then further complicates things by proceeding to conflate time and condition with geographical location, noting immediately thereafter, "and I believe it was never generally so, over all the world: but there are many *places*, where they live so now"[70]— for example, "the savage people in many places of *America*."[71]

These ambiguous and confusing characterizations of the state of nature nevertheless cohere around one feature that unites them, which is their ultimately civilizationalist character. First, as already discussed, if the state of nature is a time—an era, say, or an epoch—it is simultaneously a moment that is completely timeless, an existence lacking any dynamism or principle of change. Indeed, although Hobbes famously characterizes life in the state of nature as "solitary, poore, nasty, brutish, and short,"[72] that last adjective is simply unwarranted given that no time is possible there. However rhetorically effective it may be, lodged at the end of a litany of dreary adjectives, life in the state of nature cannot be characterized as short any more than it can be characterized as long or even average because, as Hobbes makes clear, temporality does not pertain to it.[73] However, if the state of nature is instead a *condition*, then it is one of "savagery," as Hobbes makes explicit. Bolstering the view that the state of nature is a story about humanity's prehistory, Hobbes here rehearses the colonialist trope of indigenous peoples as European humanity's ancestors or premodern childhood. Savagery is therefore associated with stalled temporality, timelessness, and the failure of forward movement or progress. Conclusively, however, when referenced as geographical location, Hobbes materializes the state of nature in "*America*" and the seventeenth-century European notion of the New World, an uncharted territory ripe for exploration and conquest. The specifications of the state of nature as premodern, timeless, "savage," and "America" make clear that the establishment of the commonwealth imposes a distinction not simply between life and death, peace and war, but also between progress and timelessness, modernity and backwardness, civilization and savagery. Each of these categorial pairs functions as a surrogate for the others; taken together, they suggest the deep implication of categories of life and death with colonization and conquest for European political theory. Once sovereignty, civilization, and peace are established as the domain of life, the state of nature, "savagery," and war are established as the domain of death. Nichols writes, "The 'savage' of the Americas thus becomes the symbolic negative—the embodiment of the state of nature itself, and thus all which is to be avoided by civilized men living in civil (political) society."[74]

The state of nature is most concrete, in Hobbes's varying descriptions of it, as a place—that is, "*America*." Immediately after declaring this, however, he concedes:

> But though there had *never* been *any time*, wherein particular men were in a condition of warre against one another; yet *in all times*, Kings, and Persons of Soveraigne authority, because of their Independency, are in continuall jealousies, and in the state and posture of Gladiators; having their weapons pointing, and their eyes fixed on one another; that is, their Forts, Garrisons, and Guns upon the Frontiers of their Kingdomes; and continuall Spyes upon their neighbours, which is a posture of War. But because they uphold thereby, the Industry of their Subjects; there does not follow from it, that misery, which accompanies the Liberty of particular men.[75]

Rescinding his prior example of native North Americans, Hobbes concedes that there never really was any such time or condition as this state of nature. Not only are native peoples not in a state of nature, then, but also, and quite literally, there *is* no state of nature because, as we have seen, *no time* is possible there. Instead, Hobbes now claims, in "all times," the situation of international relations is like that of the state of nature, because heads of state are in perpetual warfare with one another. The state of nature, then, is neither a time nor a condition nor a place but, rather, an allegory of interstate behavior. And yet, even in this new global location, anarchy does not lead to the misery of the state of nature Hobbes described earlier because, as he says, sovereigns engage in foreign wars in the interest of securing their domestic subjects (rather than their own personages, presumably). Thus *even as a metaphor* the state of nature does not exist. It is a time that is no time, a condition that cannot exist in its unconditionality, a place that is nowhere, a representation of the unrepresentable.[76]

Hobbes's vacillation, confusion, and ultimate retraction of any concrete examples of the state of nature can be productively deciphered by linking it to theories of settler colonialism, on the one hand, and Edelman's critique of futurism, on the other. Regarding the first, Lorenzo Veracini has argued that settler colonialism is distinct from other types of colonialism insofar as its seeks consistently to erase itself *as* settler colonial, to "supersede the conditions of its operation."[77] Following Patrick Wolfe's argument that settler colonialism pursues a "logic of elimination" whereby settlers seek to replace the natives and indigenize themselves post facto,[78] Veracini argues that because it aims at the elimination of the native, settler colonialism necessarily aims at its own elimination:

> The successful settler colonies "tame" a variety of wildernesses, end up establishing independent nations, effectively repress, co-opt, and extinguish indigenous alterities, and productively manage ethnic diversity. By the end of this trajectory, they claim to be no longer settler colonial (they are putatively "settled" and "postcolonial"—except that unsettling anxieties remain, and references to a postcolonial condition appear hollow as soon as indigenous disadvantage is taken into account). Settler colonialism thus covers its tracks and operates towards its self-supersession (this is why, paradoxically, settler colonialism is most recognizable when it is most imperfect—say, 1950s Kenya or 1970s Zimbabwe—and least visible in the settler cities).[79]

The truly "successful" settler colonial project, in other words, would manage to efface the native entirely, whether through genocide or assimilation or some other form of disappearance—more recently, via a politics of recognition, as Glen Coulthard has argued.[80] One way this happens is through the narration of settlement itself, which disappears the native through discourses of nonexistence, invisibility, or *terra nullius*.[81] In Hobbes, this emerges as his inability to definitively locate or circumscribe the state of nature. This is consistent with the originary imaginings of all settler polities. As Veracini observes, "It is not a coincidence that the cultural traditions of the settler polities often focus on real or imaginary locales putatively epitomising specific national attributes: the 'outback,' the 'backblocks,' and, most famously, the 'frontier.' Generally speaking, these are not specific locations, and their most important characteristic is to be always somewhere else."[82] The state of nature is one such highly abstract geographical imagining and, as we have seen, Hobbes displaces it from a time to a condition to a place to a metaphor, eventually determining that it never existed at all, even as a hermeneutic.

Of course, regardless of how Hobbes defines or determines the "state of nature," the fact of the matter is that neither settlement nor indigenous people are, in fact, "elsewhere," but ever-present facts of the here and now.[83] Yet Veracini argues that settler colonialism must nevertheless constantly imagine native peoples as elsewhere, an act of symbolic displacement that effaces the actual existence of native peoples and erases them even in their existence:

> If the indigene is fundamental to the settler relation, where the indigene is located does matter. Thus, the "real" indigence is always somewhere else; that is why, to play on Philip J. Deloria's insight, he is always "unexpected" in actual places. Likewise, indigenous peoples are generally not seen in the settler cities, the places where the settlers live. Examples abound; the main point is that discursive devices aimed at redirecting attention away from emplaced settler-indigenous relationships are indeed many.[84]

Veracini suggests that all forms of indigenous removal can be characterized as different versions of "transfer," which he argues is foundational to the settler colonial project.[85] Regardless of whether we call it transfer or elimination, however, unless and until it is accomplished, settler states engage in all sorts of contortions, both political and ideological, to obscure the native in order to naturalize conquest. In short, disappearance of the land's indigenous inhabitants and subsequent attempts to "indigenize" settlers are the means by which land expropriation is simultaneously naturalized and obscured.

Veracini presents this iterative, imaginary displacement either as conceptually embedded in the definition of settler colonialism or else as a kind of bad faith on the settlers' part, potentially implying that a guilty conscience gives rise to a host of defense mechanisms to ward off (knowledge of) conquest. In other contexts, political theorists have considered that such recursive movement is definitive of sovereignty itself, which can establish the law only via a prior, extralegal, and illegitimate assertion of force. Yet the recursive ideological contortions of settler sovereignty are neither the result of guilt nor somehow intrinsic to its conceptual definitions. Robert Nichols has already persuasively argued that the recursive character of settlement is a means of facilitating dispossession, denying the existence of indigenous peoples, and disregarding their claims to land and sovereignty.[86] So the materiality of this operation is clear. Yet what to make of the specifically *ideological* character of this recursivity? What explains the reiterative *rationales* for conquest that attempt to erase it as conquest at all?

Borrowing from Edelman, one might say that while these ideological contortions are fundamental to settler colonialism, they are also fundamental to any futurist narrativization of "life." In other words, the reason why Hobbes cannot definitively locate or circumscribe the state of nature is the same the reason why the settler state seeks ideologically to naturalize settlers as native to the lands they have conquered. It is because, to use Edelman's vocabulary, both are futurist narrativizations of the *drive*, his Lacanian term for that aspect of human existence that resists any temporal or symbolic determination. Hobbes talks about this in terms of "endeavor." But Edelman's drive/Hobbes's endeavor is what in fact defines the unending present that is the time/condition/place of the state of nature; indeed, Hobbes's state of nature is effectively an attempt at a representation of this drive/endeavor, which both thinkers are clear is *un*representable. For, while Hobbes defines the motion of human life in terms of desire and aversion, these terms are only appropriate monikers for motion once it becomes perceptible. Before it is manifest in the form of desire, it exists as "small beginnings of Motion, within the body of man, before they appear in walking, speaking, striking, and other visible actions."[87] In other words, it is only once endeavor takes an object and becomes motion toward something that it becomes simultaneously apprehensible and also properly called desire, while endeavor away from an object "is generally called AVERSION."[88]

This drive/endeavor is not only prior to or outside of representation, but it also has no intrinsic justification, much less any clear or uncontroversial narrative articulation. It simply *is*. Thus any imposition of terms onto it—in order to render it apprehensible, coherent, or legible—is precisely that, an imposition, and thus an explicitly ideological move that serves a particular political agenda. For Edelman, this act of transforming the otherwise unsignifiable endeavor of human existence into "the fictive form of a narrative"[89] is the very definition of politics. As he says, "politics is a name for the temporalization of desire, for its translation into a narrative, for its teleological determination."[90] This definition of politics explains his insistence that politics is necessarily "conservative"—because "it works to *affirm* a structure, to *authenticate* a social order"[91] in its very existence—and also destined to fail. For Edelman, futurism perpetuates "the fantasy of meaning's eventual realization," a realization that is by definition impossible insofar as endeavor itself has no intrinsic meaning and "the future" as its justification is always only ever *to come*. As the future, it is just out of reach, ever beyond our grasp, "an always about-to-be-realized identity."[92] Rather than confront its own, necessary impossibility, Edelman argues that futurism instead generates scapegoats to distract from and take the fall for it, people or places or events that become the displaced, villainized obstacles to futurism's otherwise successful realization. His name for these scapegoats is "queer." This queerness, also unrepresentable because it is another name for the drive/endeavor that politics (that is, narrativization) impossibly seeks to domesticate and resolve, takes on the figure of whatever or whoever threatens the disarticulation of the self and social order, which are ideologically presumed to be the prepolitical premises of our existence.

This futile and fantasmatic futurism is a surprisingly apt characterization of the settler state, the full realization of which would, as Veracini notes, effect its erasure. Settler colonies resort to any number of destructive forms of managing futurism's failings, of course, from transfer and removal to outright extermination through war, massacre, starvation, and disease. (There are also a multitude of cultural forms of indigenous "transfer," whether it be the usage of indigenous peoples as sports team mascots, the fetishization of indigenous religious and spiritual practices in order to deny Indianness to Indians while claiming it for settlers, or the racialization of Indians into minority populations.) Yet this anxious, reiterative activity is wholly predictable from an Edelmanian perspective and ineliminable from the structure of settler sovereignty, because the futurist narration of the drive/endeavor has rendered settlers beholden to an unsustainable temporality that must produce queerness or death in order to continue to produce meaning, survival, and civilization for itself. Settler sovereignty cannot, in other words, do without the death-native it brings into being; the native as death *must* exist in order to purchase life and survival for the settler and is the figure of queerness in this futurist scheme.

"Queerness" in Hobbes is represented, figured, or embodied by those who fail to conform to the lineaments of rationality that his particular sovereign formation takes for granted—in this case, the rational character of life and its value. Hobbes calls these figures "absurd" rather than queer, but the meaning is the same. The queer or absurd are those who do not seek to preserve themselves or flee death. Such figures barely show up in this text and are largely incomprehensible in his schema. They both instantiate death and invite it as the only proper response to their incomprehensible and insupportable rejection of the social order. For example, any remaining holdouts in the state of nature unwilling to join a majority decision to create a commonwealth must be forced to go along with them "or be left in the condition of warre he was in before; wherein he might without injustice be destroyed by any man whatsoever."[93] This is the rationalization of conquest, however abstract, unmarked, or "rational" it may seem to be. For, as has become clear, those who do not recognize the value of life are not simply absurd or irrational; they are specifically those "savage" or precivilizational people(s) who have no concept of time or established system of governance.

Of course, the "savage" as deathly threat has been produced precisely *as* that threat by the settler polity itself, which can only sustain itself via this anxious, recursive, and impossible-to-resolve dynamic of producing and eliminating the enemy of its own order, the enemy that it requires if it is to be an order at all and yet that it must eliminate if it is to "overcome" what it is. As Alyosha Goldstein observes, "United States colonialism is a continuously failing—or at least a perpetually incomplete—project that labors to find a workable means of resolution to sustain its logic of possession and inevitability by disavowing the ongoing contestation with which it is confronted and violent displacement that it demands."[94] This constant aspiration toward an unrealizable future is a promise bought at the expense of effacing the founding violence that is the institution of settler sovereignty itself. Because that foundation is impossible to leave behind, because the native has *not* been finally eliminated once and for all, because the subjects of the commonwealth remain settlers, they cannot rest. They cannot rest until the last trace of the native has been eliminated, such that settlement can become a truly legitimate commonwealth founded on the basis of a free and equal social contract of its "native" citizens.

In the face of the impossibility of this achievement, however, they must find other outlets for their anxious desire. This is how and why the settler colonial foundation of biopolitical sovereignty transforms itself into an expansionist, imperial security state that finds new enemies abroad, new obstacles to its endless expansion, thereby solving (albeit only ever temporarily and incompletely) the problem of futurist failure that constituted settlement to begin with. This transformation is immediately apparent in Hobbes's astute psychology of the life of futurist desire. Regarding desire, Hobbes claims that one seeks not simply "enjoyment" in the present or "to enjoy *once* onely, and for one instant of time." Rather, one seeks "to assure *for ever*, the way of his *future* desire."[95] If the nature of desire is such that we seek to assure satisfaction forever, indefinitely into the future, then life/desire is inevitably bound up with anxiety, on the one hand, and power-seeking, on the other. Perpetually uncertain about the prospects of successfully getting what we want, we must continually seek to enlarge our power in order to secure the objects of our desire. It is important to note that this ever-expanding sphere of influence is not the result of a snowballing or addictive sort of pleasure-seeking behavior, nor is it due to some essential will to power at the heart of human nature. It is, rather, simply what is required in order to preserve the status quo: "It is not alwayes that a man hopes for a more intensive delight, than he has already attained to; or that he cannot be content with a moderate power: but because he cannot assure the power and means to live well, which he hath present, without the acquisition of more."[96] Mere maintenance of the present, in other words, requires accumulation, undertaken in perpetual reference to an uncertain future. The successful maintenance of an indefinite present is, for Hobbes, the content of human happiness: "*Continuall successe* in obtaining those things which a man from time to time desireth, that is to say, continuall prospering, is that men call Felicity."[97]

Such felicity is impossible, of course, as Hobbes concedes in the very next sentence: "I mean the Felicity of this life. For there is no such thing as perpetuall Tranquillity of mind, while we live here; because Life itself is but Motion, and can never be without Desire, nor without Feare, no more than without Sense."[98] Hobbes acknowledges, in other words, that, based on his own futurist accounting of life/desire and in fact precisely because of it, "happiness" (that is, getting what you want) is impossible. Even supposing one were able to secure the requisite amount of power necessary to maintain the status quo, such an (impossible) achievement would mean that our desire would be satisfied, and therefore extinguished. It would mean, in other words, no longer being alive, since "to have no desire is to be dead."[99] As he explains,

> To which we are to consider, that the Felicity of this life, consisteth not in the repose of a mind satisfied. For there is no such *Finis ultimus*, (utmost ayme,) nor *Summum Bonum*, (greatest Good,) as is spoken of in the Books of the old Morall Philosophers. Nor can a man any more live, whose Desires are at an end, than he, whose Senses and Imaginations are at a stand. Felicity is a continuall progress of the desire, from one object to another; the attaining of the former, being still but the way to the later.[100]

Suggesting that (attainment of) the highest good of Aristotelian ethics is itself a kind of stasis or death, Hobbes plainly rejects the idea that the endless motion that characterizes human life could come to a halt in some fashion that does not entail death. Understood psychologically, he is making clear that human happiness—the only kind available to us in "this life"—means never *actually* being satisfied. The perpetuity of enjoyment at which desire aims is a consumption that is never, can never fully be (allowed to be) complete(d).

Hobbes's specifically futurist and expansionist understanding of desire makes clear that, rather than confront the impossibility of security, happiness, and immortality, he instead offers the commonwealth and an ever-expanding pursuit of power as a substitutive satisfaction. In other words, he both institutes life and pushes it forward via a futurist narrativization of endeavor into an insatiable, accumulative desire. Rather than face the founding violence that brought peace and "life itself" into being, Hobbes instead naturalizes this act by declaring it to be "a generall inclination of all mankind" to engage in "a perpetuall and restlesse desire of Power after power, that ceaseth onely in Death."[101] Yet while desire may push us ever forward, ever beyond the initial moments of settlement, it cannot erase that settlement or relieve settler sovereignty of the burden of conquest. This is neither because of settler colonialism's theoretical definition nor because settlers secretly feel guilty about conquest, but rather because of the impossibility of fulfilling futurism's fantastical promises. Empire functions as a kind of substitutive satisfaction to compensate for the failure of settler sovereignty to finally and fully exterminate indigenous peoples. The pleasures of endless imperial expansion—the restless desire of "power after power" in an attempt to secure the future, once and for all—relieve the burden of the failed "completion" of the settler colonial project and the impossible promise of happiness. Empire is thus the settler impulse turned outward. It is a salve for settlement in its promise of an impossible, if now-externalized, future happiness and security.[102]

Built into Hobbes's understanding of desire, then (and, therefore, the Commonwealth), is the failed teleology of futurism, which, as Edelman instructs, is fundamentally and futilely political. The reason the commonwealth cannot alleviate the anxiety that runs apace with desire is because it cannot eliminate the foundations of its existence and the basis of its regime: on the one hand, indigenous removal and dispossession; on the other, the futurist constitution of "life" and/as desire. Indigenous removal and dispossession are accomplished, therefore, not only via the exertion of violence, domination, war, famine, genocide, and disease, but also via a specifically ideological imposition of the meaning of "life" and "death" that requires an indigenous removal and dispossession that it cannot accomplish without killing itself. This intractable dilemma explains the transformation of settler societies into security states, which reformulates the indigenous threat of "savagery" and death into external, terroristic opponents of its "way of life." As Jodi Byrd observes, "Indianness becomes a site through which U.S. empire orients and replicates itself by transforming those to be colonized into 'Indians' through continual reiterations of pioneer logics, whether in the Pacific, the Caribbean, or the Middle East."[103] Empire, in other words, relocates the state of nature from the domain of the indigenous "savage" to the "wilderness" abroad, itself in need of taming and civilizing if life and its value are to be satisfactorily protected. Twenty-first-century empire is thus legible, as Byrd and others have argued, as an outgrowth of the settlement of the United States and a contemporary episode of its ongoing structure.[104]

Stephen Silliman has documented the US military's usage of "Indian country" to describe Iraq and Afghanistan in the War on Terror. While the

Revolutionary War or Civil War possess just as much "resonance in the psyche of the United States as wars for freedom, unity, and democracy," nevertheless "soldiers in the Middle East draw on the 'Indian wars' of the 19th century to inform their daily experiences in combat."[105] Silliman argues that "The efficacy of this metaphor relies not in the accuracy of the historical or cultural details . . . but on the believability and acceptability of them as part of a narrative of conquest and nation building."[106] The "Indian country" characterization serves, in other words, to naturalize the "success" of the conquest of North America by casting contemporary US empire as an inevitably victorious, if now-worldwide, battle against "savagery," this time in the form of Islam and "terrorism." Of George W. Bush's expressed desire to "smoke" Osama Bin Laden "out of his cave," for example, Alex Lubin writes,

> The invocation of the Western drama of settler colonialism has always animated American thinking about and activity in the Middle East, and Bush is merely tapping into a well of affective politics that links the United States to the Middle East as well as provides support for increased surveillance and the suspension of rights domestically. Yet, in the contemporary era of neoliberal globalization, the United States' comparative rendering of the Middle East through its own settler colonial past has been multiplied and transformed into a "global war on terror." That is, the United States' unparalleled superpower status enables it to universalize and globalize its comparative politics into a global "clash of civilizations."[107]

Simultaneously, then, as the "terrorist" obstacles to empire become projected versions of Indians, Indians become retroactively legible as the first or foundational examples of "terrorism." Of the Declaration of Independence, for example, which complains that King George "has endeavored to bring on the inhabitants of our frontiers, the merciless Indian Savages whose known rule of warfare, is an undistinguished destruction of all ages, sexes, and conditions," Byrd observes,

> The non-discriminating, proto-inclusive "merciless Indian Savage" stands as the terrorist, externalized from "our frontiers," and functions as abjected horror through whom civilization is articulated oppositionally.

This non-recuperative category, a derealization of the Other, serves as a paranoid foundation for what Jasbir K. Puar defines in *Terrorist Assemblages* as Islamic "monster-terrorist-fags," the affectively produced and queered West Asian (including South Asian, Arab American, and Muslim) body that is targeted for surveillance and destruction by U.S. patriotic pathology.[108]

The "terrorist" of today, the contemporary obstacle to empire, is the native of an alleged "yesterday," the archaic obstacle to settlement. Whether in the domain of conquest or empire, however, the failed futurism of settler colonial sovereignty produces abjected queer repositories of death that stand as a threat to the civilized life of the settler society.[109] Their interconnection is crucial; the logic that connects them continuous.

Unsurprisingly, then, Hobbes's political theory serves as a justification for what it claimed only to describe. While an unmarked self-preservation and fear of death have typically been taken to be the natural and logical preconditions of the sovereign politics Hobbes institutes in *Leviathan*, an Edelmanian approach to this text reveals them to be the premier *values* settler sovereignty ideologically seeks retroactively to (re)produce and uphold. What this means, then, is that Hobbes's entire state of nature story is an anachronism. Like all origin stories, it is fundamentally ideological and offered primarily in order to legitimate an already-existing political order and the political commitment of its storyteller.[110] The particular agenda being naturalized in Hobbes's biopolitical story of the state of nature is settler conquest, and its futurist determination is the reason why he cannot decide when and where it is, and also why settler colonial societies seek constantly to erase themselves as settler societies.[111] The insecurity lodged at the heart of settler colonialism's futurist desire renders satisfaction impossible, an impossibility that remains unacknowledged and is instead foisted onto those "savages" who refuse collaboration with its ideological ruses. *Leviathan* is thus a settler colonial text par excellence. Like Agamben in this regard, it is a rationalization of empire that ignores all those queered by its machinations. Unlike Agamben, however, it makes explicit the connection between the biopolitics of settler colonialism and that of contemporary empire, revealing the futurist temporality that links them together and renders them continuous projects.

THE FUTURE IS MORAL

Readers of *Leviathan* usually find Hobbes's claims regarding the rational character of self-preservation persuasive. They are the basis of much so-called rational choice theory in the social sciences, typically found unproblematic by undergraduates (if not reproduced by them), and they seem plausible, if not self-evident, in most mainstream US cultural and political discourse. This is symptomatic of, among other things, the unstated if nevertheless profound impact of Hobbes on American politics and political culture (and therefore his impact on the world—or, at least, everything touched by American trade and foreign policy), as well as his compatibility with and adoption by capitalism and purveyors of capitalist ideology (the social sciences prominent among them).[112]

Despite the hegemony of Hobbes's "rational" presuppositions, however, it does not take much critical reflection to recognize their obviously normative character (and thus the exceedingly narrow and nonuniversal character of rational choice theory). Hobbes tries desperately to construct a universal psychology wherein all human beings, by definition, seek to preserve life and avoid death. In the introduction, for example, Hobbes claims that his book offers a reading of the nature of "not this, or that particular man; but Man-kind," an ability that qualifies one "to govern a whole Nation."[113] This familiar European philosophical conceit—that its author has divined the true character of all humanity—and the characterization of this accomplishment as a qualification to rule over them highlight the imperial character and aspirations of this text. In typical imperial fashion, then, the existence of counterexamples to its biopolitical logic serves not to undermine Hobbes's argument but rather to bolster its universalist logic and stigmatize those who fail to conform to its mandates as irrational, absurd, or unthinkable. Recall that Hobbes declares that anyone not recognizing the value of the commonwealth, the rationality of joining it, or the legitimacy of its sovereignty (all of which are synonymous) may justly be "destroyed" because, by remaining in a condition of war, they are a threat to the life of the commonwealth and its subjects. These refusers, in other words, are also enemies. Such people are not simply figures of the "absurd" who cannot be fit into a rational schema. Rather, or additionally, their existence is *opposed* to the civilized life of peace and society, and is thus a legitimate target of elimination and death.

The "absurd," in other words, is synonymous not simply with "irrational" but also with "enemy," and even "murderer" or "terrorist." This is the specifically moralized content of the "savage," who is not simply premodern, stuck in nonlinear time, and lacking rationality, but also a mortal threat to the settler polity and its security and way of life. Hobbes is not simply outlining an empirical description of human nature here, in other words; he is elaborating an ideologically determined and explicitly moralizing characterization of life, the value of life, and the absurd and hostile threat posed by all those who do not accede to its mandates. As Tom Roach writes, "Biopower . . . operates not on the principle of taking life away, but of investing it with the highest value—promising a heaven on earth, a life worth living. Death, by contrast, is necessarily relegated to the category of pure negation and constitutes the normative framework of life's value. In short, the biopolitical state does not turn away from death; it simply mobilizes it in a different manner."[114] The mobilization of death and/as "savagery" makes clear the extraempirical and, indeed, highly normative character of Hobbesian biopolitics.

Thus it is insufficient to say, with Agamben, that native people(s) are produced as "bare life," as people(s) who are able to be killed but not sacrificed. This formulation does not adequately capture the threat, negativity, and terror that moralizingly constitute the category of the "savage" within settler sovereignty. "Savagery" is a kind of deathly negativity that disarticulates the very social itself, in a form that Edelman would describe as the "death drive" of the settler polity. Natives' existence is more than mere fodder for killing or letting die; rather, their existence is a mortal threat to the coherence, meaning, sovereignty, stability, and persistence of the settler state. This is why they must be actively eliminated: not because they are a remnant of what has been exceptionalized from politics, but rather because their continued existence embodies an out-and-out menace to the polity as such. Genocide of indigenous peoples, then, is fully compatible with a moralizing valuation of "life itself" and is the material reality of the more formal theoretical claim that sovereign biopolitics is always already a necropolitics. As noted already, in the Hobbesian schema, this is wholly "rational." That even rationality itself is caught up in the logic of conquest, or civilizationalist hierarchies of biopolitical determination, is what has been erased from the rational choice characterization of self-preservation as self-evident, obvious, or common sense. "Self-preservation" is no empirical baseline of human existence; rather, it is a moralized championing of "life" and the value of "life itself" that justifies and legitimates the genocide of indigenous peoples. It is a futurism that commits its subjects to the punitive production of queerness, which, as a settler scheme, commits settler societies to the production of the native as uncivilized, "savage," backward, and absurd, as that which can and must be destroyed if "life" and "civilization" are to endure.

In today's moment, those irrational, unthinkable figures of death inevitably produced by futurism's civilizational project seem less associated with native people(s) than with Muslims and the now-pervasive and toxic Islamophobia that is one prominent site and residuum of the War on Terror. Indeed, the widespread conflation of Islam with "terrorism," antimodernity, savagery, backwardness, a culture of death, and an irrational death wish renders "the Muslim terrorist" the contemporary US imperial queer par excellence. Just like indigenous peoples who do not recognize the sovereignty of the settler state (but ostensibly are no longer), the enemy of US empire in the contemporary form of the "terrorist" is the one who today does not accept the "civilized" rules of engagement, has no respect for human life, and obliterates all worth and meaning in the refusal to recognize the difference between "innocents" and proper military targets. The American commonwealth is the global savior of civilization, protector of life and democracy, guarantor of a civilized future. The Muslim "terrorist," by contrast, is the remorseless annihilator of life, the very emblem of futurelessness, the epitome of "savagery" in his (and sometimes her) destruction of people and places whose lives have already been determined to be valuable.

Of course, the very determination of who or what counts as "terrorist" is a political calculation. As Hobbes makes clear for anyone who cares to notice, the state is the biggest "terrorist" of all insofar as deploying violence against civilians to instill fear in the service of accomplishing political goals is its essential function.[115] Yet what is perhaps clearest about the increasingly global War on Terror is that "terrorism" is never considered to be an action undertaken by states; rather, it is what states seek to eliminate. This is perhaps an illustration of the irony that, in the Hobbesian schema, the commonwealth protects us from "death" even as it is anointed as the only legitimate source of our death. Thus, shockingly yet perhaps not surprisingly, during a three-month span in 2011, the Obama administration extrajudicially executed four US citizens living abroad:

forty-year-old Anwar al-Awlaki, his sixteen-year-old son Abdulrahman al-Awlaki, twenty-six-year-old Samir Khan (all three were living in Yemen at the time), and twenty-year-old Jude Kenan Mohammad (in Pakistan).[116] In doing so, Obama undertook the one thing Hobbes hardly bothers to forbid the sovereign from doing because he considers it so unthinkable: waging war on his own subjects. What these extrajudicial killings make clear, however, is not (simply) that Hobbes is a definitive thinker of tyranny. It also makes clear that there is no need to exceptionalize Muslims in order to kill them or relegate them to spaces of death. Rather, we need simply to recognize Islam and "terrorism" as a nihilistic death cult in order to proceed with its necropolitical elimination. This seamless transposition of biopolitics and necropolitics is not the result of an increasing politicization of bare life, but rather the logical consequence of a futurist biopolitical order that moralistically produces queers or "savage" figures of death and destruction as the inevitable and necessary by-product of its constitution and reproduction of life as such, itself the legacy of an unresolved settlement that has not succeeded in eliminating the native.[117]

I will have much more to say about "terrorism," "terrorism" discourse, and the War on Terror in chapter 5. For now, I want to suggest that understanding futurism as a biopolitical project that perpetuates "civilization" through the moralized privileging of settlers over the "savages" they seek to erase offers a basis for (re)thinking liberation and liberatory politics. Conceiving of bio/necropolitics in terms of desire and temporality allows for a repoliticization of "death," rather than the helpless relegation of it either to an all-consuming abjection beyond which it is impossible to think or exist (the Agambian reading) or to increasingly obscure scientific and medical debates about when life begins and ends (the more liberal, "reasonable" reading). Recognizing the role of futurism and desire within settler colonialism and biopolitics, in other words, suggests that any liberatory project both is and must be simultaneously "queer" and "deathly." It must be queer insofar as it insists on the otherwise unthinkable refusal of the moral principle that "the body politic must survive." It will be deathly when it becomes a praxis—an embrace of "life"-denial that menaces the settler colonial order and openly threatens its "successful" accomplishment. Queer theory is thus essential to any liberatory project of resistance to settler colonialism and US empire; explaining how and why is the task of the next two chapters.

3

FOUCAULT AND QUEER THEORY

*And if I don't say what needs to be done, it isn't because I believe there
is nothing to be done. On the contrary, I think there are a thousand
things that can be done, invented, contrived by those who, recognizing
the relations of power in which they are involved, have decided to
resist or escape them. From that viewpoint, all my research rests on a
postulate of absolute optimism. I don't construct my analyses in order
to say, "This is the way things are, you are trapped." I say these things
only insofar as I believe it enables us to transform them. Everything
I do is done with the conviction that it may be of use.*

—Michel Foucault[1]

*Where the political interventions of identitarian minorities—including
those who seek to substantialize the identities of lesbians, gay men,
and bisexuals—may properly take shape as oppositional, affording the
dominant order a reassuringly symmetrical, if inverted, depiction of its
own ostensibly coherent identity, queer theory's opposition is precisely
to any such logic of opposition, its proper task the ceaseless
disappropriation of every propriety.*

—Lee Edelman[2]

S quarely facing the character and constituents of biopolitical
sovereignty demands a rethinking of liberation and liberatory
politics. In chapter 1, I argued that Agamben's work fails as a
resource to critique US imperial power or formulate strategies of resistance
to it, due on the one hand to its reliance on Arendtian presuppositions,

which are by definition antiliberatory, and on the other to Holocaust Exceptionalism, which weighs down the analysis and renders Agamben oblivious to the apparatuses of the contemporary War on Terror. In chapter 2, I suggested that reading Hobbes and Edelman together makes clear that the biopolitics of modern sovereignty is a specifically settler colonial investment in an ideological notion of life, which it can only constitute through a moralizing, retroactive condemnation of its opposite as death(ly), "savage," and irrational. Over the course of the next two chapters, I will make the case that queer theory is both necessary and useful for theorizing projects of political resistance to this civilizational sovereign biopolitics. In this chapter, I lay the groundwork for that claim by making the more general, broader argument that queer theory is, in essence, a specifically dissident and liberatory project. To establish this claim, I turn to Foucault, Agamben's ostensible interlocutor in the discussion of biopolitics and the author of *The History of Sexuality*, vol. 1, a text often considered foundational to queer theory. Investigating Foucault's most explicitly political works of the 1970s, I suggest that the "queer" of queer theory is indebted to a Foucauldian understanding of critique that is invested not simply in dissidence but, even more robustly, in liberation, and that this Foucauldian liberatory political commitment can be seen even in some of queer theory's best-known antipolitical texts and arguments. Taking on the widespread dismissal of revolutionary desire and commitment within queer theory, I suggest that, rather than turn away from revolutionary politics toward an ethics of desubjectivation, on the one hand, or a phenomenology of affect and assemblage, on the other (two broad directions the field has taken in recent years), we can and should mine the liberatory components of Foucault's political thought for an emancipatory project that does not problematically reify either sovereignty or the subject, as many contemporary queer theory critics otherwise rightly warn against.[3]

While Foucault sees himself as offering a political theory with copious resources for thinking and enacting modes of resistance, his work has not often been received in this way, in particular by left thinkers looking for resources to theorize liberatory politics. As Foucault's work increasingly became part of the American academy in the 1990s and beyond, he was more often received as offering, on the one hand, a totalizing view of power that rendered resistance always already coopted by what it sought to refuse or, on the other, a bankrupt political theory lacking any normative basis for resistance to power, much less a critique of it.[4] My turn to queer theory may also not seem a promising avenue for theorizing radical resistance to biopolitical sovereignty. As a by-product of both poststructuralism *and* Foucault, many Marxist and Marx-inspired critics have argued that queer theory is a poor choice of resources for thinking about liberatory politics, in particular because it fails to foreground the material reality of class hierarchy and the exploitation of labor.[5] Yet, I think the story with regard to both Foucault and queer theory is more complicated. In Foucault, there is in fact a profound ambivalence regarding revolutionary desire and radical politics, an ambivalence I see mirrored in a similar tension in queer theory between its exuberant, anti-identitarian founding moments and its current, more reserved, and even cautionary tales about precisely those heady days of the 1990s. This tension, I think, can be described differently as a conflict between a commitment to emancipatory or radical politics and the knowingness of the futility, uselessness, or even damaging character of those frameworks for liberatory praxis. As I will argue in this chapter, at least one of the founding investments of queer theory was to contribute to and galvanize a radical left political project. While it is true that, by now, this moment either has been largely discredited within queer theory or is simply considered passé, what is nevertheless significant is that some of the field's leading thinkers, many of whom have come to dismiss this reading of queerness as uninterrogated liberalism or ill-founded vanguardism, nevertheless remain motivated by the very same stakes as those that founded queer theory to begin with—that is, the left or liberatory impulse. These thinkers are attentive to Foucault's critiques of sovereignty and subjectivity, and suggest the uptake of his later, allegedly more ethical writings for political projects. Yet they urge a turn to Foucauldian ethics not from an abandonment of either queerness or revolution, but rather from a sense that a revolutionary queer politics is no longer a viable possibility, whether for the field of queer theory or for political praxis. What I want to show in this chapter is not only that the liberatory impulse is the basis of queerness and queer theory, regardless of the relative unfashionable-ness of revolution, but also that a Foucauldian project of radical queer politics is not an impossibility. That is, one can be both a Foucauldian and an avatar of radical, emancipatory politics; the former need not invalidate or vitiate the latter. Indeed, this may very well be the meaning of "queer."

INSURRECTIONARY METHOD: GENEALOGY AS CRITIQUE

As is well known, in his works of the mid- to late 1970s, now sometimes referred to as his "middle" works on power, Foucault rejects sovereignty as the predominant model of modern power relations for both historical and theoretical reasons: it has been outflanked by discipline, biopower, and governmentality; it relies on an untenable view of preconstituted subjects and sovereigns exchanging power like a commodity; it imagines power solely in terms of a law that functions to constrain or repress.[6] Yet there is another reason why Foucault rejects sovereignty as inadequate to explain or describe the workings of power beyond monarchical Europe in the sixteenth and seventeenth century: remaining within its framework stymies projects of political resistance. At the beginning of his 1975–1976 lecture series *"Society Must Be Defended,"* for example, Foucault declares that "we are in a sort of bottleneck" if we seek to resist discipline by relying on the old terms and terrain of sovereignty: "Having recourse to sovereignty against discipline will not enable us to limit the effects of disciplinary power."[7] Such an observation suggests that resisting discipline is an important project for Foucault, or at least one with which he was concerned. "Truth to tell," he says, "if we are to struggle against disciplines, or rather against disciplinary power, in our search for a nondisciplinary power, we should not be turning to the old right of sovereignty; we should be looking for a new right that is both antidisciplinary and emancipated from the principle of sovereignty."[8] Similarly, the first volume of *The History of Sexuality* ends with a warning against celebrating a sexuality that only reiterates the terms of our sexual subjectification. The thrill of sexual "liberation," Foucault insists, only keeps us in thrall to "that austere monarchy of sex."[9] Instead, he evasively suggests investigating "bodies and pleasures" as an alternative to the deployment of sexuality.[10] Now, whether or not "bodies and pleasures" constitute a viable prospect for political resistance, the mention at the end of *The History of Sexuality* suggests that Foucault is at least aware of the political consequences of his critique in this text, and perhaps even specifically for what we might anachronistically call queer dissidence. He puts it even more strongly in an interview from 1977 wherein he declares that the melding of sex and truth together "ends up in fact repressing and controlling movements of revolt and liberation" insofar as it "exploits [people's] temptation to believe that to be happy, it suffices to cross the threshold of discourse and remove a few pro-hibitions."[11] In short, it is not simply for historical or philosophical reasons that Foucault wishes to dispense with the primacy of the theory of sover-eignty. It is also for explicitly dissident, political reasons that he famously declares it is time to "cut off the head of the king"[12] and "study power outside the model of Leviathan."[13]

Notably, these most definitively political of Foucault's texts are also characterized by explicit methodological considerations.[14] *Discipline and Punish, History of Sexuality*, vol. 1, *"Society Must Be Defended," Security, Territory, Population*, and *The Birth of Biopolitics* are all very much taken up with methodological concerns, specific methodological choices, and substantial discussions of method. Some of Foucault's most famous remarks about power are contained in the section "Method" in *History of Sexuality*, vol. 1, the germs of which appear already in *Discipline and Punish* and are more fully expanded upon and amplified in *"Society Must Be Defended."* Foucault describes *Security, Territory, Population* itself as a kind of "experiment" in method—his attempt to see if it was truly possi-ble to embark upon a history of the state without presuming its existence beforehand[15]—and *The Birth of Biopolitics* continues this trajectory by fur-ther unpacking neoliberal governmentality. As he considers in lecture 5 of *Security*, he is attempting to do with regard to the state what he had already undertaken with regard to the study of discipline, which he characterizes as a "triple displacement"[16] of institution, function, and object from the study of technologies and strategies of power. The point of the analysis in *Security* is to undertake these three displacements precisely with regard to the state, to demonstrate "how the emergence of the state as a fundamental political issue can in fact be situated within a more general history of gov-ernmentality, or, if you like, in the field of practices of power."[17] The point of these displacements themselves, he explains, is to deinstitutionalize power and recognize its dispersed workings *from below*, not only to under-stand and track them better but also to open up space for resistance. Fou-cault calls this "methodological precaution" an "ascending analysis of power" that begins by studying power's "infinitesimal mechanisms."[18] It makes resistance possible because it shows that "Major dominations are the hegemonic *effects* that are sustained by all these confrontations [that is, manifold relations of force]":[19]

Overall domination is not something that is pluralized and then has repercussions down below. I think we have to analyze the way in which the phenomena, techniques, and procedures of power come into play at the lowest levels; we have to show, obviously, how these procedures are displaced, extended, and modified and, above all, how they are invested or annexed by global phenomena, and how more general powers or economic benefits can slip into the play of these technologies of power, which are at once relatively autonomous and infinitesimal.[20]

These smaller, "local" confrontations and strategies of power are unstable, tractable, vulnerable, reversible. Undertaking the genealogy of power relations from below, then, rather than tracking "major dominations" from above, makes clear that major dominations are *produced* by power relations and are neither essential, inevitable, nor strictly causal agents.

The politics of this particular methodological perspective—which Foucault acknowledges *is* a perspective, rather than a normative prescription[21]—is more explicit in *"Society."* He offers a disarming preamble to this series of lectures, declaring that his scholarly research has been somewhat haphazard to this point and confessing that he has trouble explaining it according to any larger goal, project, or overall purpose. Although Foucault is hopeful that his readers have found lines of continuity in the "fragmented, repetitive, and discontinuous"[22] works of the previous years, he is clear that, from his vantage point anyway, he was engaged in "the busy inertia of those who profess useless knowledge,"[23] caught up in "the great, tender, and warm freemasonry of useless erudition."[24] Nevertheless, Foucault says, "it was not *just* a liking for this freemasonry that led me to do what I've been doing."[25] He says the work of this time is also "quite in keeping with a certain period; with the very limited period we have been living through for the last ten or fifteen years, twenty at the most."[26] The period Foucault is referring to, of course, is the great social, cultural, and political upheaval of the 1960s and 1970s, including May '68 but also the general global ferment of oppositional social, antiwar, and anticolonial movements. Foucault characterizes this period as consisting of a generalized attack—in both the intellectual and the sociopolitical arenas—against the organizing institutions of social life (psychiatry, sexual morality, prisons, the state) as well as "totalitarian theories" like Marxism and psychoanalysis. "What was it that was everywhere being called into question? The way in which power was exercised—not just state power but the power exercised by other institutions and forms of constraint, a sort of abiding oppression in everyday life."[27]

This generalized attack became possible due to what Foucault calls "the insurrection of subjugated knowledges,"[28] by which he means the scholarly excavation of "buried or masked" historical records of people and events whose existence contradicts the "functional arrangements or systematic organizations" of power,[29] as well as all those knowledges "from below" that have been "disqualified" *as* knowledges because they lack some kind of institutional, scholarly, or other elite credibility.[30] Foucault describes these latter knowledges as "what people know at a local level."[31] What links these two, otherwise disparate forms of knowledge—"the buried and the disqualified"—is that they are both archives of struggle that have "been confined to the margins."[32] They would not even have become apparent were it not for the general critical ferment of these years that resulted in "the removal of the tyranny of overall discourses."[33] In characterizing his work up to and including 1975–1976 as in keeping with and indeed part of this struggle, Foucault is effectively describing works like *Discipline and Punish* as an uncovering of the documentation of the struggles of subordinated knowledges and a facilitation of their emergence in support of their insurrection.[34]

Even more significantly, Foucault argues that this emancipatory activity is the effect of the practice of genealogy, which he opposes to "science." In both *"Society"* and *Security*, Foucault explicitly links his method with "genealogy" and characterizes his prior work as similarly genealogical. In *"Society,"* however, he presents genealogy itself as an emancipatory methodology. In these lectures, Foucault argues that sciences are institutionalized discourses that claim to account for and explain everything according to a particular rule or rubric for producing truth. Sciences treat all meaning, experience, and knowledge as grist to their mill of verification and confirmation. Foucault calls such sciences "totalitarian theories." His explicit targets are Marxism and psychoanalysis; of the former, he says: "we can deduce whatever we like from the general phenomenon of the domination of the bourgeois class."[35] Such deductions, he says, "are always possible," but

They are essentially too facile, because we can [also] say precisely the opposite. We can deduce from the principle that the bourgeoisie became a ruling class that controlling sexuality, and infantile sexuality, is not absolutely desirable. We can reach the opposite conclusion and say that what is needed is a sexual apprenticeship, sexual training, sexual precocity, to the extent that the goal is to use sexuality to reproduce a labor force.[36]

The point, however, is that the answer—whatever it is—always serves to reinforce the power/knowledge of the scientific discourse that yielded it in the first place. This "vanguard" knowledge is what is opposed by genealogies, which Foucault characterizes as "antisciences."[37] By refusing the deductions and truth mills of sciences and interrogating power from the bottom up, rather than from the top down, genealogies "are about the insurrection of knowledges . . . against the centralizing power-effects that are bound up with the institutionalization and workings of any scientific discourse organized in a society such as ours."[38]

In lecture 2 of "Society," Foucault offers five methodological precautions regarding the study of power. These precautions—effectively a further organization of material already published in the sections "Objective" and "Method" in History of Sexuality—must be read within the context in which they are presented here, namely, as understanding scholarly and archival work as engaged in a political project of struggle, overthrow, and even, dare I say it, liberation. In "Society," Foucault characterizes genealogy as "a tactic" of unearthing and describing the local knowledges that will destabilize totalitarian discourses. Its obviously political character is further characterized by him as emancipatory: "Compared to the attempt to inscribe knowledges in the power-hierarchy typical of science, genealogy is, then, a sort of attempt to desubjugate historical knowledges, to set them free, or in other words to enable them to oppose and struggle against the coercion of a unitary, formal, and scientific theoretical discourse."[39] While Foucault's skepticism regarding liberation is well known, it is difficult to know how else to describe the activity, erudite or otherwise, of facilitating this renegade disruption of "totalitarian discourses."[40]

In describing Foucault's methodology and methodological commitment as emancipatory, I am not suggesting that he is advocating revolutionary struggle as traditionally understood by political theory (Marxist or otherwise), or even that his scholarship itself constitutes a form of revolutionary activity. I mean to make the narrower and more specific claim that, methodologically, Foucault's understanding of genealogy in this period and his practice of it proceed from an essentially liberatory political commitment to voices, experiences, and knowledges that are "subjugated" or in some sense "below." Foucault is unearthing knowledges from below in an attempt at disrupting hegemonic or "totalitarian" theories, discourses that therefore reign in some sense *from above*. While this sort of vertical mapping may seem foreign to Foucault's thinking about power, just as the "insurrection of subjugated knowledges" perhaps sounds eerily like the repressive model of power relations he worked so assiduously to sideline in political thinking, it is nevertheless undeniable that Foucault uses precisely such spatialization to mark the relationship between "totalitarian theories, or at least—what I mean is—all-encompassing global theories"[41] and "subjugated knowledges."[42] So, for example, he says:

> When I say "subjugated knowledges" I am also referring to a whole series of knowledges that have been disqualified as nonconceptual knowledges, as insufficiently elaborated knowledges: naïve knowledges, hierarchically inferior knowledges, knowledges that are below the required level of erudition or scientificity. And it is thanks to the reappearance of these knowledges from below, of these unqualified or even disqualified knowledges, it is thanks to the reappearance of these knowledges: the knowledge of the psychiatrized, the patient, the nurse, the doctor, that is parallel to, marginal to, medical knowledge, the knowledge of the delinquent, what I would call, if you like, what people know (and this is by no means the same thing as common knowledge or common sense but, on the contrary, a particular knowledge, a knowledge that is local, regional, or differential, incapable of unanimity and which derives its power solely from the fact that it is different from all the knowledges that surround it), it is the reappearance of what people know at a local level, of these disqualified knowledges, that made the critique possible.[43]

In addition to the clearly verticalized positioning of subjugated knowledges as "from below" in this passage, notice also the ways that Foucault characterizes the knowers of these subjugated knowledges: "the psychiatrized, the patient, the nurse, the doctor," personages who run alongside or in tandem with "medical knowledge, the knowledge of the delinquent" and are marginalized by them. This is not so far from the way that Foucault characterizes the subjects of disciplinary power in *Discipline and Punish*—as analogously dominated by specific, "despotic"[44] techniques of power. To take only one instance of this: Foucault contrasts processes of "individualization" within feudal and disciplinary societies. To do so, he uses not only a vertical spatiality but also a similar listing of marginalized or dominated subjects:

> The disciplines mark the moment when the reversal of the political axis of individualization—as one might call it—takes place. In certain societies, of which the feudal regime is only one example, it may be said that individualization is greatest where sovereignty is exercised and in the higher echelons of power. The more one possesses power or privilege, the more one is marked as an individual, by rituals, written accounts or visual reproductions. . . . In a disciplinary regime, on the other hand, individualization is "descending": as power becomes more anonymous and more functional, those on whom it is exercised tend to be more strongly individualized. . . . In a system of discipline, the child is more individualized than the adult, the patient more than the healthy man, the madman and the delinquent more than the normal and the non-delinquent.[45]

I cite these passages to make the point that, while Foucault is deeply critical of sovereign theoretical models insofar as they imagine power as unitary, state-centric, repressive, and "from above," this nevertheless does not obviate the fact that, for him, there still exist people and knowledges who *are dominated* and therefore in some sense located beneath or "below." As he makes clear, domination subjects, and in both senses—it both produces subjects and subjugates them. However, whether the term is *subjection*, *subjectivation*, *subjugation*, or *subordination* (and Foucault uses all of these at various points), the commonality among them is the prefix *sub-*, meaning "under"; *subjugation* literally means "under the yoke." Therefore, while it is indisputable that Foucault rejects the notion that there are determinate or specific people *in* power who wield it over others the way a king wields a scepter, it does not necessarily follow that Foucault rejects the idea that there are those *beneath* strategies and imperatives of power who are dominated, subordinated, and subjectified by it. Indeed, it is that very subjectification by which we can recognize power in the first place. And, although Foucault evinces extraordinary ambivalence in *"Society"* regarding the binary conceptualization of society at perpetual war with itself, a discourse he associates with the inversion of Clausewitz's maxim that characterizes politics as war by other means, it is nevertheless the case that Foucault (admits he) was significantly drawn to this thesis and that, in the end, he rejects only part of it: the ruling part. The other part, however, he retains:

> I am obviously not saying that great apparatuses of power do not exist, or that we can neither get at them nor describe them. But I do think that they always function on the basis of these apparatuses of domination. To put it in more concrete terms, we can obviously describe a given society's school apparatus or its set of educational apparatuses, but I think that we can analyze them effectively only if we do not see them as an overall unity, only if we do not try to derive them from something like the Statist unity of sovereignty. We can analyze them only if we try to see how they interact, how they support one another, and how this apparatus defines a certain number of global strategies on the basis of multiple subjugations (of child to adult, progeny to parents, ignorance to knowledge, apprentice to master, family to administration, and so on). All these mechanisms and operators of domination are the actual plinth of the global apparatus that is the school apparatus.[46]

Beginning "from below," then, has multiple meanings: beginning not simply with the subjugated, but also with smaller and more local relations of power that are themselves appropriated, colonized, and redeployed by larger, more global apparatuses of power. Regardless of whether he means people or powers, however, Foucault's methodological and political loyalties are identical here: they lie with those below, with those subjugated and subjectified. As he puts it more pithily elsewhere, "It is often difficult to say who holds power in a precise sense, but it is easy to see who lacks power."[47]

Foucault retains this loyalty to those below because—and this is the other way in which he can be said to practice an emancipatory methodology, which returns us to the beginning of the argument—he is interested in securing a space for political resistance, for what he so often describes as resistance to the mechanisms of power itself, rather than to a specific institution (say, the prison) or a group of people (say, the ruling class). So, when Foucault describes genealogy as the insurrection of subjugated knowledges, he clarifies that this insurrection is aimed "not so much at the contents, methods, or concepts of a science" but that, "above all," genealogy is "to fight the power-*effects* characteristic of any discourse that is regarded as scientific."[48] Those effects are, to say it one more time, subjection or subjectivation, which (and this is part of Foucault's point) are inevitably bound up with and function *as* subjugation. In other words, rather than getting bogged down in determining or fixing the oppressor-enemy—which only affirms and reifies its power—Foucault instead suggests examining the very mode of power itself so as to take aim at dismantling its subjectifying effects. "Rather than asking ourselves what the sovereign looks like from on high, we should be trying to discover how multiple bodies, forces, energies, matters, desires, thoughts, and so on are gradually, progressively, actually and materially constituted as subjects, or as the subject. To grasp the material agency of subjugation insofar as it constitutes subjects would, if you like, be to do precisely the opposite of what Hobbes was trying to do in *Leviathan*."[49]

This is one way that Foucault carves out a space for intellectual activity and production within political work without thereby anointing the scholar with any special role "from above" as privileged interpreter of ideology or pedagogue of the masses. For example, in an interview from 1978 explicitly focused on method and politics, Foucault makes clear that "the problem of the prisons isn't one for the 'social workers' but one for the prisoners," because "'what is to be done' ought not to be determined from above by reformers, be they prophetic or legislative, but by a long work of comings and goings, of exchanges, reflections, trials, different analyses."[50] As Foucault rightly observes, meaningful transformation requires the knowledge and participation of those from below, those *affected* by power, not necessarily Foucault himself or people like him, much less "reformers."[51] Indeed, Foucault rejects any privileged position for the intellectual whatsoever, noting that her very implication in the academy enlists her in regimes of power she should be engaged in disrupting: "Intellectuals are themselves agents of this system of power. . . . The intellectual's role is no longer to place himself 'somewhat ahead and to the side' in order to express the stifled truth of the collectivity; rather, it is to struggle against the forms of power that transform him into its object and instrument in the sphere of 'knowledge,' 'truth,' 'consciousness,' and "discourse.'"[52] If the intellectual does have any specific role to play, her job is to problematize existing and settled conclusions to the point that those in charge no longer *know* what to do. This activity, I would argue, is *in service to* those below, even if it does not take a position as to what they should do (or what should be done on their behalf)[53] and never rises to a position of explicit advocacy. It is a kind of comradeship in struggle, "an activity conducted *alongside* those who struggle for power, and not their illumination from a safe distance."[54]

In the end, I think this is what Foucault means by critique. Critique is the careful and deliberate disruption of existing regimes of power/knowledge in order to fight their effects, "to show that things are not as self-evident as one believed, to see that what is accepted as self-evident will no longer be accepted as such. Practicing criticism is a matter of making facile gestures difficult."[55] Moreover, this commitment to critique is in no way at odds with a commitment to liberatory or revolutionary struggle. Indeed, Foucault characterizes this critical activity as in service to resistance and part of the struggle for social and political transformation; "deep transformation," he says, must be "constantly agitated by a permanent criticism."[56] Critique is therefore not removed or separate from politics or political struggle, nor is political resistance without critique unless it is supplied by the intellectual class. Rather, these activities are mutually reinforcing and even require one another in order to function. It is, in fact, difficult ultimately to distinguish them, since critique, in Foucault's view, is that which constantly resists—both the relations of power it documents and the provocation to "solve" the problems it raises therein:

> Under no circumstances should one pay attention to those who tell one: "Don't criticize, since you're not capable of carrying out a reform." That's ministerial cabinet talk. Critique doesn't have to be the premise of a deduction that concludes, "this, then, is what needs to be done." It should be an instrument for those who fight, those who resist and refuse what is. Its use should be in processes of conflict and confrontation, essays in refusal. It doesn't have to lay down the law for the law. It isn't a stage in programming. It is a challenge directed to what is.[57]

Genealogy, then, as the method of unearthing subjugated knowledges, is the method of critique, the grounds for a constant and insurrectionary challenge to "what is." Less a loyalty to a specific cause, analysis, or foundational ground, genealogy is instead a loyalty to critique or dissidence itself, which emerges in many places and forms but always and necessarily *from below*.

FOUCAULDIAN CRITIQUE AND QUEER THEORY

This critical proliferation of insubordinate knowledges that serve to challenge, destabilize, and discombobulate "sciences" or "totalitarian theories" that, in this period, Foucault calls "genealogy," looks a lot to me like, in its heyday, what queer theorists wanted to marshal for the meaning and content of the word *queer*—whether as an identity marker, a methodology for intellectual inquiry, or the name of political dissidence. That one word could mean or do all these things actually further reflects Foucault's influence on queer theory's field formation. As an identity marker, queer is of course the anti-identity marker: either the signifier with no clear or stable referent or the identification that indicates one's opposition to identity as such (and thus one's interest in undermining or undoing it). As a method, queering operates similarly: as a refusal of orthodoxy, normalization, and homogenization in the domain of knowledge, as well as a delight in revealing the hidden improprieties of disciplinarity and celebrating the perversities it is complicit in both erasing and producing. As a political praxis, queerness signals noncooperation with, if not active undermining of, regimes of normalization, which, following Foucault, are recognized to be at work effectively everywhere: at home, school, work, government agencies, public transportation, shopping malls, toilets, bars, convenience stores, airports, sidewalks, parks, movie theaters—the list goes on. The creative, visually powerful, intellectually rigorous, and entirely grassroots coalitional activism of ACT UP is often credited with both launching and giving content to this emerging notion of queerness. Exuberantly prosex and gay-affirmative activism, the brilliant tactics and actions of ACT UP performed the sexuality and the politics of what would come to be called queer. Queer theory, then, as a field that emerged at least in part from a queer struggle for survival, is knowledge of and for those who were never meant to survive, those whose deaths were acceptable, unremarkable, even necessary for the undisturbed functioning of the heteronormative order.[58]

This is a survival whose perpetuity challenges the grounds of identity, markers of propriety and impropriety, and indeed the very domain of the political itself.

Michael Warner provided what has become among the most oft-cited passages used to explain just what in the world the "queer" of queer theory might mean, in the introduction to his now-canonical edited volume *Fear of a Queer Planet*. There he writes: "The preference for 'queer' represents, among other things, an aggressive impulse of generalization; it rejects a minoritizing logic of toleration or simple political interest-representation in favor of a more thorough resistance to regimes of the normal."[59] For Warner, this definition (if, in fact, it is a definition—it certainly has been taken as such) means that " 'queer' gets a critical edge by defining itself against the normal rather than the heterosexual."[60] Warner here does the important work of distinguishing heterosexuality from *heteronormativity*, which, together with Lauren Berlant, he elsewhere defines as "the institutions, structures of understanding, and practical orientations that make heterosexuality seem not only coherent—that is, organized as a sexuality—but also privileged."[61] The political and critical target of "queer," in other words, is not heterosexuality "itself," much less heterosexual people. Following the Foucauldian injunction to examine particular tactics and technologies of power rather than look for "the headquarters that presides over its rationality,"[62] and to find these tactics and technologies by examining their subjectifying power-effects, Warner and Berlant's heteronormativity names neither an oppressor group nor specific people (much less their choices, intentions, or behavior) so much as it does a system of power and social meaning that unifies and privileges a particular sexual/social order whose "power-effects" are registered by the ways in which all of us are subjectified by it.

Queer theory has often been interpreted as the replacement field that surpassed its predecessor, gay and lesbian studies.[63] However disputed the virtues of this development may be, the nevertheless undeniable emergence of and field-defining preference for "queer" over "gay" and "heteronormativity" over "homophobia" had significant political consequences. Warner argued that queer inquiry does not *replace* antihomophobic inquiry, nor could it, since "normal sexuality and the machinery of enforcing it do not bear down equally on everyone."[64] There is still, in other words, a need and a place for antihomophobic inquiry and praxis. But this is identical with neither the mandate for nor the referent of *queer* praxis, both of which are wider and less determinate than the "more minority-based versions of lesbian and gay theory."[65] As Teresa de Lauretis, the person considered to have coined the term *queer theory* in 1990, writes in the introduction to the *GLQ* special issue on the matter,

> Today we have, on the one hand, the terms "lesbian" and "gay" to designate distinct kinds of life-styles, sexualities, sexual practices, communities, issues, publications, and discourses; on the other hand, the phrase "gay and lesbian" or, more and more frequently, "lesbian and gay" (ladies first), has become standard currency. . . . In a sense, the term "Queer Theory" was arrived at in the effort to avoid all of these fine distinctions in our discursive protocols, not to adhere to any one of the given terms, not to assume their ideological liabilities, but instead to both transgress and transcend them—or at the very least problematize them.[66]

Although, according to Warner, de Lauretis subsequently became skeptical about "queer theory,"[67] it is indisputable that this distance from and problematization of "gay and lesbian" were part and parcel of the anti-identitarian dissidence so crucial to queer's emergence. As Judith Butler wrote just after *Gender Trouble*, in a volume offered, ironically enough, as a contribution to the field of gay and lesbian studies,

> I'm not at ease with "lesbian theories, gay theories" [the book's subtitle], for as I've argued elsewhere, identity categories tend to be instruments of regulatory regimes, whether as the normalizing categories of oppressive structures or as the rallying points for a liberatory contestation of that very oppression. This is not to say that I will not appear at political occasions under the sign of the lesbian, but that I would like to have it permanently unclear what precisely that sign signifies.[68]

Eve Sedgwick, sometimes referred to as queer theory's fairy godmother, wrote memorably in 1993, the same year as *Fear of a Queer Planet*:

> That's one of the things that "queer" can refer to: the open mesh of possibilities, gaps, overlaps, dissonances and resonances, lapses and excesses of meaning when the constituent elements of anyone's gender,

of anyone's sexuality aren't made (or *can't* be made) to signify monolithi-
cally. The experimental linguistic, epistemological, representational,
political adventures attaching to the very many of us who may at times
be moved to describe ourselves as (among many other possibilities)
pushy femmes, radical faeries, fantasists, drags, clones, leatherfolk,
ladies in tuxedos, feminist women or feminist men, masturbators,
bulldaggers, divas, Snap! queens, butch bottoms, storytellers, trans-
sexuals, aunties, wannabes, lesbian-identified men or lesbians who
sleep with men, or...people able to relish, learn from, or identify
with such.[69]

For Warner, "queer" can encompass this varied and illimitable, inevitably
incomplete listing of sexual subjects because its distinct advantage is that
it points to a "wide field of normalization, rather than simple intolerance,
as the site of violence."[70] On this reading, queerness in some sense *names*
the violence and power-effects of this heteronormative social system and,
through affirmative reclamation, suggests its users' resistance to them,
both symbolic and actual. "Originally generated in a context of terror,"[71]
queer becomes the mark of refusal to regimes of the normal, a resistance
in particular to the specific regime and subjectifying effects of heteronormativity. It is, to use Foucauldian language, resistance to "the material
agency of subjugation insofar as it constitutes subjects."[72]

I will have much more to say about the connection between queerness
and terror in chapter 5. For now, the other important implication to be
spelled out from this dissident notion of queerness is, as Warner puts it, the
difficulty of "defining the population whose interests are at stake in queer
politics."[73] Given the broadening of queer beyond the minority-group identification "gay and lesbian," or even the particularities of any identity group
at all, the question then becomes who or what, exactly, queers are. Yet queer
theory refuses a definitive answer to this question as well. As Warner and
Berlant note in their essay from 1995, "What Does Queer Theory Teach Us
About X?": "Just as AIDS activists were defined more by a concern for practice and for risk than by identity, so queer commentary has refused to draw
boundaries around its constituency. And without forgetting the importance
of the hetero-homo distinction of object choice in modern culture, queer
work wants to address the full range of power-ridden normativities of
sex."[74] In other words, if queer, by definition, opposes the power-effects

of something like a material system of subjectification and social meaning called heteronormativity, then it inevitably cannot demarcate from the outset on whose behalf it advocates or whose interests it represents. This would only be possible if heteronormativity itself were static and seamlessly reproduced along some sort of determinist view of structural power and social organization by a clearly designable and unchanging enemy class of heterosexuals. But since "regimes of the normal" are multiple, dispersed, overlapping, and in flux, so too are those subjected to its regimes and normalized by it—including heterosexuals. As Warner notes, "broad visions of social change do not follow from sexuality in any way that seems obvious and necessary to all those affected by sexual politics. And why should they? If social vision were dictated in such an inevitable way, it wouldn't be politics."[75] How, then, to determine the "queers" who are the avatars or supposed beneficiaries of queer politics? Warner, at least, argues that queers are a constituency unlike any other that has hitherto graced the pages of left critical analysis: "at present there is no comparable category of social analysis to describe the kind of group or nongroup that queer people constitute."[76] He considers in turn the possibilities of class ("conspicuously useless"), status ("somewhat better," but still inadequate), and (a non-Foucauldian version of) population (which makes "the question who is and is not 'one of them' not merely ambiguous but rather a perpetually and necessarily contested issue"). He concludes: "Queer people are a kind of social group fundamentally unlike others, a status group only insofar as they are not a class."[77]

I revisit these beginning moments of queer theory not only because I think they take up a Foucauldian version of emancipatory critique, but also because they serve as an important reminder that at least one of the field's founding investments was an interest in a decisively left project of critical praxis.[78] Warner is straightforward in this regard: he intends to claim queer theory as part and parcel of "left traditions of social and political theory" in order to imagine how "queer experiences and politics might be taken as starting points" for these traditions "rather than as footnotes."[79] But Warner's view of queerness as resistance to "regimes of the normal" by now either has been dismissed within the field or seems irrelevant to its scholarly concerns.[80] This is particularly true for Foucauldian-inspired critics of dissident queerness, who use Foucault to argue against revolutionary politics and turn instead either to Deleuze or to Foucault's later, more "ethical" writings as more promising avenues of queer political inquiry. For example, Jasbir Puar offers a trenchant critique of these inaugural views of queerness as a kind of exceptionalism that inoculates queer people from complicity with power and activates "resistance" as a normative queer ideal.[81] Meanwhile, Lynn Huffer suggests that, in a US context "characterized, more or less, as better than it was before the rise of feminist and queer movements," "the exuberantly anti-identitarian queer performances of the 1990s" seem "quaintly trivial or simply irrelevant." She writes: "To the extent that some of us still consume, if only through our teaching, the subversive claims of those theoretical leftovers from the 1990s, there is no doubt that in the present our tastes have changed; many of those dishes seem to have lost, as leftovers do, both their heat and their flavor."[82]

Huffer forthrightly declares that "the queer has lost her generative promise" and has been "drained of her transformative, contestatory power." These observations, coming as they do in Huffer's groundbreaking *Mad for Foucault*, make clear that at least part of the rejection of Warner's politicized reading of queer comes from scholars eager to refound or redirect queer theory on the basis of a new reading of Foucault that leaves behind the "genealogical" Foucault of the midcareer "power years" in favor of the later, more "ethical" Foucault.[83] At stake in this rereading of Foucault and in my return to queer theory's foundings, then, is the very possibility of a left or emancipatory politics within, as part of, or integral to queer critical praxis.

RADICAL QUEER POLITICS

Maybe it is because I like leftovers, or maybe it is because I have often felt that I was born too late, having tragically missed the feminist and gay liberationist moments of the late 1960s and early 1970s, that I want to insist on this anachronistic, seemingly exceptionalist, and embarrassingly leftist understanding of radical politics as the content of queerness and queer critique. But it is also because I see this founding left impulse in queer theory as still politically useful in a way that avoids the pitfalls of sovereign politics that Foucault details but are not addressed by the turn to a Foucauldian ethics on the one hand, as Huffer proposes, or to affect and assemblage, as Puar proposes on the other.

In recitations of queer theory's founding texts and moments like the version I just gave, one essay, written in the late 1990s, is nevertheless rarely included in the canonical bibliographies of queer theory that always contain Butler, Foucault, Sedgwick, and Warner: Cathy Cohen's "Punks, Bulldaggers, and Welfare Queens: The Radical Potential of Queer Politics?" Published in 1997 in *GLQ*, the field's flagship journal, which also did much to establish queer theory *as* a field, I see Cohen's essay as clearly aligned with Warner's insofar as she is interested in demarcating a specifically "Left" politics (her capitalization) for queer theory. Diverging from Warner, however, Cohen also indicates the failures of queer theory's reading of heteronormativity when it comes to race and class. Although Cohen endorses the move to broaden the analysis of queer politics toward resistance to regimes of the normal rather than attack heterosexuality (and, by implication, heterosexual people and/or a heterosexual "class"), her essay is written at least in part out of frustration and despair at the repeated failures of what Marlon Ross calls "(white)queer theory,"[84] which continues to neglect the specificities of working people and people of color in its analysis. Cohen suggests that "queer" was initially attractive to her because it seemed to promise both a challenge to and an expansion of traditionally defined gay and lesbian (identity) politics. Unfortunately, quite the opposite occurred and, in her view, "queer" became the designation of anything "not-straight," reinforcing a thoughtless, binary view of power and oppression that relied on a single-axis identity model of politics.[85] This single-axis analysis "make[s] no room either for the analysis of oppression of those we might categorize as heterosexual, or for the privilege of those who operate as 'queer.' "[86] Instead of falling back into uncomplicated power binaries, Cohen says, queer theory must instead seek to build a Left politics that "makes central the interdependency among multiple systems of domination."[87] This "broadened understanding of queerness must be based on an intersectional analysis that recognizes how numerous systems of oppression interact to regulate and police the lives of most people."[88] The example she provides in this essay, as referenced in her title, is that of the single mother of color receiving welfare support. Although perhaps nominally heterosexual, Cohen asks whether or not this person's outsider status with regard to heteronormativity—a regulatory ideal that is substantially structured by if not founded upon white supremacy—thereby constitutes the "welfare queen" as a "queer" subject, or at least as a member of a marginal constituency called queer that resists, undermines, or falls outside of dominant heteronorms. Ultimately, Cohen suggests a coalitional politics for the meaning of queerness: a coalition of people based on one's position with regard to and relationship with power rather than one's sexual orientation. This type of queer politics allows for an analysis of heteronormativity as part and parcel of a series of interlocking oppressions that coconstitute both one another and those they subject.

Clearly an important critique of (white)queer theory, Cohen's essay can also be read as an attempt to materialize the ineffable radicality promised by queerness that Warner and Berlant outline. What is even more significant is that those who seek to dispute queerness's claim to radical or dissident politics often return to *her* essay, rather than Berlant and Warner or Butler or Sedgwick, in their repudiations. This suggests that, although not always considered canonical, Cohen's essay nevertheless makes explicit the theoretical and political stakes of Warner and Berlant's version of queerness, stakes that contemporary queer theorists remain reticent to abandon even as they critique the very version of queerness that attempts to concretize them.[89] So, for example, in her critique of queer exceptionalism in *Terrorist Assemblages*, Puar criticizes Cohen's reliance on intersectionality, suggesting that while the critique of the constitutive whiteness of queer is important and welcome, intersectionality is unable to recognize its own complicity with the liberal humanist subject.[90] As Puar writes elsewhere, in an elaboration of this argument, intersectionality remains "trapped within the logic of identity."[91] Noting the tendency of intersectional analyses to apply only to women of color and, in particular, to black women, Puar argues that intersectionality not only renders women of color ancillary to white feminism and white feminist subjects, but also reinscribes at the heart of feminist method and inquiry the commitment to the modern disciplinary subject that it should instead be working to dismantle.[92] In effect, intersectionality requires and reinstates the subject as the traversed center or crossroads of these intersecting vectors of oppression: "intersectional critique has both intervened in the legal and capitalist structures that demand the fixity of the rights-bearing subject and has also simultaneously reproduced the disciplinary demands of that subject formation."[93] Puar's critique of intersectionality here is indebted to Foucault even as it seeks to move beyond Foucault toward Deleuzian assemblage, which she offers as a more adequate roadmap of the "accidents" of bodies and affects that produce events. Assemblage, she says, "problematizes the predominance of subject formation itself,"[94] while affect may provide a "basis for the force of political transformation that does not rely on identity politics or any particular model of social movement, but a different kind of resistance."[95] Assemblage, affect, and event not only displace the "poststructural fatigue around the notion of the subject itself,"[96] but also, importantly, "work against narratives of U.S. exceptionalism that secure empire, challenging the fixity of racial and sexual taxonomies that inform practices of state surveillance and control and befuddling the 'us versus them' of the war on terror."[97] Using terms a bit foreign to Puar's vocabulary, we might redescribe her argument as claiming that intersectionality looks like a radical critique that actually functions as an accommodationist or reformist strategy, insofar as it strengthens the very formation—the disciplinary subject—the power-effects of which it should instead be documenting and contesting. In reaching for both nonintersectional *and* non-Foucauldian terms, Puar is looking to more adequately theorize relations of power and modes of resistance to it.[98]

Lynn Huffer's critique resonates with Puar's. Huffer, too, wants to resist, on the one hand, queer's exceptionalist tendencies and, on the other, queer theory's (and intersectionality's) reliance on the subject. Regarding queer exceptionalism, Huffer argues that the basis for queerness's "radical inclusivity"[99] is its claim to undecidability: "what queer theory claims, specifically, as constitutive of queer theory itself, is the instability and undecidability of the term *queer*, to the point where being 'queer' and being 'undecidable' have become virtually synonymous."[100] Echoing a now-familiar refrain, Huffer complains that, in this view, queer theory "ends up referring to everything and nothing, thereby repeating its own invisible but hegemonic subject position ad infinitum."[101] This is not unlike Puar's complaint that if queer is the always already transgressive, then queerness becomes a kind of regulatory ideal that normativizes resistance itself. Like Puar, however, Huffer is more concerned with what she sees as queer theory's staunch if largely undetected reliance on the subject. Huffer thinks the notion of queerness as undecidability renders invisible the "masculinist universalism" at work in the "we" of queer theory,[102] a "we" dependent upon "the structure of discursive power, which, like the structure that articulated the universal Rights of Man, upholds the term *queer* through the universalizing narratives of legitimation that allow the queer subject to speak."[103] Thus, Huffer concludes, explicitly referencing and returning to Cohen, "queer" can never *actually* refer to mothers of color on welfare, because these women "generally lack the discursive authority through which queer theory disseminates itself *as* theory. And these reasons are not unlike those that historically excluded all women and nonwhite men from the 'we' of the Enlightenment subject."[104]

What I find noteworthy about these two important critiques of dissident queerness is that their stakes actually seem to be much the same as those of the field's founding. In other words, both Puar and Huffer seem concerned with the same thing Warner and Cohen are concerned with: Left or liberatory politics. Puar and Huffer are worried about queer exceptionalism and queer theory's attachment to subjectivity, but they are concerned about this tendency and attachment because, on the hand, they erase or perpetuate complicity with existing regimes of power (for example, capitalism, the War on Terror, racism, masculinist universalism) and, on the other, they foreclose our ability to think beyond or outside those regimes of power. While neither Puar nor Huffer would necessarily characterize their concerns this way, in returning to Cohen's essay for their criticisms of queer, they both return to fundamentally *left* or liberatory concerns about dissident theory and politics. Queer theory's exceptionalist radicalism may be too closely tied to the subject, but the radicalism of queer theory itself—much less its commitment to an antinormal/antinormalizing coalitional politics in the service of emancipation—isn't the problem. If anything, this commitment seems to inform and even motivate their critiques of queerness and queer theory itself, however unacknowledged it may be.[105]

I see certain left Foucault scholars navigating the same quandary, as perhaps best exemplified by Jeffrey Nealon's *Foucault Beyond Foucault*. Nealon attempts to reconcile anticapitalism with Foucault's historicization of modern power by infusing Foucault's late-career turn to ethics with a hitherto underacknowledged political content. In a deft and careful reading of the "middle" Foucault, Nealon shows how Foucault's understanding of power as intensity (whether in the form of discipline, biopolitics, or governmentality) renders the standard left frame of resistance to dominant hegemons obsolete. The globalization of finance capital in particular exemplifies the biopolitical governmentality that permeates every crack and crevice of daily life. Not only, then, is being "outside" of power impossible from a Foucauldian perspective, but also, Nealon contends, it is impossible from a Marxian perspective: "the highly intensified biopower of the present day has become almost completely synonymous with so-called late capitalism."[106] This makes "resistance" to power as ubiquitous and mundane as the everyday exercise of power itself, and defeats any outmoded notion of worker struggle to overthrow the bourgeois class as the "solution" to the situation we find ourselves in. There is no distinctly privileged act of rebellion that might oppose "the system"; therefore, we would do well to stop investing in the heroic vision of the revolutionary subject who can incite class consciousness or effectively throw a wrench into the unjust workings of capitalism. Such gestures are not only futile, but already part and parcel of the biopolitical governmentality of contemporary capitalism. "Resistance," in other words, is already part and parcel of capitalism's workings.

Nealon concludes his compact book with two important questions that one suspects may have been animating the inquiry all along:

> If, as Deleuze and Foucault both hold, power, pleasure, or desire don't work through the repression or liberation of a preexisting humanist subject, but rather through incessant production of serial subjectivities, then what could it mean to "resist" power or desire? And doesn't the vocabulary of resistance, however much we nuance it, entice us unconsciously to think that resistance is a relatively stable signifying quality of authentic subjects, rather than a hazardous and uncertain attribute of an a-signifying, social relation of force?[107]

Nealon offers no answer to the first question insofar as his answer to the second is a resounding yes. Indeed, the very question of what resistance might mean in the face of the impossibility of standing "outside of" or "against" power remains important even to Nealon's rigorous defense of Foucauldian biopolitical understandings of capitalism. On the subject of resistance, then, he concludes by citing the very Foucault I have been discussing in this chapter, the Foucault of *"Society Must Be Defended,"* arguing that, when it comes to resistance, we must begin with the every-day (both the here and now, as well as the local level), which is effectively to "*respond*"[108] to the strategies and tactics of power that subjectify us. Respond, but not "resist," much less rebel, since there is no inherently resistant or liberatory act:

> It seems that if one is to take Foucault's emphasis on social force seriously, then one has to start where one is, with the provocation to respond to "today," a particular problem or set of problems, and one is forced to end with something other than a condemnation or a judgment—the tautological conclusion that X or Y is "dominating," "bad," or "false." Let's give credit where credit is due: it's really not a matter of whether anyone *believes* the bullshit served up by her boss or his elected officials, or whether this bullshit is really true or not. Those binary questions of hermeneutic depth aside, we are nevertheless left with the forceful fact this bullshit certainly does produce effects: we certainly do have to *respond*—outside the economies of representation, assured failure, moralizing judgment, and meaning.[109]

Nealon's notion of response here may well be consistent with a certain reading of Foucault's understanding of power, but I think it is insufficient from a radical or emancipatory perspective, and I wonder if Nealon unwittingly recognizes as much by inflecting his particular examples through the figures of the beleaguered worker and citizen, relying on unstated but clearly left references for power hierarchies, and insisting that these marginalized figures "must" "respond" to the "bullshit" served up by their bosses and state representatives. For this formulation raises a number of questions: Why "must" the worker or citizen "respond"? What makes "bullshit" bullshit? And why is it the boss and the government who serve it up, and the worker and the citizen responding to it? If anything, this theoretical framing suggests that the set of presuppositions animating Nealon's critique of anticapitalism is the same as those motivating Puar's and Huffer's critiques of dissident queerness: the left or liberatory impulse. The problem is not liberationist politics, then, but the fact that how we've done it or articulated it thus far seems unsustainable. The commitment to emancipation, however, to what Foucault has called knowledges *from below*, remains a commonality across all of these thinkers.

Nealon and Huffer, along with Tom Roach's careful queer reading of Foucault's politics of friendship in *Friendship as a Way of Life*, attempt to address these difficulties by turning to a reinvigorated notion of Foucauldian ethics. Puar, by contrast, turns to Deleuze, Guattari, and Brian Massumi (among others) in order to pay attention to affects, assemblages, and events. Both strategies are premised on the damaging force of queer theory's or left theory's attachment to subjectivity, and both seek either to displace it (Puar, Nealon) or else to think through an ethics of desubjectivation so as to undo it (Huffer, Roach). Yet the problem with these strategies is that they leave behind the animus of their critique of liberatory politics in the first place: *liberation*. After all, there is absolutely no reason to believe that doing away with the subject by engaging in practices of desubjectification (as Huffer recommends), turning to affect and assemblage in order to map events (rather than relying on intersectionality in order to document the violences of identity, as Puar recommends), or responding to power in a myriad of everyday modes and practices (as Nealon suggests) will have anything to do with (furthering) liberation. Indeed, all three of these tactics or strategies may pass the Foucauldian ethical test of refusing subjectivity. But there is a surprising reticence to acknowledge the liberatory commitment to people and knowledges from below as fundamental to this critique, much less recognize the important task of genealogy as facilitating the emancipation of subjugated discourses, recognitions that are crucial to ensuring that such strategies function to further liberation rather than oppression. And although words like *liberation* and *oppression* may seem anathema to a Foucauldian or even a queer theoretical vocabulary, I think they are nevertheless the unstated stakes of the founding definition of queerness as dissidence, of Cohen's important critique and reimagining of queer coalitional politics, as well as of these contemporary critiques of queer theory's founding and left politics. Acknowledging these stakes is the crucial first step on a path to thinking more clearly about how to uphold a liberatory political commitment without investing in logics of identity, subjectivity, or outmoded and potentially reductive power binaries.[110]

In addition, I do not think such a project is anathema to a Foucauldian understanding of modern power. After all, Foucault does not deny that "major dominations" exist; rather, he says they are effects, not causes, and it is precisely the commitment to emancipation that demands we begin by understanding them from the bottom up, rather than the top down.

Moreover, we know from his biography that he was a political activist who routinely engaged in antistate and anticapitalist activist work. This means, at a minimum, that even a foremost critic of liberatory politics was actively pursuing them, and also suggests that having Foucauldian commitments while retaining a principled loyalty to liberatory politics is a possible and viable practice. For Foucault, the question of politics was a question that, ultimately, could only be decided by the revolution-makers, and it is not clear how much or to what extent he considered himself one of these actors.[111] My own contention, by contrast, is that the question of politics and/as the question of revolution is consistently and critically engaged in and as queerness, which is revolutionary by definition. In the next chapter, I return to the text of *No Future* to argue precisely this.

4
SOCIETY MUST BE DESTROYED

To write a manifesto is to announce one's participation, however discursive, in a history of struggle against oppressive forces.

—Janet Lyon[1]

What would the revolutionary project and revolutionary discourse mean if the goal were not a certain, a final, inversion of relations of power and a decisive displacement within the exercise of power?

—Michel Foucault[2]

It is in their fundamental challenge to a systemic process of domination and exclusion, with a specific focus on heteronormativity, that queer activists and queer theorists are tied to and rooted in a tradition of political struggle most often identified with people of color and other marginalized groups.

—Cathy Cohen[3]

Spurious apostles of negativity hammer new idols out of their good, while the aim of queer negativity is rather to hammer them into the dust. In the process, though, it must not make the swing of the hammer an end in itself but face up to political antagonism with the negativity of critical thought. Dare we trace, then, the untraversable path that leads to no good and has no other end than an end to the good as such?

—Lee Edelman[4]

This chapter extends the argument of the previous one by reading *No Future* as a continuation and elaboration of the left political project of queer theory. I am aware of how implausible this may sound. *No Future* is typically read as an exemplar of the antisocial thesis, itself considered to be a non- or antipolitical project. Moreover, both *No Future* and the antisocial thesis have been roundly rejected by many queer theorists for their damaging and exclusionary analyses that, critics hold, pertain effectively only to the figure whom Leo Bersani identifies (himself as) in *Homos*: the "white, relatively prosperous gay man."[5] Thus the obstacles to finding a left project in *No Future* are significant and (at least) twofold: first, it is potentially apolitical if not antipolitical; second, it is a decisively nonleft project in its unduly narrow focus on the least marginal members of queer's otherwise diverse constituency.[6] On this telling, the non- or antipolitics of the antisocial thesis is actually the old and very familiar politics of an unmarked yet reified bourgeois, white— and, in this case, gay—manhood that sabotages its own capacity to engage in radical or liberatory criticism.

In this chapter, I do not seek to rescue either *No Future* or the antisocial thesis from such criticisms, which have substantial merit. Instead, I want to offer an alternative reading/appropriation of *No Future* that recuperates what *is* worthwhile about it and put it to more decisively leftist ends. That particularly worthwhile piece is *No Future*'s unabashed conflation of queerness with both revolution and death. Although that latter term *death* may sound worrisome, at least part of the aim of this chapter is to show that death is and can be liberatory, and in fact may be the very name of liberation.[7] The crucial role of "death" in the confabulation of queerness and revolution in fact helps clarify the substantial contribution queer theory offers to left theory and praxis. The discomfort perhaps summoned by an affirmative invocation of death is a clue to this contribution, which is that queer theory draws attention to a hitherto underremarked feature of oppression that any viable left political project should also reject, namely, moralism. Although I do not know if he would put it exactly this way, I take one of Edelman's main points in *No Future* to be that the future's symbolization in the form of the Child functions to *moralize* that future, and that it is precisely this transformation of a political (and thus contestable) assertion into a moral (and thus incontestable) foundational principle that makes reproductive futurism oppressive. Mining *No Future*'s revolutionary queerness thus contributes to a left project by expanding its understanding of oppression, reconceptualizing morality as one more way in which freedom is systematically inhibited, foreclosed, exploited, or denied to most people along structurally predictable, formative, and determinate axes.

Second, however, *No Future* advances this left/liberatory project by refusing complicity with the very moralism it objects to and argues must be eradicated. This is particularly noteworthy because it constitutes a rejection, in some sense, of its own argument, but also because it amounts to a left critique of the left that does not itself become a new orthodoxy that the left must then counter. In calling for a revolution that would overturn the very terms of the revolution in/for which he is speaking, Edelman queers the revolutionary project in a way that reveals not only the problems with futurism, but also the futurist dilemmas we find ourselves in when we articulate liberatory politics within revolution's terms. In this sense, it is a more consistently revolutionary project in its advocacy of an end to revolution, because it submits the moralism of revolutionary desire to the very same critique of moralism *No Future* elaborates as the enabling condition of politics. *No Future* is thus a piece of annihilatory self-criticism that also rejects utopianism as its goal, much less any other alternative, or "better" future.

It is this rejection of futurity and hope that has led to the dismissal of *No Future* as antipolitical. My own sense, however, is that this is rather a queer revolution that simultaneously queers the revolutionary project itself. Unlike traditional revolutionary longings, this is an abolitionist vision that does not install its own redemptive or utopian vision at the core of its project. It is a resounding cry for the destruction of the social order as such that proffers no recuperation or redemptive prospects because it recognizes such calls as part and parcel of the toxic political logic that reproduces queerness. Instead, the only possible longing, the only aspiration or "better" "future" on offer in this queer(ed) revolutionary project is death—of both the social order and its own cry for justice, which would itself become a mechanism for the reproduction of queerness if elevated to a futurist ideal. The distinct advantage of such a call, in my view, is the articulation of a revolutionary vision that divests itself of moralism without, crucially, forsaking its animating, radical, and wholly *queer* desire.[8]

Of course, a utopian dream or aspiration to a "better future" is typically considered essential to left projects, such that to reject it is to risk irrelevance or, worse, nihilism. However, the presumption underlying such criticisms is that utopianism and hope are by definition liberatory, while nihilism, negativity, and death are the opposite. What I hope to show in this chapter is not simply that this predictable political calculus is misguided, but also that the charge of nihilism is actually a futile and ideologically loaded complaint that the left is better off leaving aside. Actual nihilism—the embrace of no standard, norm, truth, or foundation by which to interpret and evaluate the world—is an impossibility, whether of articulation or political conceptualization (much less action or praxis), and thus is both a facile criticism and an empty threat. Its aim is not to engage seriously with the question of emancipation; instead, it serves to discipline whatever view or position it is targeting in order to maintain social control and quash dissent (a fact that is as true within left/emancipatory movements as it is outside of them).[9]

Thus we need not fear admonishment for advocating nihilism, "death," destruction, or what have you since, as *No Future* makes clear, nihilism/"death"/destruction is in fact another name for liberation itself, a negativity that I will furthermore argue in no way commits us to a centering of whiteness or bourgeois gayness. Rather, as I hope to show, it commits us to radical and liberatory resistance to oppression in its specifically *moralizing* forms, whether that be the suffocating discourses of repronormativity, the civilizationalism of settler colonialism, the racism of white supremacy, or the multicultural liberal pieties that perennially undermine and sabotage left politics. That opposition takes the form of a figuration, embrace, and even celebration of "death." But only the moralizing strictures of leftist (and other) political pieties insist that death ought not be celebrated or embraced, or that it is "immoral" or "nihilist" to do so. If queerness is or means anything at all, however, it is surely that the only "appropriate" response to such sanctimony is not deference and reticence but rather ridicule, revelry, and rioting.[10]

ANTISOCIAL MANIFESTATIONS

To date, *No Future* has by and large been classified as the latest episode of the antisocial thesis in queer theory and thus an update or reformulation of Leo Bersani's arguments in his landmark "Is the Rectum a Grave?" and the later *Homos*. Yet the intellectual genealogy of the antisocial thesis is less than clear. The "most concentrated venue" for its discussion was an eponymous 2005 MLA panel subsequently reprinted in *PMLA*, a set of events that could themselves be seen as the category's inauguration.[11] In his introduction to the published version of this panel, Robert Caserio credits Bersani with formulating the first iteration of the antisocial thesis in *Homos*, wherein "homo-ness" is cast as unfit for or at odds with human social life.[12] By contrast, Edelman and Lauren Berlant suggest it is Caserio who coined the term *antisocial thesis*, claiming *No Future* merely as one "instance" of "an emergent trend in queer theory."[13] Others see its roots in the French radical Guy Hocquenghem's work.[14] Typically, only Edelman and Bersani are named as actual expositors of the antisocial thesis, although a set of unnamed "others" is often gestured toward of whom they are allegedly representative.[15] Meanwhile, Tom Roach claims that J. Halberstam coined the term *antisocial thesis* and that its purview includes not only Bersani and Edelman, but also the likes of Heather Love, Tim Dean, and William Haver (as well as, reliably, "others").[16]

If there is some confusion regarding both the origins and avatars of the antisocial thesis, it is even less clear what exactly it argues for or asserts. Does it designate the definitional unfitness of homosexuals or homosexuality for social life, as Caserio suggests? Or is it rather a broader designation of any number of antiassimilationist queer dissidents or dissidence, as Roach implies?[17] Is the antisocial thesis a specifically psychoanalytic theory regarding the shattering of the self that attends receptive or orgasmic sex, as Halberstam's earlier work argues?[18] Or is it instead a political theory of radical queer negativity, as Halberstam's later work suggests?[19] Is it an insistence, as Edelman argues, on "the antisocial bent of sexuality as such"?[20] Or is it a specifically psychoanalytic view of the requirements of subjectivity and sexuality's role in dismantling those requirements, as Dean and Bersani might propose? Raising such questions makes it difficult to find much common ground among Dean, Halberstam, Bersani, and Edelman, whether the subject is the sexual or the political. In addition, both Dean and Halberstam have gone out of their way to distinguish themselves from Edelman, with Dean offering a thoroughgoing critique of what he sees as Edelman's misguided readings of Lacan and sexual politics[21] and Halberstam seeking a more explicitly feminist, antiracist, and anticolonial commitment from Edelman's political project of negativity.[22] Meanwhile, Heather Love's careful work on the backward feelings engendered and experienced by queer people that pose obstacles to narratives of political or sexual progress certainly evinces skepticism about politics as such, and the "negative" affects that sustain her attention block both political action and sexual activity. Yet, while Love does not offer an optimistic reading, she certainly does not present an antisocial reading, either, at least insofar as her concern is not to eradicate futurism or social relationality, but rather to fashion a "backward future" that does not require the obliteration or disavowal of "negative" feelings like "grief, regret, and despair."[23]

Even if we narrow the focus to the two seemingly indisputable proponents of the antisocial thesis, Bersani and Edelman, difficulties remain. Perhaps most significantly, these two disagree about queerness itself. In *Homos*, Bersani names homo-ness as the threat to sociality, while in *No Future*, Edelman claims any repository of futureless-ness as *queer*, whether homosexual or not, and sees sameness as what the social order coercively reproduces, not what threatens it. Bersani's privileging of sameness, in other words, is completely at odds with Edelman's repudiation of sameness; Bersani's essentialized homo-ness is in no way equivalent to or interchangeable with Edelman's anti-identitarian, antisameness queer.[24] Yet reconciling Bersani and Edelman may no longer be the point, since Bersani has by now largely repudiated the argument of "Rectum," arguing that its conclusion is "both naïve and dangerous," whether taken as an ethics or a politics.[25]

Now, if the only two agreed-upon exponents of the antisocial thesis disagree fundamentally about its basic claims, and its oft-cited progenitor is now distancing himself from one of its original formulations, there may be some reason to call the categorization itself into question, or at least to complicate or problematize it. I want to do precisely this by suggesting that *No Future* is better classified not simply as a work of biopolitical theory, as I argued in chapter 2, but also as a *manifesto*, a specific textual genre of political theory whose meaning necessarily depends on an incomplete performative relationship with its readers.[26] This reading makes sense of the distinctive rhetorical style of *No Future*, which has troubled readers from the beginning and led to a seemingly endless list of criticisms and complaints. But *No Future* is a revolutionary text. Like all manifestos, it offers a critique of politics that aims at neither reform nor accommodation, but

rather the abolition or overthrow of a system that is essentially hierarchical and exploitative at its core and therefore beyond repair. Its language is therefore at least equally aptly read as the impetuous and declar-
ative rhetoric of revolution as it is the jargon of Lacanian psychoanalytic
theory. Although Edelman has been chided for not abiding by the norms
of academic propriety in this text, due not only to poor rhetorical styl-
ing, but also to failure to cite intellectual predecessors or offer a sufficiently
psychoanalytic reading of the death drive,[27] it is precisely such demands
for propriety that obscure the dynamic nature of this text, whose form is
intimately related to its content, both of which are a demand for the
destruction of the existing order. Far from simply a contribution to antisocial queer theory, *No Future* aims to galvanize its readership to action.
As Janet Lyon argues:

> "Manifesto" derives etymologically from a Latin composite of *manus*
> and *fectus*, or "hostile hand," and this translation acknowledges the
> nascent fury embodied in the form: like a fist striking through the scrims
> of civic order, the manifesto aims to challenge false conciliation in the
> name of a truth that fills the hearts and minds of its putative constitu-
> ents. And it seeks to assure its audience—both adherents and foes—that
> those constituents can and will be mobilized into the living incarnation
> of the unruly, furious expression implied in the text. The manifesto is,
> in other words, a genre that gives the appearance of being at once both
> word and deed, both threat and incipient action.[28]

While critics are largely united in their distaste for *No Future*'s broad gestures, bold proclamations, and seeming absolutism, the radical political
commitment of its author explains its "polemical,"[29] "melodramatic,"[30]
"self-enclosed,"[31] and coercive, absolutist, militant[32] rhetoric, just as it clarifies the stakes of its otherwise totalizing and "reductive"[33] political analysis. All this is due to the fact that, in both form and content, *No Future* is
a text that has praxis as its end.

Tim Dean has offered the most sustained criticism of *No Future* on these
grounds, a critique worth examining in some detail insofar as it makes
clear the stakes of reading *No Future* as a manifesto (or not). In one of his
more forceful statements, Dean writes,

The polemical ire that permeates *No Future* seems to have been appropriated wholesale from the right-wing rants to which he recommends we hearken. This polemical quality, producing an impression of barely restrained fury, helps account for the book's appeal insofar as it generates a *jouissance* comparable to that of Edelman's antagonists. . . . Often it remains unclear whether the reader is witnessing the results of ventriloquism or spirit possession. As Edelman formulates his argument regarding conservative perspectives on queerness, his campy hybrid of fundamentalist rhetoric and Lacanian jargon conjures a spectacle of Slavoj Žižek demonically taking possession of the body of Jerry Falwell.[34]

Although Dean presents these criticisms comedically, I think he also intends them quite seriously. Dean objects to *No Future* in both form and content: formally, the rhetoric is extravagant and extreme; substantively, the text gives credence to socially conservative, homophobic points of view.[35] The combination of the two results in an irresponsible mixture of the seductive, the uncontrollable, and the homophobic. Dean is in fact so troubled by Edelman's "irrational passion" and "barely restrained fury" that he explicitly and more than once accuses Edelman of purposefully deploying an affective rhetorical style in order to persuade readers on grounds other than the rational in order to accomplish some hidden (and implicitly nefarious) purpose.[36] Yet Edelman fares no better in Dean's book when mobilizing psychoanalytic theory. In these cases, Dean similarly suspects Edelman of "using recondite Lacanian vocabulary toward some rhetorical purpose that remains unstated."[37]

It is a bit surprising that Dean, himself a literary scholar and ethnographer of barebacking subculture, is so adamant that *No Future* be both unequivocally literal and manifestly decorous.[38] Nevertheless, if Edelman *is* deliberately misusing Lacanian concepts or manipulative rhetoric to attract readers on extrarational grounds, the question is clearly why he would do so. A distinct advantage of reading *No Future* as a manifesto is that it can answer this question: Edelman deploys a specific rhetorical style because it allows him to (attempt to) accomplish his explicitly *political* project: revolution. Reading *No Future* as a manifesto not only addresses Dean's concerns in this area but also does a better job accounting for the text's attractive force, which Dean dismisses as either flattery (by generating readers' self-congratulatory identification with a vanguard class of radical queers through an "embarrassingly pre-Foucaultian conception of sex")[39] or tomfoolery (by providing a performance of queer theory in the same campy and melodramatic key as the "delusional rants" of conservative "homophobes," thereby giving readers a "kick" equivalent to some sort of *jouissance*).[40] By contrast, I would suggest that the significant appeal of *No Future* (in addition to its argument, the logical consistency and sharpness of which Dean rather downplays)[41] lies in its surprising reliance on the rhetoric and position of the revolutionary. Annunciator of crisis, documentarian of injuries and abuse, and rouser of the rabble to rise up and break free from their chains, the revolutionary undeniably seeks to stir an audience, albeit with the explicit—not hidden or dishonest—aim of galvanizing them to action. This rhetoric is neither deceitful nor manipulative; it is the whole point. Accomplishing the manifesto's goals requires more than scholarly citations or appropriate use of psychoanalytic terminology. For the task of revolution, a specifically "political voice" is needed.[42]

This reading also explains Edelman's construction of what Dean calls "a Manichean universe,"[43] wherein binary, oppositional relationships—for example, between the Child and the queer, reproductive and nonreproductive, futurity and death—demarcate opposing "sides" of a political battlefield between which the reader must adjudicate and stake her claim.[44] As Lyon argues, this gesture is definitive of the manifesto, a genre of "rigid hierarchical binaries" that "participates in a reduced understanding of heterogeneous social fields, creating audiences through a rhetoric of exclusivity, parceling out political identities across a polarized discursive field, claiming for 'us' the moral high ground of revolutionary idealism, and constructing 'them' as ideological tyrants, bankrupt usurpers, or corrupt fools."[45] So, for example, Edelman insists on affirming that "*we* are the advocates of abortion" and that "the Child as futurity's emblem must die."[46] Putting this stark either-or alternative to the reader, Edelman also indicates which is the correct option: "We choose . . . *not* to choose the Child, as disciplinary image of the Imaginary past or as a site of projective identification with an always impossible future. The queerness we propose . . . delights in that mortality as the negation of everything that would define itself, moralistically, as pro-life."[47] So Edelman does, indeed, construct a Manichean universe. But this is because the manifesto demands that its readers stake a claim, that they choose which side they're on. As Lyon notes, "The manifesto declares a position; the manifesto refuses dialogue or discussion; the manifesto fosters antagonism and scorns conciliation. It is univocal, unilateral, single-minded."[48] It is therefore perhaps not accidental that Edelman uses the f-word throughout the text (it could have been the title of the book—*Fuck the Future*—and perhaps only the last vestiges of academic propriety prevented this).[49] On this score as well, Lyon observes,

> "Manifesto" may be shorthand for a text's particular stridency of tone, as with polemical editorial writing or grandstanding letters to the editor; in these and many other instances the term refers both to the form and to the passional state (frustration, disappointment, aggressive resolve) that precedes or engenders the text. To call a text a manifesto is to announce ahead of time its ardent disregard for good manners and reasoned civility.[50]

Edelman explicitly acknowledges all this, calling his book "polemical" and naming its task as an "engagement with the cultural text of politics and the politics of cultural texts."[51] In this sense, it is actually rather difficult to separate out critiques of form from critiques of content when it comes to *No Future*, since the manifesto itself refuses such distinctions. Its form is essential to its content, which aims not primarily at subtlety, nuance, or scholarship. Rather, its content is a righteous and indignant articulation of the problems faced by an aggrieved populace, spoken in a manner that will stir them to action.[52]

Dean's reading, then, is fated fundamentally to (dis)miss the force of Edelman's argument insofar as it explicitly discounts the political.[53] This inattention to politics leaves Dean with no other conclusion than that Edelman is using outrageous rhetoric or Lacanian terminology to illegitimately bolster his authorial influence and credibility, rather than to responsibly interpret psychoanalytic theory, as he ought: "When it thus becomes unhinged from its living concepts and reduced to its often rebarbative vocabulary, psychoanalysis degenerates into a dogma whose principal function lies in producing the rhetorical effect of authority. This is acutely the case in Edelman's account of the drive."[54] In my version, however, Edelman's project in *No Future* is not primarily concerned with psychoanalysis. Rather, it is a *political* critique of *social and cultural reality*. Insofar as it is political, it necessarily takes sides; insofar as it critiques social and cultural reality, it does not speak solely the language of rationality to an academic audience for whom it might otherwise be intended. Moreover, as a manifesto, it is unavoidable that *No Future* offends the norms of scholarly presentation and the sensibilities of a professorial readership (and not only a professorial readership—Edelman's text, like most manifestos, offends the sensibilities of a great many). From the manifesto's perspective, there is not much to say about such responses except that they are apolitical, even antipolitical, if not evidence of the offended party's complicity with the dominant powers the manifesto is attacking. After all, the primary reason for the fiery tone of the manifesto is outrage at injustice, and unless and until one recognizes the problem(s) it criticizes, one is unlikely to be persuaded that there isn't much ado about nothing going on here (or even, as in Dean's case, something deceitful and unscrupulous). The urgency and scope of the problems the manifesto reveals, however, demand a response that may not respect the protocols of rational discourse. Such stridency also suggests that political mobilization is both a process and the result of something more or other than simply rational argumentation (a fact of which scholars of psychoanalysis might otherwise well be aware). Edelman, for his part, acknowledges he is dealing with a domain "where reason must fail."[55]

The other reason for the manifesto's vehemence is that it fundamentally lacks the very power it is busily engaged in performing. As Martin Puchner points out, the manifesto speaks from a position of weakness, a fact too often overlooked by those who feel threatened or discomfited by its provocations. Manifestos voice marginalized perspectives and articulate grievances of those who do not (yet) form a hegemonic social presence. Although they seek to articulate a felicitous performative—"The time is now!" "We have nothing to lose but our chains!" "The people united will never be defeated!"—the fact is that the manifesto lacks the authorizing conventions necessary to render its pronouncements true. It speaks—forcefully—but its proclamations do not have much actual force in everyday life. Originally derived from the *manifest*, "a communication, authored by those in authority, by the state, the military, or the church, to let their subjects know their sovereign intentions and laws,"[56] the manifesto seeks to usurp the official sovereign by appropriating its idiom. But it must do so from a position that is decisively not sovereign, and so lacking in effective authority. Puchner writes: "Since the manifesto speaks from a position of weakness, it must hope that the presumption of future authority, the projective usurpation of the speaking position of the sovereign, will have effects and consequence. In this sense, the theatricality of the manifesto describes a pose of authority without which it could not utter a single word."[57]

To vanquish this theatricality and *become true*, the manifesto must bring into being the very subjects it claims to address, using its "political voice" to forge what Puchner calls the "literary agency" of the manifesto in order to constitute a new sovereign(ty). As Puchner argues regarding the famous last sentence of the *Communist Manifesto*, "Workers of the world, unite!": it is "addressed to a recipient who does not yet fully exist" but who must be constituted as such in order for its claims to ring true.[58] This "creation" of revolutionary addressee happens in three ways. First, via representation: "taking the place of, or replacing someone" in the way that the fifty-two "signatories of the Declaration [of Independence] are the representatives of the people, functioning as their organs of speech and action in the manner of a proxy." Second, via performative figuration: showing, for example, the people or the proletariat by creating a figure of them in the text itself. And third, via enactment: by theatrically performing the part of the people or proletariat in order to interpellate them in real life.[59] Edelman engages in all three of these discursive strategies in order to (attempt to) constitute a revolutionary constituency. First, as the author of *No Future* and the mouthpiece of queers' grievances, Edelman represents the constituency for whom he argues. He makes this clear when offering vignettes of his own experience of *sintho*mosexuality, for example, his encounter with the antiabortion billboard in Cambridge[60] or his anticipation of hostile criticism of *No Future* from fellow scholars.[61] Second, he engages in performative figuration, albeit in a mode particular to English professors: he cites characters from nineteenth-century British novels as exemplars of the social order's abjected queerness.[62] Third, he undeniably engages in enactment, performing the radical action of the revolutionary agent he seeks to bring into being. It is this rhetorical strategy that so rankles Dean, who, as we have seen, calls this enactment a kind of "spirit possession" or "ventriloquism." Another possible interpretation, however, is that this enactment is a posture of outrage and indignation, performed theatrically on the political stage, in an attempt to rouse and move an audience of marginalized queers to action.[63] Were any of these tactics to succeed, the political project of *No Future* might stand a chance of being accomplished, and what sounds like preposterous rhetorical bravado would become, effectively, an articulation of legitimate grievances based on an empirical description of political reality. This is the tenuous gamble at work in the theatrical, political declamations of the manifesto.

All this goes some way toward addressing Dean's claim that Edelman is not simply dishonest in his use of Lacanian jargon, but that he (mis)uses it in order to manufacture his own authority. Clearly there is something true in this view, even if it is not true in exactly the way Dean suggests. As a revolutionary, Edelman must be interested in enhancing his authority. However, as the author of a manifesto, enhancing his authority means articulating and interpellating the revolutionary class of queers who can—indeed must!—rise up and overthrow the social order that oppresses them. *No Future*, in other words, is a text written for a readership that its author cannot be confident already exists, but who must be brought into being if its aims are to be realized. Edelman therefore inhabits a precarious, high-stakes authorial position that explains his text's stridency. As Puchner observes: "Political manifestos frequently overcompensate for the actual powerlessness of their position with theatrical exaggerations, and their confidence is often feigned rather than grounded in real authority."[64] While it may seem implausible to suggest that Edelman writes from a position of weakness given his stature in the academy, it remains true that, regardless of Edelman himself or the specificities of his professional position, his text, when read as a manifesto, articulates an argument that is certainly marginal and likely unacceptable to most folks carrying on outside the narrow halls of academic queer theory and cultural studies (and even to a fair number of folks toiling within them). The constituency it seeks to galvanize as yet remains to show their faces or organize on their own behalf (except in isolated instances—more on this in the next chapter). In naming queers as such (and in the particular way in which he names them), Edelman aims to interpellate the very subjects his manifesto describes as already existing. Only if they recognize themselves in this call and take to the streets will the aims of *No Future* truly succeed—a metric of success quite distinguishable from the criteria of professional prestige.

QUEERING REVOLUTION

Because the manifesto's effectivity depends on a revolutionary agent that can only emerge in the aftermath of its textual activity, Puchner rightly points out that it is bound up with futurity: "no matter how impassioned and effective, the manifesto will always remain a split second removed from the actual revolution itself."[65] Its annunciation of crisis and demand for revolt are articulated in language; however, the manifesto also and simultaneously exhorts its readers to action, undermining the complacency of the act of reading even as it articulates the command to act in the written word. Puchner argues that the manifesto's aim is ultimately to dissolve the distinction between words and deeds so that what it most wishes for will finally come into being. It is impatient "with itself, with the fact that it cannot be more than a call, a cry, a demand."[66] But because the manifesto remains, in the end, "only" a text, it inevitably fails to bring about the revolution it otherwise so boldly heralds; its very material existence attests to the ineliminable gap between its present entreaty and the future upon which it hangs its hopes. Thus, as Puchner observes, despite their radical, performative aspirations, manifestos have been decisively *in*effective at realizing their aim of closing the gap between speech and action:

> The history of communist manifestos, the fact that there exists a history of communist manifestos in the first place, is an index of postponements and failures, the failure of a final, all-transforming revolution. The absence of such a revolution makes for the melancholic tone that can be detected underneath these manifestos' aggressive surfaces. The history of political manifestos therefore has a tragic undertone, a history of disastrous postponements of the revolution, postponements to which all manifestos have contributed even as they have tried to do everything to bring them to an end.[67]

Yet manifestos are failures not simply because the revolution (communist or otherwise) has not finally or fully arrived. Manifestos are failures because they are futurist and because the future (communist or otherwise) can never finally or fully arrive. Indeed, we might say that the manifesto is an object lesson in futurism's failings. As a rhetorical form, it exemplifies futurity; as a genre, it stakes its entire existence on a time that is only ever to come; as an object, it is material evidence of the perpetual deferral of its own most fervent desire. The longing for total revolution is thus saturated by futurism and determined by it, making the manifesto a genre of inevitably thwarted and failed desire.[68] As Puchner points out, every manifesto has contributed to this history, regardless of its claims to the contrary and its most ardent intentions. The history of modernity's most radical dissent is thus simultaneously an archive of loss, deferral, and defeat.[69]

Unsurprisingly, No Future too is afflicted with the futurism it calls upon queers to abolish. All too aware of this, Edelman attempts to undermine it by refusing his manifesto's aspirational promises, insisting to readers that he cannot fulfill any dreams, theirs or his, of overcoming heteronormativity. Adamant, he proclaims that his project offers nothing, promises no future redemption, and does not speak in the language of hope. His revolutionary "solution," such as it is, is no better alternative than the status quo: "the queerness of which I speak . . . proposes, in place of the good, something I want to call 'better,' though it promises, in more than one sense of the phrase, absolutely nothing."[70] It is "nothing" in the sense that, in the face of critique, one must always proffer a solution—"Always the question: If not this, what?"—a demand Edelman rejects as yet another disciplinary recommitment to futurism and, therefore, to the production of queerness.[71] But it is also "nothing" insofar as only the nihilism of no future poses the possibility of political liberation, or, in Edelman's version, liberation from politics itself. Thus, he says, we must reject not simply politics but all hope for the future of politics, for that future and that hope are the political operation that inevitably produces queers and queerness.

This seemingly dreary argumentative conclusion has led critics to dismiss No Future as politically useless or, worse, an antipolitics of fashionable nihilism that bolsters the critic's own self-satisfaction at the expense of actual social change. Yet I simply don't think we need to take Edelman at his word regarding the rejection of politics here. For, as readers of No Future, it is impossible to ignore the fact that even the espousal of rejection is itself an espousal; to advocate the refusal of hope is still to advocate for a turn of events that has yet to occur and thus to take up a future-oriented position. Edelman may not have a proposal for a better tomorrow, but he nevertheless wrote a book he must have imagined would be read by somebody at a later date, a book that might even, perhaps, have an effect on those readers and, thus, an influence on the future. As is evident, then, even future-denial has its stakes in some kind of future. Edelman cannot help but demonstrate that even a politics of no future is both a politics and a future.

This paradox is less a logical inconsistency or performative contradiction than it is a dramatization of the hegemonic all-pervasiveness of futurism, which determines that even the demand for its destruction be articulated in its idiom. This paradox is one reason why Edelman describes his revolutionary project as "impossible," "hopeless," and "against all reason": not only is it impossible to conceive; it is impossible even to articulate.[72] After all, were Edelman able to speak otherwise than in futurist terms about the possibility of toppling futurism, either the argument of *No Future* would be invalid(ated) or else his words would be, quite literally, unintelligible. As Teresa de Lauretis observes, *No Future* is "unreadable" to the extent that it is a "a book, a task without a future."[73] Indeed, she argues that Edelman cannot be understood *now* given the epistemological hegemony of futurism, even as *now* is the only possible time for/of his revolutionary speech. That Edelman's critique of modernity must reiterate its terms in order to be understood, then, is not an objection to the critique so much as the clearest possible demonstration of it and perhaps the most powerful indictment of the stultifying logic of modernity itself.

How, then, to articulate and effect the radical abolitionism of revolutionary desire without getting caught up in the stranglehold of futurism? Futurism's inescapability means not simply that politics is irredeemable and reform insufficient, but also that the deconstructive or queer practice of subversive redeployment is a naïve delusion regarding our own ability to think and act outside or beyond futurist mandates. As Edelman simultaneously argues and demonstrates, futurism's stifling determination of the very domain of the political itself means that any and all resistance is always already coopted, while revolt is an impossibly queered space that is simultaneously named and foreclosed by the death drive. Yet Edelman's solution to this dilemma is to recommend neither capitulation to futurism nor some sort of compromise with it but rather an accession to its worst nightmares in an embrace of queerness that will destroy it from within, "short-circuit[ing] the social in its present form."[74] In other words, rather than defend society, which Edelman finds indefensible, much less deconstruct society, as a queer critique of norms might recommend, or even (dear me!) redeem society, by entreating a utopian vision that imagines the overcoming of all suffering and oppression, Edelman instead declares we must destroy society. And we do so by taking up, inhabiting, or "embracing" the very "death" that futurism inevitably produces as the queer by-product of its social ordering. He thus dismisses utopianism in the name of an immediacy that "the future stop here,"[75] challenging us to live life as an insistent presentism that will do nothing else afterward but die, and casting this alliance with death as *the* act of revolutionary resistance.

While Dean vociferously rejects this "embrace" because of its psycho-analytic impossibility, Edelman, I think, is well aware of this fact and rec-ommends it precisely for this reason, a contradiction that becomes more intelligible if understood politically rather than solely psychoanalytically. Indeed, Edelman's recommendation of this "embrace" is a clearly political position—despite what he may say otherwise—in two specific, complex ways. First, recall the historicization of Edelman's argument provided in chapter 2, wherein I characterized his version of "politics" as a distinctly modern, European, settler colonial sovereignty. An important consequence of this historicization is that, even in his allegedly non- or antipolitical advocacy, Edelman cannot actually be rejecting politics per se since, despite his own claims to the contrary, there is no such thing. Abolishing modern politics or futurist politics is not equivalent to abolishing politics as such and could only mean as much if every modernity were European modernity, if every politics were a sovereign biopolitics, and if every tem-porality were futurist. To understand Edelman's refusal of politics as a refusal of any and all politics existing anywhere is to go along with his unmarked universalist presentation of reproductive futurism as the logic of everything existing everywhere all the time, itself a frequent conceit of psychoanalytic frames.[76] But if futurism is the temporality of modern bio-political sovereignty, it immediately becomes clear that other temporali-ties are possible, even as other versions of politics must necessarily exist.[77] As Audra Simpson argues, for example, "Indigenous political orders are quite simply, first, . . . prior to the project of founding, of settling, and as such continue to point, in their persistence and vigor, to the failure of the settler project to eliminate them, and yet are subjects of dispossession, of removal, but their polities serve as alternative forms of legitimacy and sov-ereignties to that of the settler state."[78]

Historicizing futurist politics in this way means that alternative tempo-ralities or political schemas exist but are queer(ed) and represented as existential threats to it: as unintelligible, unlivable, immoral, backward, and "savage." While Edelman does indeed conflate all politics with futurism, such that his call for the destruction of politics seems to portend an unthink-able and intolerable nihilism, it is nevertheless the case that, once situated historically, the advocacy that queers accede to the deathly positioning to which they are always already relegated by reproductive futurism is not some sort of unthinkable, antipolitical vision, nor is it an advocacy of suicide or some sort of necropolitical imperative. Rather, in the context of a European modernity built on the colonization of most of the rest of the world, Edelman's embrace of death can be read as a prescription for an anticolonial allegiance to and alliance with those forms of politics and temporality that thwart, refuse, or deny futurism's colonial mandates. *No Future*'s embrace of the "death drive," in other words, is a championing of resistant futures and political systems that *show up as death from a futurist perspective* and are various surrogates for the broad, structural category he designates as "queer." In advocating for a revolution on behalf of queers and arguing for an embrace of queerness, then, Edelman is very much arguing in the name of something—not the future, of course, and certainly not life in any biological sense. But he is also not quite arguing in the name of death in a biological sense, either. Rather, he is arguing that "the dead" should "live," that is, that they "come to life" (or insistently exist) and animate the destruction of the settler order that they are always already consigned by that social order to symbolize. This is, in other words, an argument for indigenous existence as resistance to settler sovereignty. Siting and situating futurism historically make clear that Edelman's recommended accession to queerness/death is another name for radical resistance to sovereign biopolitics and that, far from nihilism, it is an emancipatory and decolonizing political recommendation of the first order. In this sense, even Edelman's own project is wedded to life, albeit a life that is unlivable *as* life, which is the status of native life within settler colonial regimes. As he says in recommendation of embracing the death drive, "political self-destruction inheres in the only act that counts as one: the act of resisting enslavement to the future in the name of having a life."[79] Edelman's opposition to the political can therefore be reread as a wholesale opposition to the sovereign biopolitics of European modernity and an imagining of the death of that political order as the content of revolutionary politics. Indeed, his suggestion of a necessary "counterproject"[80] to futurism makes clear that his recommendation of this refusal is the essential, necessary, and definitive act of political resistance, even as it is a championing of the lives and political temporalities of those determined to be emissaries of death.

Importantly, this destructive refusal is a threat that redounds back on Edelman himself and on all of us who share his habitation of futurist politics in Western modernity (or who were ourselves trained in the history of that thought). This is the second, complex way that Edelman's rejection of politics is in fact a maximally political entreaty. The tension at work in Edelman's inevitably futurist call to end futurism means that he is also and necessarily calling for the destruction of his own revolutionary project and subjective/authorial position. This is a queer revolution that queers the aims of revolution itself, divesting itself of futurism even as it speaks in its name. As a political act, it amounts "to put[ting] one's foot down at last, even if doing so costs us the ground on which we, like all others, must stand."[81] It is a revolutionary desire that seeks to dispossess revolution of its failed foundations without thereby relinquishing either revolution or its animating desire. This revolutionary discourse exceeds the parameters of revolution as it has hitherto unfolded in modernity, even as it promises a liberation from modernity's—and liberation's—moralizing constraints.

This paradoxical, queer(ed) revolution is therefore unmistakably tied to death, and in more than one way: not only because queerness is the structural position of anything antisociety and antilife; not only because it demands the destruction of all that has been construed as life (as valuable life, as worthy life, as life worth living and endowed with a future); but also because the revolutionary call to destroy society and its futurist temporality will necessarily result in the eradication of its own revolutionary demand in the process. This is why Edelman's queer political project can never recommit us to sovereignty, whether of a charismatic revolutionary leader, a vanguard revolutionary class, or a theological vision of an all-powerful monarch, much less the sovereign subject, whose very European coherence requires futurism's linear temporality. It can commit us only to the destruction of these things, as well as to the eradication of our own commitments precisely to that very destruction if, as, and when they threaten to become the next crushing futurist ideal. Edelman's formulation of the impossible yet wholly revolutionary goal of refusing futurism—a refusal achievable only in a future that lies beyond its textual articulation and summary rejection there—offers a rich and provocative articulation of a revolutionary desire that seeks to dispossess revolution of its very foundations, even as it speaks in its name.

QUEER THEORY AND/AS LIBERATION

There is a significant remaining obstacle to the appropriation of *No Future* for left politics, and that is the apt criticism that *No Future* (as well as the antisocial thesis more generally) elaborates an argument that only takes into account the perspectives and problems of privileged white gay men.[82] Indeed, many have argued that *No Future* gains its coherence and persuasive power precisely because of its disavowal of race, class, and gender, exclusions that allow for the fetishization of an "ahistorical"[83] and "weirdly atemporal"[84] queer subject. But, as José Esteban Muñoz accurately observes, "The future is only the stuff of some kids."[85] Edelman's failure to racialize the Child he seeks to destroy obscures the fact that "all children are not the privileged white babies to whom contemporary society caters," and thus the painful reality that queer kids of color are routinely harassed and murdered without troubling either futurism or the cult of the Child.[86] In arguing for a future for queer kids of color, therefore, Muñoz makes clear that reproductive futurism is a form of white supremacy. Alison Kafer makes a similar point regarding disability, arguing that Edelman's revolutionary antifuturism "takes on a different valence for those who are *not* supported in their desires to project themselves (and their children) into the future in the first place."[87] Building on Muñoz's argument that the future is the purview of only some children, Kafer writes, "some populations are already marked as having no future, as destined for decay, as always already disabled."[88] Kafer therefore rightly notes that the Child is not simply white, but also able-bodied, and thus that "disabled children are not part of this privileged imaginary except as the abject other."[89] The problem, in other words, is not simply that Edelman takes the Right's worldview seriously, as Dean has it. It is rather (or also) that he does so by duplicating its universalist errors and reproducing oppressions the left otherwise seeks to dismantle, such as white supremacy and ableism.

The sharpest and perhaps most synoptic critique of *No Future* in this vein is that Edelman ignores the fundamentally privileged positionality involved in rejecting survival and futurity themselves as political agendas. Indeed, it seems particularly cruel and benighted to dismiss futurist movements and political struggles when they are so often waged precisely by those who were never meant to survive. Survival is a premier value of freedom struggles, quite far from an oppressive insistence on the reproduction of sameness at the expense of the present. As Muñoz argues, in rejection of Edelman's insistence that the future stop here, "Heteronormative culture makes queers think that both the past and the future do not belong to them. All we are *allowed* to imagine is barely surviving the present."[90] Whether it is black people's fight against chattel slavery in the United States or, as my next chapter will consider, a fundamental tenet of indigenous resistance to settler colonialism, the demand for and commitment to survival in these cases are an insistence on a future that is denied and violently destroyed at every moment. As Angela Davis puts it, "Not all people have survived enslavement; hence [the black woman's] survival-oriented activities were themselves a form of resistance."[91] The oppressed's fights for survival are fights for what is unthinkable and for all practical purposes impossible: the continued existence and flourishing of (in these cases) black and indigenous life. They are essentially liberatory insistences on life as it has not been allowed to be lived or recognized as credibly livable.[92]

Queer theory has perhaps been slow to take up its connection with traditions of the oppressed or to explicitly position itself *as* a tradition of the oppressed. Key to such a positioning, however, is the recognition that futurity and survival do not mean the same thing in mainstream or canonical political theory—or even, as this discussion makes clear, mainstream (and canonical?) queer theory—as they do in traditions of the oppressed. In their early article "What Does Queer Theory Teach Us About X?," Lauren Berlant and Michael Warner observe, "Sometimes the question of what queer theory teaches us about *x* is not about politics in the usual sense but about personal survival. Like feminist, African American, Latina/Latino, and other minority projects, queer work strikes its readers as knowledge central to living."[93] This crucial observation indicates the necessity of liberatory knowledges and studies for the survival and flourishing of marginalized, subordinated, and oppressed people(s). Reading that politics of survival from the position and perspective of precisely such "minority projects"—rather than how they are inflected within, by, and for those already in positions/traditions/structures of hegemonic power—is key to ensuring that queer theory is and remains a liberatory body of thought.

What's clear is that Edelman simply does not do this. As critics rightly contend, the focus and concrete material referent for the queerness he champions in this text are reliably white, male, and gay.[94] Nevertheless, his text's argument is a liberatory one, if intentionally repurposed and read from the perspective of the oppressed. In this view, black and indigenous folks, the disabled, and queer youths of color are not *excluded* from reproductive futurism so much as they are *queered* by it. As Chandan Reddy argues,

> There is nothing in Edelman's argument that wouldn't allow one to suggest that all kinds of embodied cultural formations could be sinthomosexuals. Indeed, Edelman argues that as homonormativity becomes more the rule than the exception, the sinthomosexual is not absorbed but displaced onto other cultural subjects and figures—two that come to my mind are the illegal alien and the so-called Muslim fundamentalist.[95]

I will have more to say about the extension of Edelman's argument to the "Muslim fundamentalist" in the next chapter. For now, what is important to recognize is that futurism provides a useful map of the determination of all "enemies" of the social order, whether those enemies be *sinthomosexuals*, indigenous peoples, people of color, or the disabled—"queer" is merely their structural, catchall designation. Although Edelman himself prominently neglects to cite these additional applications, critiquing futurism from the more comfortable position of someone subject to its most privileged (if still objectionable) manifestations, I nevertheless think his analysis is a liberatory one that can be repurposed for solidarity with people and knowledges from below. It is certainly a self-critical dissent with a host of perhaps unintended but nevertheless radical consequences that links it to the kind of work that, as I argued in chapter 3, articulates the political stakes of dissident queer theory. Indeed, once this resituation and perspective is taken into account, it does not require too much theoretical convolution to recognize Edelman's critique as in accord with those of Muñoz and Kafer rather than at odds with them.

To reinforce this claim, I want to follow Lynne Huffer and Jasbir Puar in their critiques of queer theory and revisit Cathy Cohen's formative essay, "Punks, Bulldaggers, and Welfare Queens: The Radical Potential of Queer Politics?" In this piece, Cohen argues for a rethinking of marginal positionality in terms of one's relation to power, rather than in terms of a binary categorization of queer vs. straight. She cites the prohibition of slave marriages and the long history of obsession with black women's reproductive choices in the United States as examples of ostensibly heterosexual people inhabiting positions outside the bounds of normative sexuality because of race, class, and property status. In arguing for a more capacious, intersectional queer politics that is accountable not simply to the question of who is and who isn't heterosexual but, more broadly, to the question of what each of our relationships with and proximity to power may be, Cohen writes:

> As we stand on the verge of watching those in power dismantle the welfare system through a process of demonizing the poor and young—primarily poor and young women of color, many of whom have existed for their entire lives outside the white, middle-class heterosexual norm—we have to ask if these women do not fit into society's categories of marginal, deviant, and "queer." As we watch the explosion of prison construction and the disproportionate incarceration rates of young men and women of color, often as part of the economic development of poor white rural communities, we have to ask if these individuals do not fit society's definition of "queer" and expendable.[96]

Edelman's understanding of queerness in terms of futurism and its flouting by "deviants" echoes Cohen's understanding of "queer" as a kind of non- or antinormativity based on one's proximity to power. Both are structural determinations of oppression rather than reified identity categories of exclusion and difference. If we read *No Future* as a manifesto and locate its argument within a tradition of the oppressed, futurism becomes legible as a specific, historical form of oppression in relationship to which "queers" are retroactively produced and positioned. Crucially, because the key characteristic of queerness is a temporal (not identitarian) one, having "too many" babies is just as much a threat to America's future as not having any at all in this framework—it just depends on which queers we're talking about.[97] Indeed, as Andrea Smith argues, in a critique of Edelman that also happens to demonstrate the force of his argument,

> An indigenous critique must question the value of "no future" in the context of genocide, where Native peoples have already been determined by settler colonialism to have no future. If the goal of queerness is to challenge the reproduction of the social order, then the Native child may be already queered. For instance, Colonel John Chivington, the leader

of the famous massacre at Sand Creek, charged his followers not only to kill Native adults but to mutilate their reproductive organs and to kill their children because "nits make lice." In this context, the Native Child is not the guarantor of the reproductive future of white supremacy; it is the nit that undoes it.[98]

Smith has it exactly right here, even if this is not a consequence of his writing that Edelman might have foreseen and even as Smith may not seek an anticolonial reading of *No Future*. The indigenous child is, indeed, already queered, just as it is absolutely the case that not all babies symbolize America's future. As Muñoz and Smith cogently argue, kids of color and indigenous children are deemed degenerative of the social order and worthy of neglect, punishment, and outright elimination. Historicizing futurism as the temporality of European modernity and situating Edelman's critique of it within a tradition of the oppressed not only make room for liberatory critiques of a marked and very specific settler survivalism, but also allow liberatory and social justice scholarship to incorporate the constitutive role futurism plays in constituting oppression—in this case, the racist and civilizationalist oppression of people of color and indigenous people respectively—and their moralized justifications in terms of "welfare queens" or "nits" and "lice." The specific futurist oppression I have focused on in this book is biopolitical sovereignty; however, as the discussion of Cohen makes clear, it may be possible to apply it to a broader logic of American nationalism that also stigmatizes or queers black and brown people. Indeed, what my amended rendering of the logic of futurism alerts us to is the fact that slanders like "savage," "queer," and "welfare queen" are the inevitable and moralizing effects of the functioning of modern politics itself.[99]

This focus on power and the targeting of resistance at its systematic roots is at odds with a more inclusionist vein of left critique of Edelman as evidenced, for example, by J. Halberstam's championing of queer failure. Halberstam has been a consistent critic of Edelman's failures of inclusion, arguing that he relies upon an "excessively small archive"[100] to make his case, a camp archive bound up with the affects and experiences of a narrow set of canonically and stylistically white gay men. Halberstam, by contrast, emphasizes not only the lowbrow but also various axes of political marginalization such as class, gender, and nation that he thinks are neglected by Edelman, arguing for an understanding of negativity as "queer failure": the resistance to, refusal of, or incapacity for being attuned to the disciplinary norms of success, health, and well-being so prized by the heteronormative, neoliberal, adultist order. As Halberstam sees it, queer people and lives emblematize and often instantiate failure insofar as they neglect or refuse to conform to standard timelines, genders, and expectations of appropriate behavior.[101] He thus argues for a queerness that champions "failing, losing, forgetting, unmaking, undoing, unbecoming," and "not knowing," all of which "may in fact offer more creative, more cooperative, more surprising ways of being in the world."[102] These modes of failure not only are queer practices for Halberstam, but, taken together, constitute a form of political resistance, "a way of refusing to acquiesce to dominant logics of power and discipline".[103]

> There is something powerful in being wrong, in losing, in failing, and . . . all our failures combined might just be enough, if we practice them well, to bring down the winner. Let's leave success and its achievement to the Republicans, to the corporate managers of the world, to the winners of reality TV shows, to married couples, to SUV drivers. The concept of practicing failure perhaps prompts us to discover our inner dweeb, to be underachievers, to fall short, to get distracted, to take a detour, to find a limit, to lose our way, to forget, to avoid mastery, and, with Walter Benjamin, to recognize that "empathy with the victor invariably benefits the rulers." All losers are the heirs of those who lost before them. Failure loves company.[104]

Yet this valorization of queer failure leaves us neither refusing nor dissenting from the political logic of success and failure. Instead, we remain within it and simply side with a more inclusive (and apparently oppositional) cast of Democrats, workers, reality TV show losers, single people, and compact car drivers because they are potentially "more creative, more cooperative, more surprising." It is not difficult to recognize this version of queer failure as a recuperation of the hopeful logic of futurism itself, wherein "failure" is just as indebted to the terms of the political as is "success." Halberstam simply reverse-valorizes these terms (which he seems to read as surrogates for the political categories of powerful and powerless), championing the worthiness not of "winning" but rather "creative," "cooperative," and "surprising" losing.[105] Although Halberstam's celebration of queers as those who refuse to grow up seems like a more dissident version of queer failure and a "truly political negativity,"[106] Edelman aptly diagnoses it as the negation of a particular political position, rather than the negation of politics (or futurism, or success and failure, or the essential and constitutive logic of politics) as such.[107]

Thus the problem with *No Future*'s critique of oppression isn't exactly its failure of inclusion of multiple axes of identity and oppression. That's not to say this isn't a problem, but it is to say that focusing only on the failure of inclusion as the major problem with this text obscures the radical content of Edelman's critique as well as the specificity of its failure to be as radical as it could be. The problem with *No Future* is not its failure of inclusion—itself a hallmark liberal value unworthy of left aspiration, anyway—but rather that it does not link its queer theory to traditions of the oppressed or solidify the connection between queer theory and left social theory, as Warner and Cohen differently entreat. Moreover, rectifying *No Future*'s failures of inclusion would neither vanquish futurism nor eliminate the oppressions Edelman's critics rightly fault him for overlooking. This is because racial or other "inclusion" within the hegemony of reproductive futurism would not be any more liberatory for queer youths of color, the disabled, or black and brown people than the current hegemony of the white Child. Instead, it would render futurism multicultural and diverse, strengthening it by transforming it into a stultifying liberal ideal of difference amid sameness. Liberal multiculturalism, however, is a deeply inadequate model for emancipatory politics. It erases hierarchies of power and oppression and thus cannot analyze with any clarity the regimes of ableism and white supremacy (much less adultist successfulness) that left projects are interested in dismantling. Thus thinking about antifuturism from a left perspective requires eliminating futurism, not asking for permission to be included within it as equal participants.

QUEER THEORY AND/AS ANTIMORALISM

It may still seem ridiculously unlikely that *No Future* can (or even should) be read as making an antioppression argument in favor of revolution. As Shannon Winnubst has written,

To call for a politics without a future in this contemporary world of increasing imperialism and ongoing violence should strike all of us as odd or indulgent at best, perverse at worse. We already know a word for such a politics—nihilism. And writing from the material luxury of a white citizen of the U.S., I find such a call particularly noxious: what perspective but the most privileged and comfortable would gallantly proclaim the necessary disavowal of the future?[108]

Not only does the label *nihilism* emerge here, but so, too, significantly, does the descriptor *perverse*. A term for insubordination that is explicitly inflected by, in, and through sexuality, *perverse* is another name for *queer* that can also, not coincidentally, be used in disciplinary philosophy simply to mean irrational or absurd. The deliberate reclaiming of *perverse* by queers and queer theorists as a badge of pride is an open defiance of the moralizing strictures transmitted by the term, moralisms that clearly bleed into the otherwise unmarked or "objective" realms of epistemology and philosophical knowledge. It is thus no accident that Winnubst defines anti-futurism as perverse, for that is precisely what it is. The point of *No Future*, however, is that perversity is to be celebrated—in my version, its embrace is a form of political praxis.

Noting Winnubst's (surely unwitting) use of *perversity* as a term of disparagement here is no mere quibble, but rather a symbolically important entry point into the conversation regarding queer theory's distinct contribution to left politics, and that is its opposition to moralism(s) of all sorts. Although much attention has been paid to the specifically Childish version of the future Edelman opposes, what too often gets missed is the fact that the particular *content* of that future is much less problematic than the dogmatic insistence on that future's irrefutable value and worth, an insistence that secures its own hegemony via the exclusion, abjection, and negation of those who deny or defy it. Futurism's oppressiveness, in other words, resides in its totalizing demand that everyone worship at its altar (the altar of, as Edelman puts it in one place, the Futurch)[109] and that anyone refusing refuge in its sanctuary is "whatever a social formation abjects as queer."[110] While Edelman calls this operation reproductive futurism, I think a broader and more useful designation for this oppression and its punitive effects is *moralism*. Moralism can take any number of forms, of course; in this book I have focused on specifically biopolitical versions— "savagery," as I argued in chapter 2, and "terrorism," which I will discuss in chapter 5. Nevertheless, insofar as morality is and functions like one of Foucault's "totalitarian discourses" or what Nietzsche calls "the ascetic ideal," it is a discourse of truth and sociality that "permits no other interpretation, no other goal; it rejects, denies, affirms, and sanctions solely from the point of view of *its* interpretation."[111] Not only this, but it is a regime of truth that exists primarily in order to punish. Both Nietzsche and queer theory at their best recognize that morality and its idealizations *are* politics and in fact serve power's authoritarian function of condemning all those who fail to comply with its mandates. Swathed in the invisible clothes of uprightness, responsibility, dignity, and worth, both Nietzsche and queer theory recognize the emperor's nakedness, understanding all too well that only a sheer sanctimony shrouds his imperiousness as morality. That morality unveiled, however, is better understood as a political tool that segregates populations according to manufactured idealizations of merit or worth in order to stigmatize, demean, ostracize, and punish those deemed undeserving by its measure. In Foucauldian language (and minus the emperor), morality serves the normalizing and disciplinary functions of power, stigmatizing, ostracizing, and punishing some in the name of abstract and coercive ideals such as the common good, social welfare, law and order, and the protection of children.

It is this sort of moralism and functioning of morality that I read *No Future* as a whole to be rejecting. This aligns Edelman not simply with Nietzsche, a perhaps unlikely forebear of queer theory, but also with Gayle Rubin, an indisputable founder of the field.[112] Her justly famous essay from 1985, "Thinking Sex: Notes Toward a Radical Politics of Sexuality," is known for, among other things, a set of charts that visually map the myriad ways in which various forms of sexual activity are hierarchized and (de)valued.[113] It is also known for Rubin's indexical listing of the many obstacles that impede the construction of a radical politics of sexuality. These five obstacles are (1) sexual essentialism (the presumption that sexual desire is an innate, presocial drive); (2) sex negativity (the belief that sex is dangerous, unhealthy, destructive, or depraved); (3) the fallacy of misplaced scale (the exceptionalizing of sex to the point that it becomes burdened with "an excess of significance");[114] (4) the domino theory of sexual peril (the fear that sex must be contained or else it will leak out and spread and destroy everything); and (5) the lack of a concept of benign sexual variation (as Rubin puts it, "One of the most tenacious ideas about sex is that there is one best way to do it, and that everyone should do it that way").[115] Among other things, these five obstacles offer a useful map of the many ways in which sex and sexuality are moralized and, in calling for their elimination, Rubin effectively authorizes and demands a strictly political, nonmoral(ized) analysis of sex and sexuality.

Of course, Rubin writes mostly in terms of "value," not morality per se, noting the ways in which medical, legal, social, and religious discourses classify and rank different forms of sexuality and sexual activity. But she sees clear continuity across these different classificatory and ranking schemes, and she does at times use morality as a way of describing them. This is, in my view, the common element that gives these ranking regimes their power and coercive force. It is by now a commonplace that the seemingly more scientific or "objective" categories of pathology and neurosis are medicalizations of formerly moral categories and, as such, carry punitive and normalizing force. (Rubin suggests, for example, that the most recent edition of the American Psychiatric Association's *Diagnostic and Statistical Manual of Mental Disorders* serves as "a fairly reliable map of the current moral hierarchy of sexual activities.")[116] And whether religious, scientific, philosophical, or lesbian feminist, Rubin calls all such frameworks for ranking and classifying sex "systems of sexual judgment."[117] A central premise of the argument of "Thinking Sex," then, is that politics and morality are mutually exclusive endeavors, and that we must refuse the moralization of sex and sexuality if it is to remain a site of contestation, interrogation, and dissent, rather than an uncovering of nature, value, or truth.[118] These latter terms—*nature, value, truth*—are different modes of insulating otherwise contestable claims from interrogation or critique. Nietzsche has taught us that much, and further instructed that this act of insulation is simultaneously the operation of moralism, which attempts to bypass politics altogether even as it asserts its own will to power. As Judith Butler similarly pointed out in her early, embattled defense of poststructuralist feminism, the determination that a premise is beyond question because it resides in the realm of nature or truth is a quintessentially political act: "To establish a set of norms that are beyond power or force is itself a powerful and forceful conceptual practice that sublimates, disguises, and extends its own power play through recourse to tropes of normative universality."[119] In this same essay, she noted that "this movement of interrogating that ruse of authority that seeks to close itself off from contest . . . is, in my view, at the heart of any radical project."[120]

To follow on Butler and Rubin, then, and also borrow from Rubin's terminology a bit, I want to suggest that queer theory's contribution to left politics is its claim that morality itself can be considered a "vector of oppression."[121] Recognizing with Nietzsche that all moralities are more or less elaborate systems of punishment and cruelty, Edelman's queer political theory is a critique of oppression insofar as it recognizes the operation of morality as the production of queerness and a reproductive stranglehold on the lives of everyone else. This is why, as Michael Warner observed in 1993, it cannot be determined in advance who or what queers are or what constituency they name, even as we can be sure that queerness is a radical, indeed "fundamentalist" resistance to the hegemony of the social order. As I have argued here, queerness entails a rejection of moralism and the moralist pieties about survival and preservation that constitute political, social, and subjective intelligibility. It is no accident, then, that queer theory focuses on and emerges from sexuality, itself a privileged locus of morality and moralisms of all sorts, as "Thinking Sex" aptly documents. This emergence, however, is also an astute recognition of the political importance of desire and a crucial argument for the foregrounding of desire as integral to liberation and liberatory politics. Perhaps unsurprisingly, then, both Rubin and Edelman make the case for the seriousness, relevance, and import of political analysis of sex/uality and its importance to politics. Compare, for example, the opening of "Thinking Sex" with the opening of Edelman's essay "Ever After." First Rubin:

> The time has come to think about sex. To some, sexuality may seem to be an unimportant topic, a frivolous diversion from the more critical problems of poverty, war, disease, racism, famine, or nuclear annihilation. But it is precisely at times such as these, when we live with the possibility of unthinkable destruction, that people are likely to become dangerously crazy about sexuality. Contemporary conflicts over sexual values and erotic conduct have much in common with the religious disputes of earlier centuries. They acquire immense symbolic weight. Disputes over sexual behavior often become the vehicles for displacing social anxieties, and discharging their attendant emotional intensity. Consequently, sexuality should be treated with special respect in times of great social stress.[122]

And then Edelman, more than twenty years later:

> At a moment when violence as a first resort accentuates the fault lines of
> empire; at a moment when words like *democratization* accompany a bru-
> tal power grab that winks at torture, insists on secrecy, and trivializes
> civil liberties; at a moment when the poor and the powerless find their
> voices ventriloquized by the institutions that enforce their subordination;
> at that moment, which is also every moment, we're invited to consider
> queer theory's moment and to ask whether recent work in that field can be
> thought of as "after sex." In so framing the question addressed by this
> special issue of *SAQ*, I have no intention of trivializing, discrediting, or
> dismissing it. I mean, instead, to underscore its genuine importance and
> to indicate what its stake is. I also want to fix a point of reference for my
> claim that the governing logic of the social insists on this "aftering" of
> "sex," insists on the movement away from its all-consuming and unmas-
> terable intensities and toward engagement with a world whose hold on us
> depends on such an "aftering."[123]

While the terminology and theoretical approaches of Rubin and Edelman
clearly differ, they nevertheless both insist on the importance of sex/uality
to politics and refuse to abandon it, leave it behind, or somehow surpass or
transcend it in order to move on to "more important" issues. Even more,
both Rubin and Edelman suggest that consideration of sex/uality must be
central to any interrogation of politics. What's clear for both thinkers is
that a radical politics of sexuality and a radical sexual politics depend upon
not separating the two out as somehow exclusive endeavors and conclusively refusing to engage in moral judgments when it comes to both.[124]

For Nietzsche, moralism is a weapon of the weak, and that is how and
why it is objectionable. From a queer/left perspective, however, moralism is
the means by which morality is institutionalized; it is, in other words, the
perpetuation of oppression. And as Cohen, Rubin, Butler, Nietzsche, and
Edelman make clear, politics is not a moral enterprise. Politics is a question
of power: who has it and who doesn't. It is not a question of right and wrong
or good and evil, and only becomes so with the oppressive injection of
morality into its sphere, a place it resolutely does not belong (if, indeed, it
belongs anywhere at all). Moralism is both anathema to liberation and

inapplicable as a critique of liberation struggles that articulate themselves in terms of survival and futurity, since the very definition of abjection is to have no future and that status is itself the consequence of futurism's moralizing machinations. Thus the struggle against such elimination, the struggle for survival on the part of those never meant to survive, is itself a resolutely antimoral, antifuturist, indeed "deathly" and destructive (if not nihilist and perverse) endeavor.

In offering a politics of solidarity "from below" that embraces any and all queers, defined as "all so stigmatized for failing to comply with heteronormative mandates,"[125] a structural and political positioning rather than an identitarian one, *No Future*'s revolutionary project rejects the moralized economy of scarcity that says that the future is reserved only for those committed to self-sacrifice. Far from imprisoning queer people in a deathly here and now, as Muñoz asserts, *No Future* instead condemns the present as held hostage to a mythical, hegemonic, and coercive survivalism that comes at everyone's expense. On this point these two actually agree; as Muñoz writes, "The present . . . is impoverished and toxic for queers and other people who do not feel the privilege of majoritarian belonging, normative tastes, and 'rational' expectations."[126] The only addition to make here would be to point out that *no one* receives the payoffs promised by futurism, not even the white and upright (since it is a ruse, a governing fantasy, a tool to secure docility and obedience, whose pathologies explain its aggressive and expansionary character), while those who refuse or fail to follow futurism's mandates are queered as the social order's death and destruction. Moreover, this axis of oppression unfolds on the terrain of desire, always impossible to satisfy, that consequently produces the political scapegoating of queers. Rather than wishing that all of us might somehow be included within it, gaining the privilege of becoming white and upright and finally satisfying our desires once and for all, or instead championing some cordoned off group of oppositional queers and condemning "breeders" for upholding repronormativity, *No Future* instead suggests we go to the root of the problem and abolish the very dynamic that produces the great white hope of futurity and the deathly threat of queerness itself. This is far from vanguardism and much more in line with an "everything for everyone" emancipatory vision than multiculturalist humanism or any one of its liberal reverse discourses, much less a fatal futurist revolution that would install a new sovereignty at the heart of queerness.

No Future thus potentially offers a liberatory queer politics that could not be further from the elitist posturings of the moralist guardians of the social order, even if it does make the frightening and potentially "melodramatic" decision to take their discourse seriously and respond to it in kind. It does so, however, precisely in order to discredit and discard this discourse once and for all. In the next chapter, I attempt exactly the same thing with the discourse of "terrorism," taking seriously its most moralizing claims in an effort to destroy them or, what is the same thing, to begin to materialize its greatest fears in and as queer terror.

5

QUEER TERROR

Either you are with us or you are with the terrorists.

—George W. Bush, September 5, 2001

*What is at stake today is nothing less than the survival of our
civilization.*

—Benjamin Netanyahu, September 20, 2001[1]

*Impossibly, against all reason, my project stakes its claim to the very
space that "politics" makes unthinkable: the space outside the
framework within which politics as we know it appears and so outside
the conflict of visions that share as their presupposition that the body
politic must survive.*

—Lee Edelman[2]

To exist is to resist.

—Palestinian/indigenous liberation slogan

A major point of *Queer Terror* has been to put forward the notion that "life itself" is not a given or self-evidently natural, empirical, or biological category, but rather an ideological determination vested with specifically moralized content. In chapter 1, I showed the ways that Arendt characterizes political or proper life as a freedom from embodiment that is subsequently taken up and moralized by Agamben into a specifically Holocaust Exceptionalist Eurocentrism that simultaneously perpetuates and obscures US empire. In chapter 2, I used Lee Edelman to read Thomas Hobbes in order to show that this moralization of life proceeds simultaneously with and on the basis of a settler civilizationalism that characterizes "death" as both nihilism and threat, simultaneously absurd and hostile. In chapters 3 and 4, I argued that queer theory is a critical left project opposed to this moralizing endeavor, which means that, insofar as "life itself" is the premier civilizational value of our moralized settler society, queer theory is a project that is fundamentally anti- "life," an anticolonial alliance with "death," an unthinkable absurdity and perverse, nihilist opposition to all futurist notions of security, happiness, health, and wholeness.

In work that is very important for this study, Jasbir Puar has astutely documented the steady alliance of LGBTQ people with this moralized value of life. Her pathbreaking *Terrorist Assemblages: Homonationalism in Queer Times* documents the transition, well under way in the United States, whereby queerness has become less and less a symbol or determination of death—whether in the form of nonreproductivity or HIV/AIDS—and increasingly a marker or aspirational symbol of life, in nationalist and consumerist forms of liberal multicultural citizenship and domesticity. Her shorthand term for this transition is *homonationalism*, and she argues that it entails the assimilation of some gay and lesbian subjects into the mainstream of American normalcy, respectability, and citizenship simultaneously as Arabs and Muslims (and all those held to be such) are "queered" in the figure of the "terrorist," a personification of monstrosity, excess, savagery, and perversion.[3]

Put into the terms of this book, Puar's argument might be characterized as demonstrating that "life" has become the premier moralized category of US imperial discourse, even for or in relation to queerness and queer people. Foucault effectively predicted as much, noting that the "right to life" has increasingly become the only dissident political vocabulary available to counter biopolitics.[4] What distinguishes my appropriation of Edelman from both Puar and Foucault, however, is its replotment of biopolitics from the domain of (state) racism to that of settler sovereignty, which establishes life "itself" not through biology but rather through the moralization of desire. This shift has significant consequences for understanding the problem of "terrorism," which is primarily a phenomenon of neither racialization, as Foucauldian biopolitics might have it, nor queerness as sexual deviance, as Puar might have it, but, rather, of a civilizationalist moralizing of settler life as the only life worthy of protection and preservation.

This is not to say that "terrorism" and Islamophobia have nothing to do with race.[5] But it is to say that the specific moral traction at work in the category "terrorist" lies not simply in the racialization of this category or the construction of a racialized Islam as the enemy. It also relies on the construal of Islam, "terrorism," or, sometimes, "Islamic terrorism," as fundamentally the enemy of civilization, an instantiation of nihilism, and the embodiment of evil.[6] Contra Foucault, this is not primarily a biological designation. "Terrorists" are the enemies of "civilization" not (simply) because they pose a biological threat to the population, but rather (or also) because they portend an unthinkable destruction, an annihilation so thoroughgoing and profound that the vocabulary of theology is resorted to in order to adequately capture the devastation they proffer. Biological threats may be insidious; they can be contagious, malignant, recalcitrant, and uncontainable; they may spread in the form of cancers or plagues. But they are not wicked or evil, the distinguishing hallmark of the "terrorist."[7] The kind of death the "terrorist" both represents and portends, then, is not exactly the infiltration and spread of disease so much as the unthinkability of total destruction and the elimination of everything known, valued, sanctified, and secure. "Terrorism" threatens a destruction that is by definition unknowable and unimaginable, and, as such, exceeds the determinations of biology or medical science. It is a disintegration that is existential, generating a panic other and deeper than the fact of mortality. It is a destruction that cannot be borne by the "living," threatening a disarticulation so total that it exceeds the cessation of biological life typically demarcated by the word *death*, a nihilism so baffling it can only be described by its detractors in the supernatural language of evil.

What explains this hypermoralization of the "death" of "terrorism" is the settler/civilizationalist specificity of the "life" that must be protected from it. As I argued in chapter 2, the War on Terror can be understood as a continuation of the US settler colonial project and a morphing of that project into a new and specifically securitized, expansionist empire. Seen in this light, the native becomes the original "terrorist," just as the "terrorist" becomes today's imperial, outward projection of the native.

The championing of life that seemingly commonsensically anchors the moralizing discourse on "terrorism" is, therefore, not an unmarked or somehow universal valuing of "life itself." Instead, and as this chapter will seek to demonstrate, this "life" is better understood as the lives and well-being of a specifically settler America—and, perhaps surprisingly, Israel, in an alliance all too often construed more broadly as simply "the West" or "democracy." This civilizationalist vision of "life" entails that any refusal of its imperial imperatives is construed as everything that "terrorism" is understood to be in both right-wing and popular discourse alike: unthinkable, annihilatory, antilife, irrational, "savage," and evil. This is the colonial moralism specific to "terrorism" discourse, and it purchases the innocence of the "West," the existential threat posed by "terrorism," and, consequently, its moral intractability as what must be unconditionally opposed by decent, upright, innocent people.[8]

"Terrorism," then, can be understood as the contemporary settler state's moralized imperial name for the unthinkable indigenous remainder that, in the insistence *on* remaining, challenges the settler state's claim to sovereignty, security, and civilizational value. Indeed, indigenous peoples' continued existence not only challenges settler sovereignty's claim to legitimacy and "first"-ness, but is the harbinger of that sovereignty's death insofar as they become legible to it *as* existing. Such existence gives the lie to triumphant conquest narratives and thus threatens to dissolve the very parameters of political intelligibility of settler biopolitics. The (im)moralization of indigenous peoples' persistence *as* indigenous, and consequently as refusers of settler sovereignty's imposition, into the impossible-to-comprehend category of nihilist evil that devalues life—that is, into "terrorism"—is thus an important reminder that "terrorism" is not the name of a particular form of political violence so much as a premiere ideological tool by which resistance to empire and colonization is illegitimated out of existence. This use of "terrorism" as an epithet to manage, control, stifle, quash, and punish resistance to empire and settler colonialism is particularly clear in the smearing and punishment of Palestinians and the Palestinian liberation struggle (in both Palestine and the United States), but it is not unfamiliar with regard to indigenous North American people(s) either, as when it surfaced in 2016 as indigenous and allied water protectors were surveilled, policed, and brutalized by state and private security forces as they fought the installation of the Dakota Access Pipeline on tribal lands in North Dakota. The activities of this entirely nonviolent movement (which included, among other things, peace encampments, prayer vigils,

and marches insisting on the importance of water for life) were characterized as "terrorism" and "jihadism" by security forces and were dealt with
using anti-"terrorism" weaponry, tactics, and strategies gleaned from the
War on Terror.[9] As these examples demonstrate, "terrorism" requires no
actual connection with violence at all in order to qualify as evil or credibly
threaten civilization. To be a "terrorist," one need not commit an act of
violence—political or apolitical, legitimate or not—but, rather, persevere as
an indigenous person, be (perceived as) Arab or Muslim, or mount some
explicit or forthright challenge to the civilizationalist valuing of settler lives
(for example, in the form of advocating for the existence and endurance of
indigenous people[s]). *Queer Terror* therefore argues that George W. Bush
got one thing right—however unwittingly—in his infamous if prophetic
synopsis of War on Terror logic that one is either with "us" or with "the
terrorists." Rather than respond to Bush's ultimatum by standing with "us"
and condemning "terrorism" in a sanctimonious display of settler survivalism, as he explicitly entreats, or standing with "us" by valiantly seeking some
sort of liberal compromise wherein we defend "moderate" Muslims and
condemn "terrorism" as extremism and by definition abominable, as he
implicitly entreats, a queer practice of antimoral revolutionary dissent
instead suggests providing Bush the only answer to his ultimatum that is
clearly off the table and choosing the only choice that is truly unchoosable. If
the only options are, as Bush says, to side with a futurist, settler, and imperial "us" (whether as avowed advocates of empire or its collaborationist
liberal compromisers) or with a queered, "savage," and "terrorist" other, the
choice, I think, is clear: we must choose to stand with the "terrorists."

A note of clarification before I proceed further: this chapter is not an
examination of "terrorism" as a predetermined subject/object of inquiry
(whether in terrorism studies, international relations, political science, or
any other academic field). Nor does it attempt to explain, justify, or even
account for every instance or application of the term *terrorism* by the US
government, much less by other states throughout history or the globe.
Rather, this chapter undertakes a very specific and targeted interrogation
of the production of "terrorism" as a moralized term for threats to American lives, security, and "ways of life." This interrogation reveals the continuity between US empire and US settler colonialism, which is a punishing
moralism that purchases the life of some at the expense of everyone and
the targeted elimination and death of indigenous people in particular and,

in the contemporary moment, Arab and Muslim people (and all those who "look like" them), people whose "very subjectivities [are] cast in the form of destruction and terror."[10] In this I follow Nadine Naber, who understands Arab and Muslim immigrants to the US as forming "diasporas of empire"[11] and similarly observes,

> Post–September 11 federal government and media discourses have created an arbitrary "potential terrorist" subject—intrinsically connected to "Islamic fundamentalism" and "terrorism." I use the term "dominant U.S. discourses" to refer to systems of meaning about the "war on terror" produced among the federal government's policy makers, the defense industry, the corporate media, and neoconservative think tanks. In the demarcation of boundaries between good versus evil and between "those who are with us" and "those who are with the terrorists," dominant U.S. discourses on "terrorism" and "Islamic fundamentalism" have provided "definitions of patriotism, loyalty, boundaries and . . . belonging" [here she is quoting Edward Said]. They have also sparked nationalist sentiments that articulate subjects associated with "us" as those who are to be protected and those associated with "them" as those who are to be disciplined and punished.[12]

This chapter (and this book) will therefore not engage with questions about, say, left-wing "terrorism," whether or not ISIS is or can be credibly construed as an anticolonial actor, or the (il)legitimacy of violence as a tactic in liberatory struggles. I offer neither an endorsement nor condemnation of what is commonly named or considered to be "terrorism" here, much less the use of violence to advance political ends. To find such an endorsement or condemnation in this chapter would be to miss its point entirely (and to wish for me to provide such endorsement or condemnation will inevitably court disappointment). This is no evasion but rather a insistence on reckoning with the actual stakes of the terminology of "terrorism," which does not designate a somehow neutral or preexisting empirical category of political violence, but rather functions to secure an imperial, settler colonial order via surreptitious moralism, both of which *Queer Terror* definitively rejects and seeks to overturn. To participate in any conversation premised on the notion that "terrorism" is somehow "real" or objective within these political and discursive confines is to collude with empire, while to argue over the relative merits of violence for liberatory struggles simply moves the conversation back a step from focusing on "terrorism" to focusing on "violence" as the lurking, essential immoralism that can never, by definition, be unproblematically advocated. I do not believe it is inherently immoral to advocate violence; however, this is not tantamount to an endorsement of violence as such and can only be construed in this way by readers intent on taking what they want from this chapter (and this book as a whole) in order to evict its author from the social world of meaning and representation she is explicitly seeking to critique. Such a move would only prove my argument yet again, however, in its dogmatic and moralizing mimeticism of settler-imperial logic. By contrast, I suggest we follow Asma Abbas, who defines political violence as "violence that one is compelled to make sense and meaning out of."[13] This amoral approach to thinking through and evaluating important political questions is an admirable model for moving liberatory inquiry outside of the domain of "terrorism" discourse altogether, which is one thing *Queer Terror* aspires to do. In short, this book is offered as an outright refusal of the "morality of violence" and "legitimacy of terrorism" conversations because they are premised on a colonial and imperial oppression that I reject, one that I believe emancipatory politics and political movements also rightly reject. If that nevertheless looks or sounds to some readers like an endorsement of "terrorism," it strikes me that this is neither accidental nor in any way an objection to its argument.

"TERRORISM" AND/AS EVIL

Both too little and too much is said when a person or act is labeled "terrorist." Too little is said because there is, in fact, no established or even widely-agreed-upon definition of what "terrorism" actually is. Experts of all sorts—be they academics, pundits, NGOs, or political elites—do not agree on a working definition of "terrorism" and in fact have repeatedly failed to come to any consensus regarding just what, exactly, "terrorism" might be.[14] This definitional evasiveness is not due to the inherent difficulty of defining a field's core concepts—for example, "literature" in English, "value" in economics, "power" in political science—a generative difficulty that opens new lines of research and continually spurs the creation of new knowledge. Rather, the impossibility of defining "terrorism" is due to the particularly moralized way it developed and took shape in the latter half of the twentieth century, which reduces discussions and disagreements about "terrorism" to moral debates about who is good and who is evil (since moralism is extremely effective at closing down conversations and suppressing intellectual inquiry). Since the mid-1970s, in fact, "terrorism" has been deliberately produced as both an identity category and a moral epithet. In both cases, its definitional distinctness is its evil: a "terrorist" is an evil person and "terrorism" is an evil act. As a result of this genealogical trajectory, "terrorism" has come to name a peculiarly abominable form of political violence, a violence that is evil not because it is committed by a specific actor (for example, the state or a nonstate group or cell) or because it is a specific kind of violence (for example, it targets civilians or uses human shields) but rather because it targets and threatens people and places that otherwise ought rightfully to be protected. The perennial cliché that orbits the problem of "terrorism," namely, one person's "terrorist" is another person's freedom fighter, is a complaint about the partisan application of the term, which is considered to be the primary obstacle to its clear definition. But the problem with "terrorism" is not that it is applied in an inconsistent or partisan manner. Rather, the problem is that it functions moralistically in order to condemn whatever it is considered to name. This is the single and remarkable *consistency* that makes "terrorism" impossible to further define, leaving it a simultaneously over- and underdetermined phenomenon that can function only in an ideological manner.

The status of "terrorism" as a definitionally fraught, morally overdetermined category did not begin with 9/11, even if the United States' more official War on Terror did. As Nadine Naber argues with regard to Arab American history, in a point that is also apposite to the problem of "terrorism," 9/11 did not constitute "an essential break or rupture" with a prior, unmarked past but is, rather, better understood "as an extension if not an intensification of a post–Cold War U.S. expansion in the Middle East."[15] Even the language of a "war on terror" predates 2001, with both Nixon and Reagan having declared their participation in this fight. However, both "terrorism" and the "War on Terror" did not catch on with such widespread and fervent ideological power until after 9/11, one reason for which may be the civilizationalist moralism of 9/11 discourse itself, which insists that this day "changed everything" or that "the world was not the same" after 9/11, an echo of the exceptionalism that I argued is sometimes attributed to the Holocaust.[16]

The Cold War roots of "terrorism" extend back to both the United States' imperial ventures in Latin America and its self-proclaimed struggle against totalitarianism. In the former arena, "terrorism" was part of a larger military and international relations discourse of insurgency and counterinsurgency, understood by both scholars and political elites at that time to be one tactic among many that any party to a conflict—states included— might employ.[17] In the latter arena, "terrorism" emerged from what would later become the neoconservative movement as a variation on "terror," itself argued to be the signature political technology of totalitarianism. The sprawling postwar movement against "totalitarianism," taken up by pundits, scholars, philosophers, critics, novelists, and political elites alike, attempted to link the Soviet Union under Stalin with Nazi Germany under Hitler as exemplary of an unprecedented new form of expansionist polity that threatened the civilized world and the Western and democratic way of life via its distinctive wielding of terror as a political tactic to remake human nature.[18] Meanwhile, on the world stage, the emergence of "terrorism" as a prominent term in the discourse of Western states was concomitant with the rise of anticolonial nationalist movements throughout the rest of the globe.[19] Central to arguments taking place at the United Nations at this time, for example, was the status of the political violence committed by both parties to such conflicts: the violence committed by national liberation movements, which the Western states by and large wanted to condemn as "terrorism," and the violence committed by colonial and Western powers, which the Soviet and unaligned states wanted to condemn as "terrorism." Hence, from the very beginning of its explicit emergence into both American and international political discourse, "terrorism" has functioned as a crucial arbiter of the line between savagery and civilization.

Enter Benjamin Netanyahu, a long-standing Israeli politician who has built his career in part on a dogged promotion of the anti-"terrorism" platform.[20] In 1979, Netanyahu hosted an influential international conference on "terrorism" in Jerusalem, organized under the auspices of his Jonathan Institute, an Israeli think tank named for his brother, killed in Operation Thunderbolt at Entebbe. This landmark conference "was convened to begin the formation of an anti-terror alliance in which all the democracies of the West must join."[21] Such an alliance was necessary because the conference's participants were unsatisfied with the "easy moral relativism" characterizing the UN debates happening at this time, wherein "One man's terrorist is another man's freedom fighter."[22] The conference therefore set out to establish that "a clear definitional framework exists, regardless of political view,"[23] proclaiming that "terrorism" is "the deliberate, systematic murder, maiming and menacing of the innocent to inspire fear in order to gain political ends."[24] This definition of "terrorism," conference-goers maintained, makes clear its fundamental alliance with both tyranny and totalitarianism, its constitutive "abhorrence of freedom and a determination to destroy the democratic way of life,"[25] and makes it, as Netanyahu's father insisted, "an offshoot of Nazi philosophy."[26] "Terrorists" refuse to distinguish between civilians and noncivilians and usurp political power via antidemocratic means. They are thus threats to the Western and democratic way of life and explicit attacks on that way of life. According to Netanyahu Jr., at the conference this definition "was shown persuasively to be, beyond all nuance and quibble, a moral evil,"[27] or, as Paul Johnson put it, "intrinsically evil, necessarily evil and wholly evil."[28]

While Netanyahu Sr. is incorrect to say that this definition is not political or influenced by a particular point of view, he is wholly correct to note that its clear association with and overdetermination by moralism diminish its ability to mean more than one thing, a semantic debilitation that might be seen as this conference's central purpose. Morality, in other words, was the crucial tool by which refusal of or resistance to US/Israeli political and economic dominance was rendered the proper domain of "terrorism" and thus disqualified as anticolonial, anti-imperial, nationalist, or liberatory, while the lives of US and Israeli citizens were classified as "innocent." Of course, such moralization erases the role of US and Israeli policy in, as well as its relevance to, the phenomenon of "terrorism," dehistoricizing and tarnishing any resistance to such policies with the taint of illegitimacy and inhumanity. Thus, by 1984, the year of the Jonathan Institute's second international conference on "terrorism," Netanyahu Jr. could credibly argue, "The root cause of terrorism lies not in grievances but in a disposition toward unbridled violence. This can be traced to a world view which asserts that certain ideological and religious goals justify, indeed demand, the shedding of all moral inhibitions. In this context, the observation that the root cause of terrorism is terrorists is more than a tautology."[29]

Lisa Stampnitzky has carefully documented the transformation whereby "terrorism" has today become an identity that provides its own explanation, a characteristically immoral act committed by a specific type of immoral person. The roots of this view are evident here, in 1984. The "disposition toward unbridled violence" that Netanyahu claims is the cause of "terrorism" marks the term's rise as both an identity category and a form of savagery or barbarism; the "more than" tautology of his observation signals the premier definitional attribute of "terrorism," its evil. As Netanyahu explains, it is not simply that "terrorism" is an evil act or behavior, but rather that "terrorists" are themselves evil, presumably either as representatives of an evil principle at work in the human order (a metaphysical and potentially theological claim) or as followers of an evil ideology that subordinates everything—morality in particular—to its own aims (a psychologizing political claim). Regardless, the only way that the statement "the cause of terrorism is terrorists" is not an empty tautology is if it is also an ontological statement about the existence of evil itself, which becomes flesh in the body of the "terrorist."[30] Netanyahu's father, again a contributor to the second conference, puts it the most starkly of anyone:

> The terrorist represents a new breed of man which takes humanity back to prehistoric times, to the times when morality was not yet born. Divested of any moral principle, he has no moral sense, no moral controls, and is therefore capable of committing any crime, like a killing machine, without shame or remorse. But he is also a cunning, consummate liar, and therefore much more dangerous than the Nazis, who used to proclaim their aims openly. In fact, he is the perfect nihilist.[31]

The "terrorist" here is both premoral and precivilization, thus in effect prehuman, calling to mind the prehistoric members of Hobbes's timeless state of nature. And yet, despite his primitiveness, the "terrorist" is more cunning and dangerous than even the Nazis, who at least made plain their genocidal intent. Unlike Nazis, "terrorists" lie about their deeds, mendaciously suggesting they pertain to national liberation or ending colonialism. "Terrorists" therefore know full well they are committing murder, but couch it in liberatory rhetoric so as to deceive good and innocent people. Alluding to Nietzsche, Netanyahu Sr. concludes that the terrorist is the "perfect nihilist."

The participants in both of these "international" conferences consisted almost entirely of Americans and Israelis. Their influence with regard to the formation of "terrorism" was significant not simply at the level of the political elite, but also at the level of mass public discourse. Indeed, both conferences received extensive media coverage and were widely influential.[32] The publication of the 1984 conference in the mass-market paperback *Terrorism: How the West Can Win* facilitated its widespread distribution and review by mainstream press and journalists.[33] Hence it is worth remembering the other major impetus of the first conference and the theme of Netanyahu's essay from 1984 and the 1984 conference proceedings as a whole: the formation of an imperial alliance to counter this "terrorist" threat. As Netanyahu insists, the West must stand firm in its resolve to counter "terrorist" evil, and, in eerie anticipation of the twenty-first-century War on Terror, he cautions against "the acquisition of weapons of mass destruction by the principal terrorist states of the Middle East—Iran, Libya, and Syria."[34] He also makes clear that, in addition to hating freedom and destroying democracy, the goals of "terrorists" additionally include the "sapping" of the "political will" of "democratic societies."[35] "Terrorists" achieve partial success in this area when their actions are misunderstood as motivated by legitimate grievances or when states' retaliatory violence is condemned as part of a larger and unproductive "cycle of violence." These understandings evidence the success of "terrorists" because, in both scenarios, there is a failure to recognize the clear and necessary difference between "terrorist" violence and state violence. The former is immoral and lawless; the latter is upright and legitimately undertaken in order to protect innocent people. Thus, Netanyahu repeatedly asserts, the West must be unafraid of responding aggressively to "terrorist" threats. Indeed, much of his essay is devoted to a defense of military aggression as a rightful, legal, and legitimate response to "terrorism." And he concludes it with a call to the United States to unite the Western democracies together in a single front against global "terrorism," since the United States "alone has the capacity to align the West in this matter, alone can credibly threaten the offenders, and alone can impel the neutrals to shed their neutrality." Almost daring the United States to assume an exceptional role in the future fight against "terrorism," he entreats,

The United States appears to be moving precisely in this direction, albeit sometimes at a maddeningly slow pace. America encountered terrorism in the middle 1960s. By the middle 1970s, it realized it was its principal target. By the middle 1980s, it began thinking seriously about taking action. The more America resorts to action, such as punishing terrorists and their backers, the greater the number of states which will join the effort to combat terrorism. Allies and adversaries alike, the entire world in fact, are waiting to see the depth of American resolve.[36]

Returning to the theme of strength and lassitude, Netanyahu concludes, "The West can win the war against terrorism, and fairly rapidly. . . . But it must first win the war against its own inner weakness." Thus not only is "terrorism" unequivocally evil, but it requires a specifically US-led imperial mobilization in order to stop it, a military mobilization that is, by definition, antievil, antinihilism, and resolutely "prolife."

"TERRORISM" AND/AS TOTALITARIANISM

By the time of the Jonathan Institute's second international conference, not only has the evil of the "terrorist" been firmly established vis-à-vis the innocence and uprightness of the settler state and its citizens, but his ineffable Muslim-ness is coming into view, side by side with a distinct US-Israeli alliance in the shared cause of democracy and "the West"[37] and the notion that Jewish people are among the primary targets of "terrorism." Although the instigating role played by the Soviet Union in orchestrating international "terrorism" remains a prominent theme continued forward from the first conference, its power in this regard is now rivaled by "Arab nationalism" and "Islamic fundamentalism" as the premiere "wellspring" of terror; hence, Netanyahu now asserts in 1984 that "terrorism is thus uniquely pervasive in the Middle East, the part of the world in which Islam is dominant."[38] Notably, the term *totalitarian* is still in use, primarily by the American contributors, albeit this time to link Arab and Muslim countries with the communism of the Soviet Union and, therefore, by definitional association, the Nazism of 1940s Germany. By the time of this second conference, then, the "ideological source,"[39] political culmination, and ultimate beneficiaries of "terrorism" have all become identical: communist totalitarianism. "Terrorism" is totalitarian both in its refusal to acknowledge distinctions between civilians and noncivilians and in its use of violence as a "first resort"[40] for resolving conflict. In addition, "terrorism" is the premier tool of totalitarian regimes and is sponsored by totalitarian regimes, specifically the Soviet Union, its satellites (such as Cuba and North Korea), and the emergent Arab states (Libya, Syria, and, although not Arab, Iran). Hence the "fiercely anti-West" PLO comes in for special scrutiny throughout the second conference as a kind of culmination and exemplar of the totalitarian Communist/Arab "terrorist" threat, "the pivotal link" between "the Soviet Union and the Arab World."[41] As then Secretary of State George Schulz put it, "If freedom and democracy are the targets of terrorism, it is clear that totalitarianism is its ally."[42] In Senator Daniel Patrick Moynihan's words, "The totalitarian state is terrorism come to power."[43] Or, as Netanyahu sums up, "Modern terrorism has its roots in two movements that have assumed international prominence in the second half of the twentieth century, communist totalitarianism and Islamic (and Arab) radicalism."[44] In short, "terrorist" states are "built on the foundations of Marxism and radical Islam."[45]

In the United States, then, the moralized fight against totalitarianism that effectively defined twentieth-century neoconservative discourse in the United States broadens and expands in collaboration with Israeli power-brokers to include Arab and Muslim countries and peoples, exporting the civilizationalism of antitotalitarianism to a new global battle, the fight against "terror," and expanding the target of "terrorism" to include Jewish people among its immediate or foremost victims. The discursive slide from totalitarianism to "terrorism"—evident in George W. Bush's famous fake phenomenon "Islamo-fascism" (itself derived from neoconservative opinion-makers who played a significant role in consolidating civilizationalist antitotalitarianism in the United States)—transfers the conjoined Nazi/communist threat of totalitarianism to, and transforms it into, the new Arab/Muslim threat of "terrorism."[46] So, for example, in his address to the nation on September 20, 2001, President Bush said of al-Qaeda, "We have seen their kind before. They're the heirs of all the murderous ideologies of the 20th century. By sacrificing human life to serve their radical visions, by abandoning every value except the will to power, they follow in the path of fascism, Nazism, and totalitarianism."[47] Distinctive as Bush's rhetoric of good and evil may have seemed, then, in the wake of 9/11 and

an unprecedented act of violence against the United States, the discourse
he employed to explain and characterize it was in fact the result of decades
of conservative and neoconservative attacks on communism, decolonization, and the New Left within the United States, as well as an Israeli-led
international effort to delegitimize anticolonial violence as by definition
evil and immoral.

Importantly, the "terror" that at least Arendt was referring to when discussing totalitarianism was the concentration camps of Nazi Germany, a
phenomenon she had difficulty transposing onto Stalinist Russia.[48] Nevertheless, the emergence of "terrorism" from neoconservative totalitarianism
discourse integrates it almost seamlessly into a similarly civilizationalist
struggle of democracy vs. tyranny, West vs. East, Enlightenment vs. darkness and barbarism. Communism, then, like national liberation, anticolonial struggle, or any other "theory of grievances,"[49] becomes leftist cover for
what is the always inexcusable and barbaric, inherently antidemocratic,
irrational, and immoral violence of "terrorism." Indeed, in arguing that
"terrorism" is both the premier tool of totalitarian regimes and the means of
bringing new totalitarian regimes into existence, "terrorism" becomes the
new Nazi threat—to Europe, to America, to Jews, indeed to the entirety of
the West and its civilization. This is how, discursively at least, Israel becomes
subsumed into the West as part and parcel of its civilizational and imperial
project via the project of fighting "terrorism." This project consolidates the
US-Israeli alliance as part of a shared democratic and Western civilization
that is equally menaced by the same threat, a threat that even Netanyahu
acknowledges is "a seemingly bizarre collaboration between Arab and
Islamic radicalism and communist totalitarianism."[50] A conflagration of evil
and anticivilizational movements, ideologies, and people, America and
Israel are threatened by, alternatively and yet strangely simultaneously,
totalitarianism, Communism, and "terrorism." As Netanyahu rather bril-
liantly sums up,

The antagonism of Islamic and Arab radicalism to the West is frequently
misunderstood. It is sometimes explained as deriving from American
support for Israel. But the hostility to the West preceded the creation of
Israel by centuries, and much of the terrorists' animus is directed against
targets and issues that have nothing to do with Israel. Indeed, the relationship is most often the other way around. Middle Eastern radicals

did not develop their hatred for the West because of Israel; they hated Israel from its inception *because it is an organic part of the West.* That is, because Israel represents for them precisely the incarnation of those very traditions and values, foremost of which is democracy, which they hate and fear.[51]

It is not, then, that "terrorists" are responding to or resisting US and Israeli empire and colonialism. It is rather that "terrorists" hate Israel because it is *"an organic part of the West,"* that is, because it is democratic and civilized. And terrorists hate democracy and civilization, because (as we have seen) they are evil. Indeed, this is what evil effectively means. Emptying oppositional politics of any content whatsoever, "terrorism" becomes another word for savagery and nihilism, for the negation of the West and everything it ostensibly stands for: freedom, democracy, and the American way.

As the avid Israeli participation in producing the discourse of "terrorism" and Netanyahu's contributions in particular make clear, the futurism of US empire pertains not simply to its own sovereignty; it is also tied to that of the state of Israel, a relative latecomer to the settler colonial enterprise.[52] For Edward Said, this is symptomatic of what he calls "the common discourse of enlightened American liberal democracy. It is the complete hegemonic coalescence between the liberal Western view of things and the Zionist-Israeli view."[53] Such a coalescence had terrible consequences for Palestinians, as he explains:

> By the middle of the twentieth century . . . there was a willing identification between Western liberal discourse and Zionism. The reasons for this identification are complex (perhaps there is even an acceptable justification for it), but for the Arab Palestinian the concrete meaning of this hegemonic relationship was disastrous. There are no two ways about it. The identification of Zionism and liberalism in the West meant that insofar as he had been displaced and dispossessed in Palestine, the Arab had become a nonperson as much as the Zionist had himself become the *only* person in Palestine.[54]

Not only did this alliance function to constitute Israelis as people because of the fact that it constituted Palestinians as (a) nonpeople, but it also did so through an explicitly moralizing frame wherein "Zionism and Israel were associated with liberalism, with freedom and democracy, with knowledge and light, with what 'we' understand and fight for" while "the obstacles to Zionism and/or Israel are nefarious, stupid, or morally indecent and—this is crucial—they are not to be heard from directly. Only Zionism can speak for them."[55] Unsurprisingly, then, just as with America's War on Terror, which deploys the discourse of "terrorism" to moralize its imperialist expansion and warfare throughout West Asia as the protection of innocent life, so too is the Israeli discourse of existential and demographic threat crucial to that state's perpetuation of its settlement, occupation, and ethnic cleansing of Palestine. Based on the Holocaust Exceptionalist premise that Jews cannot be safe from extermination without a sovereign ethnocratic state, Zionist "terrorism" discourse makes clear that Israel's future, its way of life, and indeed its very existence require a cyclical eradication and rehabilitation of the deathly threat it faces for its continued security and existence.[56] As we saw in chapter 2, this endless circuit of annihilation and rehabilitation of the mortal enemy is the recursive structure of settler colonialism, which also explains why there is something rhetorically interchangeable about all of Israel's alleged enemies: whether it be Nazis, the Arab world, Palestinians, the PLO, Islam, Hamas, Hezbollah, or Iran, the "terrorist" who threatens its existence is wholly necessary to the perpetuation of Israeli "civilization." The interchangeability of "terrorism" with Nazism illustrates this most dramatically and is the most distinctive religious and civilizationalist slander offered to smear the Muslim/Arab figure of "terrorism" by conservatives and Zionists alike: not simply mendacious or tyrannical, the "terrorist" represents the West's exceptional example of annihilation par excellence—the Holocaust—a figuration that casts the West as victim of unprecedented oppression and simultaneously reinforces the ostensible solidarity between "Western civilization" and Israel as emblem of the Jewish people, who are themselves cast as eternal victims of genocidal violence. As Jin Haritaworn, Tamsila Taquir, and Esma Erdem note, the frequent conflation of Islam with Nazism in European and American political discourse creates "a basic equivalence between 'Muslim = Nazi' and 'Muslim = Evil,' in which specific persons, relationships and events appear ultimately interchangeable."[57] It is perhaps gratuitous to point out the Holocaust Exceptionalism underpinning this analysis, in which an intra-European genocide is figured as the most unthinkable and intolerable episode of human history, an assertion that erases the foundational colonial violence that produced Europe as Europe (and indeed "the West" as the West) to begin with and recuperates America and Israel as "innocent" lives victimized by "terrorism." It is nevertheless worthwhile to point out that, despite these conservatives' frequent invocations of Nietzsche as immoralist bogeyman, their reversal of strong and weak and transmogrification of these into the categories of oppressor and oppressed in fact exemplify the logic of slave morality he so trenchantly critiques, and are the means by which righteousness is purchased for an otherwise reactionary and contemptible cause.[58]

"TERRORISM" AND/AS QUEERNESS

In *Terrorist Assemblages: Homonationalism in Queer Times*, Jasbir Puar analyzes "terrorism" as a function of biopoliticized queerness. She argues that queerness articulates "terrorism" as racialized and sexualized savagery, on the one hand, as it simultaneously upholds and sustains US nationalism and imperialism via the assimilation of certain gay and lesbian subjects into the mainstream of American respectability and citizenship, on the other. Her name for this dual process is *homonationalism*. As a queer biopolitics, homonationalism disciplines and (re)produces homosexuality as white, American, patriotic, and upwardly mobile, while simultaneously designating people of color, immigrants, and Arabs and Muslims as both heterosexual and yet dangerously "queer"—as "terrorists" or "failed and perverse" bodies that "always have femininity as their reference point of malfunction, and are metonymically tied to all sorts of pathologies of the mind and body—homosexuality, incest, pedophilia, madness, and disease."[59] Neither an identity nor a defining behavioral activity (for example, homosexuality), queerness, as Puar elaborates in this text, is a biopolitical tactic that functions to define and divide populations through processes of racialization, a "management of queer life at the expense of sexually and racially perverse death in relation to the contemporary politics of securitization, Orientalism, terrorism, torture, and the articulation of Muslim, Arab, Sikh, and South Asian sexualities."[60]

Puar's use of queerness in this text in a formation she calls "queer as regulatory" is, in fact, a rearticulation and application of Foucault's understanding of racism as explained in *"Society Must Be Defended,"* wherein he states that racism is "primarily a way of introducing a break into the domain of life that is under power's control: the break between what must live and what must die."[61] In *Terrorist Assemblages*, queerness functions as this "break." Queerness is the biopolitical caesura that divides the population into those whose lives must be fostered and protected—for Puar, the gay patriot—and those who must be eradicated if the body politic is to survive—the queer/perverse "terrorist." On this reading, "the contemporary U.S. heteronormative nation actually relies on and benefits from the proliferation of queerness."[62]

Puar's account of queerness veers from any simple conflation with gay and lesbian subjects. For her, queerness functions as a biopolitical determination regarding which populations are sifted out and accorded recognition, regulation, benefits, and rights, while leaving others to degenerate, die off, or be killed. Queerness therefore does not name an inevitably resistant category for her. Rather, queerness is both a regulation of life and an apparatus of death, both a biopolitics and a necropolitics. There is a continuity between these two queernesses, to be sure, but also, and simultaneously, a radical break between them—the radical break between what must live and what will be allowed to die or outright targeted for death. Neither "type" of queerness, however—neither the biopolitical nor the necropolitical—could make a claim to any sort of opposition or dissidence, because queerness is neither in favor of nor opposed to anything in this schema. It is rather the mechanism by which populations are determined, demarcated, targeted, regulated, and surveilled (or not). Queerness exists, therefore, on both "sides" of the biopolitical operation, as both a regulation of life and an apparatus of death.

By contrast, however, and on the basis of my appropriation of Edelman for a dissident reading of the "queer" of queer theory, I have suggested that queerness is neither a tactic of biopolitics nor itself a biopolitical project, but rather *the abjected necropolitical by-product* of biopolitics, itself circumscribed and dictated by futurism and its mandates. In other words, the biopolitical project is *futurism*, and queerness is simultaneously one of its prerequisites and primary effects. Queerness is the premise upon which the moralized value of life, survival, and "civilization" is based, as well as the by-product of this moralist valuing in the form of queered populations determined to be "savage," antisocial, and deathly. This usage retains the abjection associated with queerness that Puar recognizes in the queered "terrorist" figure, but invests it with a resistant or dissident content that she would likely reject as a form of queer exceptionalism.[63] Indeed, Puar is doubtful about the dissident reading of queerness, both because she thinks it can become a regulatory ideal in its own right and because the mere fact of being a queer person doesn't exempt anyone from complicity with hierarchy and violence. Yet the queerness I am proposing in this book is a structural categorization, not an identificatory one. Anyone outside of or opposed to the logic of futurism is *by definition* queer, a determination that escapes identitarian categories and yet is inescapably determinist. On this account, queerness is indeed exceptional; it is, in fact, always exceptional, but not because it is some kind of vanguard political position or because it evades complicity with hierarchy and injustice. Rather, queer is exceptional because it is the name of what must be abjected from the social order in order for it to coherently constitute itself *as* a social order. Queerness, that is, cannot *but* be dissident, negative, and antisocial. Queerness is exceptional not because it is superior to any other political position or immune to political critique, but rather because it is the name of what the social order must exclude in order to maintain its existence and integrity *as* the social. Queerness, by definition, is the exception to sociality.[64]

Puar's apt and still-relevant critique of queer exceptionalism is more applicable, I think, to the everyday dynamics at work in classrooms, organizing sites, and politicized queer spaces of all kinds, wherein the importance of queerness and queer subversion often can become elevated into a disciplinary or regulatory ideal, at least in the United States. But I find it less apposite to queerness as a theoretical concept, particularly in its role in founding the field of queer theory. Puar potentially acknowledges such a distinction when she writes that queerness is "the *modality* through which 'freedom from norms' becomes a regulatory queer ideal that demarcates the ideal queer."[65] In other words, theory construction and development can often be (mis)translated into clear-cut demands regarding political programs, platforms, or positions in everyday life. Thus a theoretical conceptualization of queer as political dissidence can unwittingly result in a championing of the "queerest" of queer people—someone who is not simply free from norms, as Puar suggests, but, even more, is antinormative to the greatest degree possible (whatever that might mean in any particular context)—such that they are, in their very existence, a threat to the social order in themselves and ultimately unintelligible to it. Familiar as such dynamics are, however, they are neither an adequate instantiation of theory in this case nor, as Puar is arguing, a substitute for actual politics.[66]

This book's notion of queer dissidence—of queerness's inevitably anti-social *political* positioning—does not and should not be taken to mean that queer people (homosexual or otherwise) are inevitably transgressive of an unchanging social order, or that the kind of sex or gender one has is itself a form of political praxis. As Eric Stanley observes, "there is, and must be, an antagonism between *queer* as an optic, a way to read and to act against normative and normalizing power, and *queer* as a sexual and/or gendered identity."[67] "Queer" in my account is a form of dissent or refusal insofar as it designates those abjected by the social order as anathema to its existence, coherence, and perpetuity. Queerness becomes a praxis when the abject affirm that abjection rather than seeking to negotiate, reason with, or conform to the social order that produced it. While this has clear historical precedent and exemplars among specifically gay, lesbian, bi, trans, and queer-identified people, this is not to mistake LGBTQ people themselves for political dissidents per se.[68] It is also a queer exceptionalism that cannot reproduce disciplinary norms, social hierarchies, or purist political pieties. Stanley continues,

> There is also the critique that queer theory, as a field and/or methodology, can normalize antinormativity, against its own aims. Or an argument that in its reach to be infinitely antinormative it produces, by way of excess, new normativities. I think, however, this would be a misreading inasmuch as queer, under my definition, like all deconstructive projects, continues to evade those forms of legibility. Queer, then, becomes a placeholder for a horizon and a way to speak toward that which remains beyond representation but also threats [sic] representation itself.[69]

Stanley's notion of queer as "placeholder" here resonates with queer as "structural position" in Edelman. That structural position is indeed the space of unintelligibility, the ever-present challenge to meaning and coherence that haunts every such endeavor toward meaning and coherence. It therefore cannot become a regulatory or disciplinary mode itself (except via misinterpretation) because, as soon as it materializes or becomes intelligible, it flees into the abyss of dissidence and unintelligibility inevitably opened up by the very move toward concretization.

"Queer" is one name for this fugitive form of dissident critique, and *Queer Terror* is an attempt to politicize this critical version of queerness offered by Edelman in a continuation of the liberatory impulse I see as having sparked the emergence of queer theory in the 1990s by situating it explicitly within an inquiry or tradition of the oppressed. As the rest of this chapter will illustrate, the name of this unthinkable, antirepresentational, antinormative queer threat to social meaning and intelligibility in the era of the War on Terror is "terrorism," which consequently can be understood as a resource for dissident praxis. The connection between "terrorism" and queerness is most clear in the commentary and discourse of the Right, particularly those who have made their careers on the manufacture and popularization of virulent, toxic Islamophobia. Taking a page from Edelman's playbook, then, the rest of this chapter is offered as a kind of study in and reflection on the Right's discourse on "terrorism" (which, as I'll suggest, is more or less the generalized discourse on "terrorism" in the United States overall and therefore not exceptional) in order to show the queer/ed threat to imperial and settler social meaning that "terrorism" instantiates and embodies. Taking this rhetoric seriously by no means entails endorsing its moralizing condemnation of anticolonial struggle as evil, much less believing in its allegedly objective, rational, and clearly determined category of political violence (that is, "terrorism"). It does, however, require recognizing the implicit truth upon which the conservative viewpoint is built, a truth that Edelman also recognizes and also does not endorse: conservatives are acutely aware of "the fragility of a civilization" (or any other consolidated identity) and that it can be "destroyed by malign forces."[70] Their consequent impulse toward preservation is neither stupid nor basely politically instrumental; it is, however, an impulse that disperses itself ideologically through a moralized insistence on elite survival at the expense of everyone else as the only thinkable and credible political position, a moralism that stigmatizes, punishes, and eliminates those who reject their survivalist framework because such rejection constitutes an attack on their own and their worldview's mortality. The conservative morality of survival is thus not simply a particular(ly) hegemonic position, but also a wall against dissent and the means by which such dissent is evacuated of political content by characterizing it as insupportable threat—as unreasonable, corrupt, immoral, unthinkable, indefensible, and perverse. Such moralization makes "terrorists"—Muslims, Arabs, and all those who "look like" them—deserving of elimination by definition. It is the contention of this chapter and of *Queer Terror* as a whole that if this is the case, then the only credibly emancipatory response to such punitive sanctimony is to declare our queer allegiance to the "terrorists."

"TERRORISM" AND/AS DISSIDENCE

In 2011 and 2015, the liberal organization Center for American Progress (CAP) released two reports on what it calls the Islamophobia Network in America.[71] The first, titled *Fear, Inc.*, documented a small group of seven foundations that funded "five key people and their organizations" to the tune of some $40 million from 2001 to 2009. These five people and organizations produced misinformation about Muslims (for example, that President Obama was one, or that he was controlled by them, or that Muslims were seeking to take control of the US government through the implementation of Sharia law) and Islam (for example, that it is a totalitarian doctrine, that it requires lying and violence), misinformation that ascends to national prominence "through effective advocates, media partners, and grassroots organizing."[72] Their second report, *Fear, Inc. 2.0*, documents the continued existence of the Islamophobia Network and the transformation of its discourse during the Obama era in anticipation of the 2016 presidential election, including the anti-"terrorism" training of US police officers and media coverage of the Boston Marathon bombing.[73]

Based entirely on publicly available records and tax returns, the information provided in the CAP reports and its description of this Islamophobia Network are both credible and persuasive. Hardly a conspiracy theory, CAP isolates the Islamophobia Network's key players, debunks the misinformation it spreads, and shows the connections between its big foundation donors, online bloggers and journalists, academic "experts," political pundits, and government officials. As Moustafa Bayoumi importantly points out, however, the CAP reports do not explain how or why the rhetoric and misinformation of the Islamophobia Network have had such traction in US public discourse. Why, in other words, does the Network's Islamophobia work so well? What is it about this discourse that so successfully influences public opinion, generates campaign contributions, and turns people out to the polls? The CAP reports offer a careful assessment of the political goals and interests of the few folks who run it. But what about those who are swayed by its rhetoric? As Bayoumi writes, "*Fear, Inc.* . . . makes a convincing case, but it also assumes that people can be directed to act by the network and not by their own desires or for their own reasons."[74]

Bayoumi suggests that Islamophobia works because it plays on white, Christian Americans' fears of becoming, sooner or later, a minority in "their own" country. By contrast, in his now-classic analysis, Edward Said suggests that twentieth-century US Islamophobia is an outgrowth of the historical Orientalism that understands Islam as "not only a formidable competitor but also a latecoming challenge to Christianity."[75] More recently, S. Sayyid has argued that Islamophobia is an attempt to ward off any erosion of "the West and non-West framework" in which "societies and histories . . . are narrated (and narrate themselves) as Westernising and those whose hegemonic constructions represent them as already Western."[76] All of these analyses are surely important parts of the story. But they have yet to adequately grasp the depth or texture of the fear of Islam they diagnose or what might explain its psychic and political traction. Indeed, my own sense is that the problem may not be "fear" at all exactly, as the Hobbesian discussion of settler psychology in chapter 2 made clear. While a popularized misunderstanding of Hobbes makes him the political theorist of fear and thereby anoints fear as the political emotion of conservatism (frequently counterposed to its championed liberal opposite, hope), what Hobbes actually argues is that the savagery of uncertainty and indefinite insecurity in the state of nature leaves us in a motionless state he characterizes not as fear, but rather *despair*. Recognizing this specific subjective anguish in settler colonial biopolitics was only one of the correctives offered in chapter 2 to standard accounts of biopolitical death. The other was the recognition that settler sovereignty simultaneously *moralizes* these psychic and subjective states into irrefutable designations of value and worth(lessness), such that "life" and "survival" become interchangeable with value and inviolability, while "death" (along with its subjective experience, "despair") becomes the name for antivalue, absurdity, enmity, and annihilation. When it comes to "terrorism," then—closely related to if not inextricable from the problem of Islamophobia in the United States—the rhetorical effectiveness of this discourse lies not simply in white supremacist anxiety, historical reticence regarding Islam's competition with Christianity, or an undue attachment to a "West and the rest" framework, but also in its moralization of civilizational survival and immoralization of any dissent from or refusal of that project as an unpredictable and perverse savagery that renders all happiness, security, and futurity impossible. This is what compels about "terrorism" discourse, and it explains why Islamophobia is a racist formation that is not exhausted by the framework of racism and therefore how it is that Muslims have become such a political football in American public discourse and political life.

To see this moralism and its effectivity at work, I want to turn first to a now-infamous three-and-a-half minute video documenting an exchange in 2010 between a University of California Davis undergraduate and David Horowitz following a lecture he had given there.[77] Horowitz is one of the better-known popularizers of Islamophobic misinformation, particularly on college campuses. He is famous for, among other things, organizing "Islamo-Fascism Awareness Week" on college campuses across the country.[78] As this exchange reveals, Horowitz's provocative discourse is not somehow outside the bounds of political reasonableness, as many might want to suggest, but is rather illustrative of the presuppositions that constitute it. That is, the exchange between the student and Horowitz is not a dispute between two extremists, but rather a clarification of the basic premises that animate and sustain the contours of the political in the United States that well-meaning liberals would prefer to ignore or elide. Perhaps unsurprisingly, this is a constitution of the political that purposefully and systematically abjects the Muslim as "terrorist." Indeed, this short if dramatic confrontation amply illustrates the impossibility of speaking as a Muslim in opposition to American imperialism without always already being relegated to the *position* of the "terrorist," a logic that Edelman describes as futurism and that I think astutely maps the biopolitics of US settler sovereignty.

The video begins with the student introducing herself as Jumanah Imad Mousa Ahmed Albahri, an articulation of her full Arabic name that includes her grandfather's and father's names. She then identifies herself as a member of UC Davis's Muslim Student Association (MSA) and asks Horowitz what evidence he has for his claim that MSAs both at the

University of California and across the United States are linked with what he calls "jihadi terrorist networks."[79] Worth noting are that the student is wearing hijab and that her coming forward to address Horowitz as she does is already a kind defiance, insofar as Horowitz has already equated Islam with "terrorism" and "jihad" during his talk and thereby provisionally set the terms of further discussion. Understanding full well that to be Muslim or Arab is to be a "terrorist," Albahri nevertheless steps into the predefined role supplied for her and affirms that it applies, merely by stating her own name.[80] Rather than addressing Albahri's question, however, Horowitz instead responds with his own question, asking, "Will you condemn Hamas, here and now," as a "homicidal, terrorist organization?" In the terms of this book project, Horowitz can be understood as asking Albahri to make clear whether or not she is, in fact, a part of the US settler order or external to it. Is she an immoral, "savage," "terrorist" threat to the project of "life," itself aligned with both US and Israeli dictates regarding survival and political futurity? Or is she rather the deathly threat he already suspects her to be, someone aligned with the "terrorists" who are against "life," against the United States, and thus against the future?

Consistently more astute than Horowitz, Albahri answers cannily, "Are you asking me to put myself on a cross?" Fully aware of the constraints that render Horowitz's question a reflection of the impossible social and political dictates governing Muslim lives in America after 9/11, Albahri instead references a Christian metaphor of self-sacrifice to make clear that, regardless of her response, she (knows she) is always already guilty, always already a "terrorist," inevitably—because of (the visible markers of) her Muslim religion—cast as the spectral threat of death and annihilation produced by the current moment's post-9/11, futurist imperial logic. And she perhaps deploys this metaphor also as a reproach, for no redemption will come from her accession to the terms of this debate. She cannot, in other words, speak outside the terms Horowitz presents. As she well realizes, she is always already queer(ed)—as a Muslim/"terrorist," she represents the dissolution of the social order, the "queer" who portends "death." Answering Horowitz's question *at all* legitimizes this framing presupposition, for even to answer "yes" and present herself as a "good Muslim" still shores up the constitutive suspicion of Islam and affirms its inherently threatening character. Albahri can either say "no" and, in affirming support for Hamas, render herself a "terrorist" sympathizer and expose herself even further to the machinations of the post-9/11 US security state, or answer "yes" and speak in the only words allowed to her—words that designate her status as legitimately targeted for death. In both cases, the answer is the same insofar as the question's premise is that Islam is a menacing threat to civilization.

Unperturbed, Horowitz concludes that Albahri's response indicates her support for Hamas, explaining that "If you don't condemn Hamas, obviously you support it." When the student tries to explain that her answer to any question about Hamas is constrained by the threat of arrest and indefinite detention by Homeland Security, he ignores her, listing other MSA students who have similarly "refused" to "condemn" Hamas. Unwilling to allow anything but a yes or no answer to his question, Horowitz then ups the ante, restating the question to Albahri this way: "I'm a Jew. The head of Hezbollah has said that he hopes that we will gather in Israel so that he doesn't have to hunt us down globally."[81] Horowitz then raises his voice and speaks directly into the mic, demanding: "*For it or against it?*" Seeming to grasp the depth of the situation, Albahri replies coolly: "For it." Surprised to receive such a direct answer, a pleased Horowitz thanks Albahri for "coming and showing everybody what's here."

Now, among certain narrow groups on both the Left and the Right, this video went viral. However, it was not really talked about much on the Left, despite how painful it was to watch. This silence is due, I suspect, at least in part to the fact that Albahri's answer seems to confirm all the horrifying presuppositions upon which Horowitz and the Islamophobia Network rely, presumptions that liberals and progressives want to say are mere fantasy or bigotry: Muslim = "terrorist" = Nazi. What is disturbing about this video, however, is not Albahri's response, but rather the overarching discourse and political logic that constrain and prevent her from answering in any other way than to smear Islam as "terrorist." In other words, her "For it" answer is effectively no different from the "Against it" answer Horowitz seeks, since both answers affirm the constitutive "terrorism" of Islam and take "terrorism" to be a credible designation of political violence, rather than a manufactured ideological category used to stifle anticolonial and anti-imperial dissent and moralize it out of existence. This is why Horowitz's question is impossible to answer and also why the video is so upsetting to watch: it shows the complete abjection of Muslims and Islam and/ as "terrorism" as this abjection unfolds within the confines of ostensibly free and reasonable discussion on a university campus. Indeed, if anything is disturbing about this video, it is its naked illustration of the hegemony of this political logic, which defines contemporary US culture. The imperial futurism of US and Israeli politics dictates that Albahri cannot do or be anything else than a "terrorist." Her response that she is "For it" merely makes explicit the entire animus of the social order, which is neither her fault nor an accurate representation of her own political position, the latter of which is of course impossible to render legible.

In the wake of some amount of media coverage of this exchange (for the most part in right-wing astroturf media, blogs, and Zionist news sites) and multiple demands from Zionist organizations that Albahri be censured or expelled, Albahri released a public statement regarding her answer to Horowitz's question. In it she states unequivocally, "I do NOT condone murder, I do NOT condone genocide, and I do NOT condone racism under any circumstance whatsoever against Jews or anyone else" (original emphases).[82] As if (she knows) these emphases will nevertheless fail to convey her meaning, she then goes on to explain her "For it" response by stating, first, that she did not hear the entirety of Horowitz's question and, second, that she was unable to provide a simple yes or no answer to the question of support for Hamas (both then and at the time of her statement) because she wanted to distinguish between "supporting Hamas" and supporting the Palestinian liberation struggle: "I am not a member of Hamas, nor have I ever given support to Hamas, nor do I agree with their actions or stances wholesale, but I refused to offer Mr. Horowitz a blanket condemnation of Hamas that night. I felt that doing so would be a blanket condemnation of the Palestinian cause." In other words, it is not simply that she is Muslim that makes her a "terrorist." She is also an advocate of the Palestinian cause, and one cannot advocate on behalf of Palestinian liberation without being anticivilization, antilife, and, it must be recognized, anti-Jewish. Albahri understands this, writing that "*any* answer that I would provide" to Horowitz would be construed as "anti-Semitic, genocidal hate speech in order to further his political agenda" (original emphasis). There is thus an almost tragic irony underwriting Albahri's forthright statement. Even as she attempts retroactively to fit her understanding of and advocacy for Palestinian liberation within the terms of settler futurism, she recognizes the impossibility of doing so, even in a "moderate" or "reasonable" manner that explicitly condemns murder, genocide, and anti-Semitism. Although she does not express it this way, she recognizes that support for the Palestinian cause and proud Muslim self-identification are conflated in the US and Israeli imaginaries with "terrorism," precisely *because* their existence threatens the settler-imperial order that would disappear natives or allow them to appear only as death and destruction. Thus it is no surprise that her statement did not appease anyone who complained about her initial answer, instead only serving as further evidence of her irredeemably "terrorist" nature. Indeed, Horowitz continues to show this video clip in his addresses at college campuses to this day as evidence of the genocidal Nazism of Islam, MSAs, and Palestine solidarity activists.

The clip featuring Albahri and Horowitz is by now rather dated. Yet the same line of questioning uncannily emerged once again during the Israeli war on Gaza in 2014, known as Operation Protective Edge. Although the disparate impact of both casualties and destruction in this war was, both at the time and to this day, indisputable (a fact that holds true for this particular war as well as the entirety of the Zionist/Palestinian "conflict"), Operation Protective Edge was nevertheless deemed justifiable by much of the Israeli public (who actually wished Netanyahu had gone further) as well as most Americans because of the "terrorist" threat posed by Hamas. So, in a surreal replay of Albahri's interrogation, Yousef Munayyer was "interviewed" on Fox News, along with Zuhdi Jasser, founder of the American Islamic Forum for Democracy (AIFD).[83] At the time, Munayyer was executive director of the Palestine Center; Jasser is a regular guest commentator in right-wing media outlets and frequently claims that the United States is being infiltrated by radical Islam.[84] The occasion for this joint interview, in a segment titled "Sympathy for the Terrorists," was a Council on American Islamic Relations (CAIR) press release demanding that the US government condemn "Israel's unjust and disproportionate use of force against the Palestinians in Gaza" during Operation Protective Edge. Notably, the host Sean Hannity observes, there is no mention of Hamas in the statement, which he finds astonishing given that they "were the ones who started this conflict." For Hannity, CAIR's statement raises the question as to "Why," in his words, "America's largest Muslim so-called civil rights group [is] showing sympathy to terrorists?" This is the question that Jasser and Munayyer have been invited to discuss.[85]

As quickly becomes clear, however, Hannity is not terribly interested in hearing Munayyer say much of anything. Although Munayyer is the focus of the interview and the main addressee of Hannity's questions, as soon as

Munayyer makes any move in the direction of situating Israel's war on Gaza in any sort of historical or political context, Hannity cuts him off, at one point explaining that, by doing so, Munayyer is "justifying the terrorists" and "making a rationalization for rockets and kidnapping and murder and you wanna blame the victims in this case." Jasser then pipes up and blames Hamas for having begun the war; additionally, he asserts that there is "gender apartheid" in the Gaza Strip along with rampant church burnings and declares that Hamas's "doctrine is fascist and genocidal against Jews." At this point, Hannity turns directly to the camera and says, "I want to ask Yousef a question: Is Hamas a terrorist organization?" Like Horowitz, Hannity proscribes any answer that exceeds one word because it is "a simple yes or no question." Each time Munayyer attempts to answer, then, because it does not take the form of either "yes" or "no," Hannity cuts him off and accuses him of evading the question. Only once, when Munayyer is finally given a moment to articulate a sentence, he begins with the following: "It's very telling to me, and it should be telling to your viewers, as well, by the way, that the moment you have a Palestinian voice on your program, who begins to explain the legitimate grievances of Palestinians. . . ." But at "legitimate grievances" Hannity once again interrupts, yelling at Munayyer, "Is Hamas a terrorist organization?" and demanding, "Answer! Answer the question!" to which Munayyer replies, "Am I a guest on your program or am I on a witness stand?" Without irony, Hannity replies, "Yes, you're a guest, but you don't get to filibuster."

Munayyer finally relents under the force of Hannity's interrogation and says that yes, the US government considers Hamas a terrorist organization. But this only provokes Hannity further, causing him to demand, "Do *you* consider Hamas a terrorist organization? I didn't ask what the United States thinks; I asked what *you* think! Can you hear?" At this point, Munayyer encourages Hannity not to yell at him, to which Hannity responds, "OK, I'll ask you nicely." Twinkling his fingers in the air, batting his eyelashes, and smiling, Hannity asks in a singsong tone, "Is Hamas a terrorist organization?" He cannot maintain this performance for long, however, and quickly reverts back to demands. Munayyer tries to change tactics, saying to Hannity, "Let me ask *you* a question." But, in addition to not being allowed to filibuster, Hannity tells Munayyer that he is also not allowed to answer a question with a question. By this point, Hannity is again yelling at Munayyer and again asks the same question—Is Hamas a terrorist organization?—but he adds on to it this time, "What part of this can't you get through your thick head? *Is Hamas a terrorist organization? Yes or no?*" And with this final discursive escalation the two are at an impasse, with Munayyer insisting he has answered Hannity's question, and Hannity remaining disgusted and dissatisfied. Jasser then again interjects, saying that Hamas uses children as human shields, launches rockets at civilians, and starts wars, while organizations like CAIR attempt to portray "terrorists" as victims when precisely the opposite is the case. Wearily, Munayyer sighs, "Do I get to say anything?" Hannity promptly replies, "You had your chance. You didn't say Hamas is a terrorist organization. Goodbye."

Now, Hannity's question differs from Horowitz's, at least superficially, insofar as he does not ask Munayyer to condemn Hamas as a "terrorist" organization but merely to confirm its "terrorist" status. Given the moralization of "terrorism" as the name of what seeks to destroy Western/US-Israeli civilization, however, to label a person or group "terrorist" is by definition to condemn it. As Lisa Stampnitzky has shown, even in the academic realm of social science research, offering explanations of "terrorism" is still relatively taboo. Explanation is too close to exoneration, and suggests that "terrorism" is comprehensible, thinkable, even rational.[86] Thus what is consistently more important when discussing the problem of "terrorism"—whether in academia or on Fox News—is less its meaning or explanation than its unconditional condemnation. Even Human Rights Watch, while conceding that "there is no single definition of terrorism under international law" and that "many of the definitions used by countries are overly broad,"[87] nevertheless begins its report on the FBI's abusive prosecution of "terrorism" cases against US Muslims by obligatorily declaring, "Terrorism entails horrifying acts, often resulting in terrible losses of human life."[88] As Ghassan Hage remarks, "perhaps the most important aspect of the classification *terrorist*" is that "it forces us to normalize certain forms of violence and to pathologize others."[89]

By contrast with Albahri, Munayyer refuses to answer the question. Unlike her, he does not, even by accident, explicitly avow any commitment to the destruction of the Jews or Israel or the United States. However, he doesn't have to. Indeed, he doesn't have to answer the question at all. Simply by virtue of being Palestinian, he is already condemned as a "terrorist," "terrorist" sympathizer, or "terrorist" excuse-mongerer. As illustrated all too literally, the only way he can speak *at all* is to align himself in some way with the settler-imperial project that relegates the existence of Palestinians and Muslims to incarnations of death and destruction—as his companion guest on the program, Zuhdi Jasser, makes clear. This same inevitability of condemnation is evident in the clip with Horowitz and Albahri, which ends with Horowitz telling her she is wearing a "terrorist neckerchief"—that is, a keffiyeh—as if he needed some further, external confirmation of her "terrorist" nature. Although he does not cite her hijab, it was this that clued him in to her being Muslim; her wearing of a globalized symbol of the Palestinian liberation struggle, the keffiyeh, makes clear that her hijab is not innocent, that she is not even a "good Muslim," that she cannot be or say anything except "terrorism" and death. The impasse produced on Fox News by Munayyer's nonanswer only further illustrates the impossibility of speaking or knowing or just simply *being* outside the constraints of settler futurism. And the fury Munayyer's nonanswer engenders in Hannity forecasts the punishment that attends any attempt to flout or deviate from those constraints.

Now, it may seem absurd to suggest that Albahri or Munayyer or Palestinian civilians in Gaza are "terrorists," just as it now seems equally absurd to suggest that homosexuals pose inherent pedophilic threats and augur species annihilation due to their perverse, nonreproductive lifestyles. Yet, just as the latter claims were credible and widely accepted on the basis of their moralizing celebration of children and childhood (and functioned simultaneously to authorize the criminal punishment, ostracism, violence, segregation, discrimination, and murder of queer people and all those perceived to be such), so, too, is the former claim widely credible on the basis of its moralizing celebration of settler life in the form of American freedom and Israeli democracy (and it functions simultaneously to authorize the surveillance, torture, disappearance, deportation, targeted killing, and death of Muslims and Arabs and all those who "look like" them). But this is not simply a case of ideological overreach. It is also an accurate depiction of how Muslims, Arabs, and Palestinians show up within a futurist frame. Indeed, in some very real sense, Albahri, Munayyer, and Palestinians in Gaza *are* "terrorists," just as much if not more so than any officially declared "terrorist" organization. Their dissent, their indigeneity, their continued existence and refusal to comply with the futurism of settler sovereignty are very real threats to "civilization"; if they were not, there would be no need to monitor, yell at, pacify, punish, surveil, and murder them.

As Stampnitzky shows, not only was there an elaborate, international effort to produce "terrorism" as the evil threat to Western civilization, but as CAP documents, there is an enduring, coordinated, and well-funded effort to keep that definition in place and intact via a noxious discourse of Islamophobia. The evidence of the success of these efforts is abundant, in the form of Islamophobic anti-"terrorism" law enforcement in the United States,[90] the criminalization of speech that is critical of Israel,[91] the vast surveillance of Muslim people in the United States,[92] and the electoral victory of Donald Trump via, among other things, his promises to ban Syrian refugees, institute a Muslim registry and ban, and move Israel's capitol to Jerusalem. The targeting and punishment of Muslims and all those in alliance with "Muslim" goals—that is, undermining Zionism and US settler-imperialism—make clear how serious and real this threat of "terrorism" truly is, even if it is not exactly the same threat Islamophobes imagine it to be. Why, otherwise, would there be such a vast, well-funded machinery of pundits, policymakers, think tanks, organizations, and opinion-makers invested in producing and reproducing this discourse? Why else is the United States engaged in such protracted monitoring, surveillance, incarceration, entrapment, and deportation of US Muslims? Why, indeed, did Israel go to such catastrophic excess in its vicious assault on the Gaza Strip in 2014 (and, before that, in 2012, and before that, in 2008 and 2009)? These are not mistakes. They are purposeful efforts at containment and pacification in order to preserve the existing futurist order. Rejection of that order is *correctly* understood as an existential threat.

Moreover, any response to such seeming absolutism that attempts to sift out the "real" terrorists from the imposters, the bad Muslims from the good Muslims, only upholds the futurist logic of US imperialism and reinstalls it at the heart of any project of resistance. Regrettably, both CAP reports rely on just such a distinction, and it is reproduced in Moustafa Bayoumi's otherwise admirable book *This Muslim American Life*. For example, the first *Fear, Inc.* report complains that the Islamophobia Network undermines America's ability to fight "terrorism,"[93] which they insist is empirically real and also Islamic ("Across the globe, there are terrorists killing in the name of Islam")[94] but nevertheless overemphasized, a focus that occludes the vast numbers of "moderate" Muslims living quiet, assimilated, American lives. These moderate Muslims should not be alienated by Islamophobic discourse and policy since, CAP disturbingly recommends, "the largest single source of initial information to authorities about the few Muslim American plots has come from the Muslim American community."[95] In their second report, *Fear, Inc. 2.0*, CAP laments the viciously Islamophobic anti-"terrorism" trainings provided to US police officers for the same troubling reason: "it drives a wedge between law enforcement and Muslim communities and creates endless red herrings that make detecting actual terrorist plots more difficult."[96] CAP is overall quite eager to distinguish between good Muslims and bad Muslims, praising George W. Bush for differentiating between "radical Islamist groups abroad who seek to kill Americans and the overwhelming majority of peaceful Muslims,"[97] criticizing the Religious Right for making "no distinction between moderate and radical Islam,"[98] and insisting that the Islamophobia Network should be resisted (only?) insofar as it attempts "to equate mainstream American Muslims with the perverted brand of Islam promoted by ISIS." [99] Relegating the likes of Horowitz and Hannity to a "fringe" that bears no connection with "mainstream" America, CAP expresses consternation that their first *Fear, Inc.* report was taken to suggest "that the United States is indeed hostile to Muslims and Islam," when in fact "the Islamophobia network that CAP identified in 2011 is not indicative of mainstream American views."[100] Bayoumi similarly intimates a distinction between good and bad Muslims, describing the writings of the extrajudicially murdered US citizen Anwar Al-Awlaki as "lunatic ravings"[101] while positioning himself as a patriotic American[102] and qualifying his critique of American Islamophobia as by no means impugning the character of the nation overall, which is "of course" not "an Islamophobic country."[103] Bayoumi condemns "terrorism" in all the loaded, moralized words used by the Islamophobia Network (for example, "horrific, immoral, and nihilistic").[104] And both Bayoumi and CAP emphasize the importance of facts in coming to grips with Islamophobic assumptions about "terrorism," with Bayoumi insisting that "the automatic association of Muslim Americans with terrorism has become completely institutionalized and thoroughly commonsensical, even though it flies in the face of the evidence"[105] and the CAP reports emphasizing the importance of "providing the public with fact-based knowledge, rather than shrill, fear-based attacks."[106]

Surely well intentioned, both CAP and Bayoumi nevertheless reproduce the allegedly "fringe" discourse of the Islamophobia Network and the brokers of "terrorism" discourse in their own, anti-Islamophobic research, albeit in a liberal key. Making a distinction between "moderate" and "perverted" Islam concedes that Islam is always, by definition, a potential problem and responds to Islamophobia by attempting to correct its "ignorance, disinformation, and sweeping generalizations"[107] rather than rooting out its origins in civilizationalist hatred of indigenous existence and anticolonial dissidence. Indeed, the claim that only some Muslims are "radical" or "terrorist" not only concedes that Islam itself is a threat but actually echoes key arguments and talking points advanced by the Islamophobia Network itself (talking points that CAP documents in its own reports).[108] Meanwhile, echoing the Right's condemnation of "terrorism" as immoral, nihilistic, and evil shores up the moralizing parameters of "life" and "death" that constitute the "civilized" order of US and Israeli settler colonialism. Conceding the importance of "facts" in any adjudication of either "terrorism" or Islamophobia suggests that "terrorism" is, as CAP says, "real," rather than an ideological determination wielded moralizingly in order to stigmatize, punish, and eliminate anti-imperial and anticolonial dissidence, while it affirms the contingent if nevertheless undeniable link between "terrorism" and Islam, the latter of which is always already guilty, either potentially or actually. Bayoumi correctly observes that the United States is afflicted by what he calls "War on Terror culture," which he defines as "the deep institutionalization of George W. Bush's simplistic proclamation that 'either you are with us, or you are with the terrorists.'"[109] This is exactly right; in this statement, Bush synopsizes the futurist logic of US settler sovereignty. But, Bayoumi continues, it is "as if there can be no other options, as if one can't oppose the horrors that the War on Terror delivers and the murderous nihilism of terrorism simultaneously."[110] What Bayoumi misses, however, is that this, too, is exactly right. There are *not* other options, which is precisely the point Bush, Horowitz, Hannity, and all the other members of the Islamophobia Network make clear, in a discourse that is not at all "fringe" but rather firmly institutionalized, as Bayoumi observes, in US political culture. As illustrated in the exchanges with Horowitz and Hannity, whether one affirms or denies that Hamas is a "terrorist" organization, merely answering the question accepts the host of unspoken premises impacted in the term's settler and imperial genealogy, premises that limit and foreclose any other answer than condemnation of "terrorism" as evil. To accept the terms of "terrorism" in this way—by conceding, for example, that most Muslims are moderate, that not all Muslims are "terrorists," or that not all "terrorists" are Muslim—is to align oneself with that settler-imperial project that sets the terms of who and what a "terrorist" is to begin with. Such an alignment does not threaten empire but rather advances it in a familiar liberal key of tolerance and inclusion. It is this benign multiculturalism that asks "moderate" Muslims to condemn "extremists" and understands Islamophobia to be primarily a problem of "scapegoating based on religion, race, or creed"[111] rather than an effect of racialized imperial domination and the by-product of colonial settlement.[112]

Rather than fall for this moralist ruse and be coopted by the liberal lure of evidence-based rationality and the free exchange of ideas, any critical dissent from the War on Terror must recognize that the domain of those "reasonable ideas" is itself governed by the morality of settler civilizationalism and is duplicated in liberal discourses that fail to grapple with the deeper roots of Islamophobia and "terrorism" discourse. Rather than avoid or evade the association of Islam with "terrorism" and the associations of "terrorism" with nihilism, evil, and death in an attempt to secure a place at the table of rationality, liberty, and the American way, the only possible option for any truly dissident opposition to settler-empire is to affirm a position *outside* this stultifying social order, a position that is impossible to affirm as such because its only meaning and existence are antimeaning and antiexistence. Dissent from War on Terror culture is not effected by saying that Muslims aren't really evil, much less by engaging in some sort of liberal humanist argument that declares a respect for different faith traditions and praises "moderate" Islam. Rather, dissidence is effected by embracing precisely what is determined to be unembraceable, unthinkable, unreasonable, or immoral—the refusal of settler colonialism and the War on Terror. Only this constitutes an actual threat to the social order that declares that you are either with it or against it. In being against it, one necessarily declares oneself a "terrorist." But let's be clear: only the "terrorist" is *actually* against "civilization."

To ally oneself with "terrorism" in this way is not to declare an intention to murder people, hijack airplanes, or behead journalists, but rather to resist and reject the racist, civilizationalist moralism that underpins the structural and ideological positioning of the categories of "life" and "death" within US settler sovereignty and its expansionist imperial project. To

choose "death" in this scenario means to reject its civilizational imperatives. Such a formulation may sound simplistic or reductive. It is no less
accurate for all that; that these are the explicit meanings and stakes of the
War on Terror and its global order is made especially clear in the explicit
discourse of the Right to which I am paying so much attention in this
chapter. To take one final and profoundly illustrative example: In 2014,
Ayaan Hirsi Ali was interviewed by Mike Huckabee on Fox News during
Israel's brutal and unrelenting war on the Gaza Strip.[113] The CAP reports
do not mention Hirsi Ali as a prominent contributor to the Islamophobia
industry, but Bayoumi correctly profiles her as one of a handful of native
informants who claim "to reveal the true nature of Islam to Western audiences, promising an insider message of telling it to you like it is" (and it
is, of course, almost uniformly bad).[114] During the approximately twenty-
minute interview, Huckabee asks Hirsi Ali why she, as a Muslim, was nevertheless supportive of Israel—both generally and in particular during
this specific war. Hirsi Ali explained:

> I support Israel primarily because it is not only a democratic and free
> government in that region where there is a lack of that, but Israel is based
> on a creed of life, life before death. And they are facing enemies that
> want to annihilate not only Israel, but eliminate all Jews. And the ene-
> mies of Israel believe in a creed of death. For them, life is transitional.
> And so the life of their own children, the life of their own mothers, the
> life of their own wives, and fellow civilians, it doesn't matter that much,
> because they're looking forward to death so that after death something
> wonderful is going to happen. And people don't see this basic difference.
> And it's so important to see this. If you don't see that, then you don't
> understand the conflict. I vote for life, so I vote for Israel.

Now, to be clear, Operation Protective Edge was by far the worst of Israel's
military attacks on Gaza in the history of either's existence, and resulted
in the death of approximately twenty-two hundred Palestinians, more than
five hundred of them children. It was Israel's third attack on the Strip in
almost six years, each of which came after the Israeli historian Ilan Pappé
had already described Israel's "normal" treatment of Palestinians in Gaza
in this period as "incremental genocide."[115] During this indiscriminate[116]
massacre, Israel bombed people in their homes, on beaches, in cafés,

mosques, hospitals, schools, UN shelters, and disabled persons facilities. Dead bodies piled up so quickly during this short war that Gazans were warehousing corpses in ice cream freezers, both because the morgues and hospitals had run out of space and because these were in increasingly short supply due to their systematic destruction by Israel. Family homes, schools, hospitals, factories, and entire neighborhoods were knowingly reduced to rubble by IDF forces.[117] What is so striking, then, about Hirsi Ali's answer to Huckabee is that even as Israel was then engaged in a massacre, the extent and atrocity of which were unprecedented even for this brutal regime and which is itself eligible for designation as an act of genocide in its own right, Hirsi Ali can without any discernible dissonance declare that it is a regime that stands on the side of life. Her argument here is a crude if extremely clear elaboration of the biopolitical logic of settler sovereignty I explicated in chapter 2. The evidence of Netanyahu's contributions to "terrorism" discourse is here in the presentation of Israel as a democracy and "terrorism" as a threat specific to Jews and akin to Nazism in its aspiration to Jewish annihilation. But what's even more clear is the way that the contours of both US empire and Zionist colonization are distilled down to their basics: Israel (along with the United States) is on the side of "life." They are cultures of life; they value life; they fight in the name of life; they seek to protect, nurture, and enhance life. Pitted against them is the culture of death: Islam, Arabs, "terrorism," "fundamentalism." This sanctimonious condemnation of "terrorism" is the necropolitical flipside of the settler moralization of life. The genocidal eradication of Palestinians, just like the genocidal conquest of native North America, is *justified*, and it is justified precisely because and in the name of "life," a term that clearly refers only to settler lives, the lives that matter. Settler sovereignty is a biopolitics for settlers and a necropolitics for natives; it allows for and in fact facilitates the self-righteous championing of genocide as a "creed of life." Huckabee concludes this segment of his interview with Hirsi Ali by asking her if there is any use in attempting to negotiate with Hamas in order to try to end the then-ongoing Israeli war on Gaza. Hirsi Ali's answer is clear: "There is no common ground with an enemy that not only believes in death, but that only believes in your elimination." George W. Bush couldn't have said it better.

"TERRORISM" AND/AS QUEER/RESISTANCE

Back in the United States, at roughly the same time as Hirsi Ali's interview, Professor Steven Salaita was fired by the Board of Trustees of the University of Illinois at Urbana-Champagne (UIUC) for his now-famously "uncivil" tweets criticizing Israel's assault on Gaza in 2014. I do not seek to rehash that controversy here. I only want to consider one of the most infamous of Salaita's tweets by way of concluding this chapter: "You may be too refined to say it, but I'm not: I wish all the fucking West Bank settlers would go missing."[118] Now, the threatening nature of such a longing is perhaps clear. Tweeted in the wake of the abduction of three Israeli teenagers subsequently found murdered by a rogue faction of Hamas in the West Bank, many interpreted Salaita's tweet to be saying that he wished the same fate upon Israeli settlers. At an event at Brooklyn College, however, Salaita explained this tweet rather differently:

> So, "oh, he meant that he wanted them murdered, or he wanted them kidnapped." No. I *didn't* mean that, actually. I meant that I want them to go missing. Am I a shrinking violet on Twitter? I'm not passive aggressive. If I would have wanted them murdered or kidnapped, I would have said "murdered" or "kidnapped." All right?
>
> And when I say "go missing," I wish—you gotta understand that there's a long, long, long tradition of people who've been colonized wishing that their colonizers would go away. You might not like to hear it, but it's true. They don't like you. They don't want you there. Please, read *The Wretched of the Earth*, and read what Frantz Fanon has to say about what the native says about the settler. All right? That comes directly out of that framework.
>
> Think about the ghost dance in the 1890s, in the lead-up to the Wounded Knee massacre. Right? The ghost dance was an articulation of the desire that all the settlers go away.[119]

Salaita here connects Palestinians' rejection of Israeli settlers with indigenous North American tribes' rejection of European settlement and characterizes his tweet as part of that anticolonial tradition.[120] The immediate reception and interpretation of this tweet as a call to violence, however, make clear that one need not commit or even advocate violence in order to be guilty of threatening the US-Israeli order with "terrorist" annihilation. Considered "uncivil," the master term of Salaita's dismissal from the university, his tweeted longing for colonists and colonialism to "go missing" makes clear that the stakes of settler sovereignty today remain much the same as those of the "initial" conquest, and that to oppose settler sovereignty is indeed to be uncivilized, "savage," violent, nihilistic. Salaita continues,

> It [negative response to the tweet] seems to be oriented in a discursive community or political community where the very thought of not accepting the presence, right, or the power of the colonizer is a sort of personal rejection that they simply cannot tolerate. But it's one that, if we're gonna understand the situation clearly, right, we need to confront the [fact that] Palestinians do not want Israeli settlers on the West Bank. And we want them to go away. All right? That's what that tweet was saying, and I can understand why people reacted strongly to it, but it's a sentiment that you will find on every single street corner, on every single village or city on the West Bank.

Ghassan Hage observes that "people often expect the colonized, because they are victims, to be 'nice' people. . . . Western colonialism has often produced and still produces some of the worst living conditions created on the planet. And yet the people who try to rise above these living conditions are somehow expected to be chic, humanitarian, cosmopolitan—even aesthetically appealing."[121] Hage gets something right here but also fails to take the analysis further to interrogate the ways in which "nice"-ness itself is a value of the civilized used to stifle, silence, and delegitimate anticolonial dissent. His first ambit is better: Salaita's tweet wasn't very nice but, then again, colonization isn't very nice. Moreover, to insist on nice-ness as the criterion for resistance is effectively to say that the colonized ought not to resist at all, since you can be sure that resisting colonization will definitely not seem very "nice" to the colonizer. Thus a political critique is reduced to rudeness or "incivility," which allows it to be justifiably expelled from polite, rational, and indeed "civil" discourse. As Salaita writes in his book about his hiring and firing at UIUC, *Uncivil Rites*, however, "We have a language with which we speak of Israel. To accommodate normative sensibilities is to forfeit the only power we have over the colonizer: the ability to reject its rapacious demands and, in so doing, its very existence."[122]

The counterpoint to Salaita's longing that the settlers "go missing" is the revolutionary refrain of the Palestinian cause and the rallying cry of indigenous struggles everywhere: "to exist is to resist." This slogan can be seen graffitied in more than one place on the Palestinian "side" of Israel's enormous, twenty-six-foot-high wall that slices through the West Bank in jagged, aggressive strokes. To see one version of it as a tourist requires passing through the enormous, airport terminal–like Qalandiya checkpoint, where one is greeted, on the Israeli "side," by an enormous sign tacked onto the wall by the Ministry of Tourism, visible only through multiple loops of barbed wire, entreating "Peace Be with You" in English, Hebrew, and Arabic. The Orwellian impact of this encounter is perhaps one's only preparation for the flood of graffiti, paintings, images, and protestations spray-painted on the Palestinian "side" of the wall, none above approximately five feet, highlighting the enormity and oppressiveness of this twenty-six-foot-high concrete barrier. There this slogan can be seen on a mural proclaiming boldly in red, "To Exist Is to Resist," inscribed within the folds of a keffiyeh covering a face of which only big, long-lashed, brown eyes can be seen.[123] The meaning of the slogan is clear: for an indigenous people, subject to ethnic cleansing and systematic dispossession since 1947, the commitment to stay put and remain, to simply *exist*, is itself a form of resistance. This political resistance is, as Ali Abunimah writes, largely ignored by mainstream media—and, I would add, by politicians, scholars, and other "experts"—caught up in the frenzied identification of Arabs and Muslims with violence and "terrorism":

> One of the things that the violence-obsessed media coverage conceals is that nonviolence is and has always been integral to Palestinian resistance. The word for it in Arabic is *sumud*—steadfastness. When Israeli walls and roadblocks prevent people from moving, and yet children and old women, workers, students, mothers each day, every day climb hills and mountains to get where they need to go, that is *sumud*. When Israeli occupation forces uproot trees and farmers replant them, that is *sumud*. When Israel uses every administrative and legalistic means to force Palestinian Jerusalemites to leave the city for good, but

instead they stay, even if it means being painfully separated from family members in the West Bank, that is *sumud*. Millions of Palestinians practice nonviolence every day, yet this is ignored by the media and by politicians and is totally invisible to the vast majority of Israelis.[124]

In other words, even mere survival can constitute "terrorism." As Scott Lauria Morgensen notes, "The normative function of settlement is to appear inevitable and final."[125] Palestinians, in exercising *sumud*, in continuing *simply to exist*, are resisting the imperative of settler colonialism that seeks to disappear them from the land and from history. In remaining, they flout the conceits of the colonizing, occupying nation. Further disarticulating futurity from reproduction, here it is clear that Palestinian *life* is the site of death within Israeli futurism (as it says underneath "To Exist Is to Resist" on the wall, "*Viva Palestina*"). This is confirmed by the discourse of "demographic threat" that circulates routinely in various Israeli and Zionist circles by academics and politicians alike.[126] As Ali Abunimah consistently points out, the thoroughly militarized country of Israel, known to possess hundreds of nuclear weapons, is nevertheless profoundly threatened by Palestinian babies, whose existence and birthrate are invoked as the dissolution perpetually menacing the "Jewish state" and threatening its demographic annihilation.[127]

The slogan of Palestinian *sumud*, wherein existence *is* resistance, makes clear how and why the very existence of Palestinians—much less their biological reproduction—is understood as threatening, as "terrorist," as requiring reflexive condemnation, destruction, and murder. For they are reminders that the sovereign biopolitics of US/Israeli empire is not what it claims. It is not a benevolent protector securing life and futurity for all, a global regime of security and freedom. It is a civilizationalist project that weeds out those ineligible for its protections and deserving of its violence in the name of the civilized "life" it protects and all those who value it. Given these options, Edelman's point is that there is no future in this futurist scheme. There is no choice here worth choosing. The only choice is, as Palestinians demonstrate, perseverance and, as Albahri and Salaita make clear, avowal of the aspiration to be rid of that futurist project once and for all. As Edelman puts it, "The queerness we propose, in Hocquenghem's words, 'is unaware of the passing of generations as stages on the road to better living. It knows nothing about "sacrifice now for the sake of future generations." . . . [It] knows that civilisation alone is mortal.' Even more: it *delights* in that mortality as the negation of everything that would define itself, moralistically, as pro-life."[128] Edelman's suggestion that queers wed themselves to the taint of death and destruction with which they are always already tarred suggests that our alliances and solidarities must be precisely with these queers and, as a consequence, with a vision of the future that promises no more or less than the certainty of annihilation of the present. This is an embrace of death, to be sure, but it is an embrace of the death of empire and its settler colonial origins, the only radically queer response to its travesties and abuses. It is an affirmation of the survival of the presumptively dead, the always-already-disappeared, and those who allegedly never were because their existence is too terrifying to confront, in the name of decolonization and dismantling empire. Today, these queers are Muslims and Arabs; tomorrow it may be somebody else. But it will inevitably be someone, because futurism is a definitive logic of modern sovereignty; the War on Terror is merely the latest of its episodes. Redeeming Edelman's political promise, which he insists is neither political nor promising, let's declare that we, too, are queers, bent on the annihilation of the social order and its ceaseless reproduction of specters of nihilism and death. We choose *not* to choose empire or the endless futurism of colonial domination. We choose to stand on the side of "terrorism."

NOTES

INTRODUCTION

1. Address to the Nation, Atlanta, GA; https://georgewbush-whitehouse.archives.gov /infocus/ramadan/islam.html.
2. Nietzsche, *Twilight of the Idols*, "The Problem of Socrates," §2.
3. Foucault, "Questions of Method," 236.
4. Bayoumi, *This Muslim American Life*, 122.
5. Smith and Kauanui, "Native Feminisms Engage American Studies," 244.
6. See the agenda-setting volume edited by Haritaworn, Kuntsman, and Posocco, *Queer Necropolitics*, as well as the work of Jasbir Puar, whom the editors of and contributors to this volume cite as formative in opening up this line of inquiry: Puar, *Terrorist Assemblages*, as well as her essay with Amit Rai, "Monster, Terrorist, Fag." See also issue 3 of *Darkmatter: In the Ruins of Imperial Culture*, entitled "Racism in the Closet: Interrogating Postcolonial Sexuality" (2008), www.darkmatter101.org/site/category /issues/3-post-colonial-sexuality/, and Kuntsman, "The Soldier and the Terrorist."
7. Mbembe, "Necropolitics."
8. The archive from which queer necropolitics scholars draw is vast, and includes queer of color critique, women of color feminism, postcolonialism, critical race theory, Afro-pessimism, Marxism, and abolitionisms of all kinds.
9. Edelman, *Homographesis*.
10. I discuss the antisocial thesis at length in chapter 4.
11. Social death is how Orlando Patterson famously characterizes the existence of the slave in his definitive study *Slavery and Social Death*. In *Red, White, and Black*, Frank Wilderson argues that social death characterizes the (non)existence of black people as such, who cannot, ontologically, be distinguished from slaves as the abjected nonhumans upon which the modern world has been constituted. Cf. Sexton and Copeland, "Raw Life."
12. In *Cruel Optimism*, Lauren Berlant describes "slow death" as "the physical wearing out of a population in a way that points to its deterioration as a defining condition of its

experience and historical existence" (95) and seeks to decouple biopolitics from sovereignty to locate it more distinctly "within spaces of ordinariness" (99).

13.   Eric Stanley explains "overkill" as "a term used to indicate such excessive violence that it pushes a body beyond death" (for example, multiple stabbings or gunshots, removal of body parts or postmortem decapitation), the particular punishment directed at queer (and other abjected) people insofar as they constitute an ontological absence: "The temporality of violence, the biological time when the heart stops pushing and pulling blood, yet the killing is not finished, suggests the aim is not simply the end of a specific life, but the ending of all queer life. This is the time of queer death, when the utility of violence gives way to the pleasure in the other's mortality. If queers, along with others, approximate nothing, then the task of ending, of killing, that which is *nothing* must go beyond normative times of life and death." Stanley, "Near Life, Queer Death," 9.

14.   Haritaworn, Kuntsman, and Posocco, "Introduction." 8.

15.   Haritaworn, Kuntsman, and Posocco, 19.

16.   Haritaworn, Kuntsman, and Posocco, 20.

17.   For an argument that makes this claim from the opposite direction, showing how Nietzsche's revitalization of the body is a revolutionary position he himself recognizes to be impossible in a *décadent* modernity, thereby rendering him both an advocate of "death" and an unwitting progenitor of the project of queer theory, see Schotten, *Nietzsche's Revolution*.

18.   Nietzsche, *Beyond Good and Evil*, §6. On the relevance of autobiography—to Nietzsche, to philosophy, and in particular to left/radical politics—see my *"Ecrasez l'infâme!"*

1. THE BIOPOLITICS OF EMPIRE

1.   Arendt, *The Human Condition*, 121.

2.   Agamben, *Homo Sacer*, 179.

3.   Mamdani, *Good Muslim, Bad Muslim*, 11.

4.   A special issue of *South Atlantic Quarterly*, edited by Alison Ross, dubbed this "The Agamben Effect."

5.   Agamben, *Homo Sacer*, 6.

6.   As Andreas Kalyvas observes, "At a moment when, amidst the emergence and consolidation of new transnational, global institutions, the concept of sovereignty has been declared obsolete, Giorgio Agamben seeks to remind us of its lingering presence. Sovereign power, he argues, remains a constitutive, even paradigmatic, feature of modern politics." Kalyvas, "The Sovereign Weaver," 107.

7.   Butler, *Precarious Life*, 61.

8.   Kathrin Braun notes that Arendt's work offers "a rich and in-depth analysis of the specific features that constitute modern biopolitics, so that we can read Arendt as a theorist of biopolitics *avant la lèttre*," an "aspect in Arendt's work [that] seems to have been widely overlooked." Braun, "Biopolitics and Temporality in Arendt and Foucault," 7.

9. See Foucault, *The History of Sexuality*, 1:143.

10. Agamben, *Homo Sacer*, 9.

11. Agamben, 4. That both Foucault and Arendt omit this important event from their work is symptomatic of what Agamben calls, rather enigmatically, "the difficulties and resistances that thinking had to encounter in this area" (4; cf. 120).

12. Agamben, 120.

13. Arendt offers versions of this argument in *The Human Condition* and *On Revolution* as well.

14. Agamben, *Homo Sacer*, 4–5. This suggests the importance of subjecting Agamben's claims about his relationship with Foucault to close critical scrutiny; it also implies that Arendt is a crucial contributor to the discussion of biopolitics.

15. Agamben, *Homo Sacer*, 6, emphasis added.

16. Aristotle, *Politics*, 1252b28–30.

17. For example, in another text, Agamben offers a close reading of an excerpt of the *Nicomachean Ethics*, which presents a clearly tripartite schema of nutritive, sensitive, and intellectual life, yet nevertheless comes to the same bifurcated conclusion as *Homo Sacer*, namely, that properly political life is activity that excludes "the simple fact of living, of bare life." Agamben, "The Work of Man," 5. By the time of volume 3 of the *Homo Sacer* series, Aristotle has dropped out entirely and he simply asserts that "the place of the human is divided." Agamben, *Remnants of Auschwitz*, 134. For criticisms of Agamben's Aristotle interpretation, see Finlayson, " 'Bare Life' and Politics in Agamben's Reading of Aristotle," and Dubreuil, "Leaving Politics."

18. Arendt has her own specific philosophical worldview that, while it may depart from an Aristotelian starting point, does not remain there insofar as, among other things, it does not remain tied to the particularities of ancient Greek society.

19. See, for example, Arendt, *Human Condition*, 96–97.

20. Arendt, 24.

21. Arendt, 37.

22. Arendt, 36–37; cf. 24–25, 30–31.

23. Agamben, *Homo Sacer*, 7.

24. Kalyvas notes that Agamben's account of the "biopolitical body, which cannot be escaped since it cannot be negated or even transformed, seems literally to hover outside of time. The eternality of the biopolitical body defies historical time." Kalyvas, "Sovereign Weaver," 113. For Alexander Weheliye, this ahistoricism allows Agamben to imagine the impossible notion of "an indivisible biological substance anterior to racialization" (Weheliye, *Habeas Viscus*, 4), accomplishing "a conceptual feat that race as an analytical category cannot: it founds a biological sphere above and beyond the reach of racial hierarchies" (52).

25. Arendt also contrasts labor with work, distinguishing between activity that exhausts itself in consumption and activity that exhausts itself in use (and thus creates something more permanent and "worldly"). Although Mary Dietz suggests it is reductive to read Arendt as offering a dichotomous reading of the vita activa solely in terms of labor and action ("Feminist Receptions of Arendt"), as Hannah Pitkin correctly notes, it is

Arendt herself who emphasizes this oppositional dyad (*The Attack of the Blob*, 168). Indeed, while *The Human Condition* does have a triadic structure, Arendt devotes extremely little time to work as the activity of homo faber and it is, in the end, neither her focus nor her interest in this text.

26. Arendt, *Human Condition*, 31.
27. Arendt, 82–83, 121.
28. Arendt, 105–106.
29. Arendt, 111.
30. Arendt, 115, 120.
31. Arendt, 119.
32. Arendt, 115.
33. Arendt, 119.
34. Arendt, 215.
35. Arendt, 118.
36. Arendt, 160.
37. Arendt, 144.
38. Arendt, 117, 212.
39. Arendt, 146–147, 214.
40. Arendt, 160.
41. Arendt, 212, 214.
42. Arendt, 115.
43. Arendt, 105–106.
44. Arendt, 81.
45. Arendt, 101.
46. Arendt, 118.
47. Arendt, 119.
48. Arendt, 84.
49. Arendt, 46.
50. Arendt, 45.
51. Arendt, 121.
52. Arendt, 133–134. It is worth noting that in his reading of the human *ergon* in Aristotle's *Ethics*, Agamben offers a strongly Arendtian reading of both politics and "work." Modernity, he argues, has reconceived the proper activity of "man" as the care of biological life, a consequence of the essentially aporetic legacy of Aristotle, who allowed for properly human life as thinking and activity on the basis of its biopolitical exclusion of *zoē*: "The 'work' of the living being in accordance with logos is the assumption and the care of that nutritive and sensitive life on whose exclusion Aristotelian politics had defined the *ergon tou anthrōpou*." Agamben, "Work of Man," 6.
53. Margaret Canovan rejects the idea that Arendt is a "romantic conservative" because, although her critique of modernity in *The Human Condition* takes the form of a "fall from grace" narrative, she nevertheless has no love of any supposedly lost community and does not long for any sort of "return to nature." Canovan, "Hannah Arendt as a Conservative Thinker," 12–13. As Canovan correctly notes, for Arendt, "recent times

have seen too great a surrender to nature on the part of human beings, and that what has endangered or destroyed the human world is precisely an 'unnatural growth of the natural'" (14). But two different notions of nature are at work here: one is the nature of biological or bodily processes—associated with what is primal, first, or instinctual—and the other is the nature of Aristotle, which is associated with telos, completion, and ends. Arendt's claim regarding the "unnatural growth, so to speak, of the natural" (Arendt, *Human Condition*, 47) is that the first has come to dominate the second inappropriately, such that life's bases have become its ends or purposes. The result is that the natural hierarchy—of both human activities and human beings—has been overturned. If nature is understood in this dual sense, then Arendt quite clearly takes a romantic conservative position in *The Human Condition* as Canovan construes it.

54. Arendt, *On Revolution*, 104. Canovan alters this sentence by tacking "in the absence of material abundance" onto the end of it. Canovan, "Arendt as Conservative Thinker," 20. Yet there is no warrant for this addition, which traffics in the very modern hubris Arendt critiques in *The Human Condition*—that is, the notion that we ever could be freed from the necessities of life's biological demands. Arendt is not making an observation about human behavior under conditions of scarcity; she is making an observation about the fundamental conditions of embodied human life, which hold even under conditions of abundance (wherein humans would still have to procure food, clean their bodies, and dispose of its waste), and therefore does not eliminate the necessity of labor.

55. Arendt, *Human Condition*, 119–120.

56. In his classic, cross-historical study, Orlando Patterson cites "the extremity of power involved" and "the peculiar role of violence in creating and maintaining that domination" as the first of three factors that define slavery as a distinct social position (the other two being what he calls "natal alienation" and generalized social dishonor). Notably, labor is not definitive of enslavement, raising even further questions about Arendt's qualified endorsement of slavery. Patterson, *Slavery and Social Death*, 2.

57. Arendt, *Human Condition*, 215.

58. Elsewhere Arendt does, however, acknowledge the "known disadvantages of slave labor, such as lack of initiative, laziness, neglect of tools and general inefficiency." Arendt, *Origins of Totalitarianism*, 193.

59. See Elisabeth Young-Bruehl's definitive biography of Arendt, *Hannah Arendt: For Love of the World*.

60. Falguni Sheth writes memorably about Arendt being the sole exception to the rule of her graduate coursework in political theory that race was not to be discussed or theorized. Sheth, *Toward a Political Philosophy of Race*.

61. Arendt, *Origins of Totalitarianism*, 192.

62. Strangely, Achille Mbembe seems to accept this analysis in his famous essay "Necropolitics." He qualifies Arendt's logic as racialized (if not racist) by stating that "In the eyes of the conqueror, *savage life* is just another form of *animal life*, a horrifying experience, something alien beyond imagination or comprehension" (24, original emphases). Yet he overlooks the fact that Arendt seems largely to endorse this racialized

(if not racist) reading of savagery, seeing as she does in this historical episode not an example of the *construction* of racialized distinctions between civilization and savagery, but rather confirmation of her view that remaining within the domain of labor or nature dooms one to a life of enslavement (Mbembe, "Necropolitics"). For a useful critique of Mbembe's problematic subsumption of enslavement to colonialism and consequent oversight of the antiblackness constitutive of slavery, see Sexton, "People-of-Color-Blindness."

63. Arendt, *Origins of Totalitarianism*, 194. Cf. Arendt's lament that the "perhaps worst" aspect of imperialist massacres—which in the Congo, for example, reduced the native population "from 20 to 40 million . . . to 8 million people"—was not the massacres themselves but rather "the triumphant introduction of such means of pacification into ordinary, respectable foreign policies" (185), not to mention her concern in *On Violence* that the dwindling power of European imperialism means an uptick in the use of violence that will, ultimately, return home and treat the residents of the metropole just like the "subject races" abroad (Arendt, *On Violence*, 53–54).

64. Arendt, *Origins of Totalitarianism*, 300.

65. In this sense, Arendt is a case study in antiblackness. As Kathryn Gines makes clear, Africans are Arendt's savages par excellence, about whom she effectively adopts Joseph Conrad's description in *Heart of Darkness* (which she seems to accept as a reasonable source of anthropological information) and from which she amply quotes in her attempt to describe the Dutch settlement of southern Africa (see Gines, *Hannah Arendt and the Negro Question*, esp. chap. 5). Indeed, "those African savages" were so horrifyingly uncivilized that they "frightened Europeans literally out of their wits" (Arendt, *Origins of Totalitarianism*, 206) such that "when European men massacred them they somehow were not aware that they had committed murder" (192). This was different, however, from the killing of "Indians and Chinese," for which "there could be no excuse and no humanly comprehensible reason. . . . In a certain sense, it is only here that the real crime began, because here everyone ought to have known what he was doing" (206). Frantz Fanon is more direct: "The Negro symbolizes the biological." Fanon, *Black Skin, White Masks*, 167.

66. As Wendy Brown long ago observed, Arendt evinces an "extraordinary level of horror at 'the natural,'" which conditions her belief regarding "its danger to political life." Brown, *Manhood and Politics*, 28. William Connolly notes Arendt's failure to recognize the political constitution of disgust, which she seems largely to take for granted as self-evident (a premise that he argues undermines her larger project of cultivating an explicitly political sensibility). Connolly, "A Critique of Pure Politics."

67. Arendt, *Human Condition*, 119–120.

68. Arendt, 64.

69. Arendt, 71.

70. See Arendt, *Origins of Totalitarianism*, 301–302.

71. Arendt, *On Revolution*, 58–62.

72. Arendt, for example, 58–59, 84. Arendt's disgust with the body is much more explicit in this text, where her horror of embodiment takes the form of her horror at poor

people who, unlike those better off, are more subject to their bodies: "poverty is abject because it puts men under the absolute dictate of their bodies" (50).

73. To Arendt, "the distinction between private and public coincides with the opposition of necessity and freedom, of futility and permanence, and, finally, of shame and honor." Arendt, *Human Condition*, 73. In one place, she says that the private must remain hidden because of its association with birth and death: "The non-privative trait of the household realm originally lay in its being the realm of birth and death which must be hidden from the public realm because it harbors the things hidden from human eyes and impenetrable to human knowledge. It is hidden because man does not know where he comes from when he is born and where he goes when he dies" (62–63). While no logical relationship exists among the terms Arendt relates in this sentence, it is nevertheless the case that both what is "impenetrable to human knowledge" and where "man" comes from have all too often been construed as the same thing by Western philosophy: woman or the female body.

74. Arendt, 72.

75. See, among others, Bordo, *Unbearable Weight*; Gatens, *Imaginary Bodies*; and Schotten, *Nietzsche's Revolution*.

76. See, for example, Gilman, "Black Bodies, White Bodies"; Somerville, "Scientific Racism and the Invention of the Homosexual Body"; Stepan, "Race and Gender."

77. Arendt, *Origins of Totalitarianism*, 301.

78. Here, at least, Arendt is at pains to show that the condition of "savagery" is actually worse than the condition of enslavement (*Origins of Totalitarianism*, 302). In this now-canonized chapter of *Origins of Totalitarianism*, "The Decline of the Nation-State and the End of the Rights of Man," Arendt compares the stateless person to, by turns, the criminal, the slave, and the "savage," concluding that the criminal is the best-off insofar as "he" is entitled to equal protection of the laws (unlike the stateless person, to whom no laws can be said to apply and who is deprived of legal equality) and that the slave, unlike the "savage," is actually part of civilization and, therefore, to some degree human: "To be a slave was after all to have a distinctive character, a place in society— more than the abstract nakedness of being human and nothing but human" (297; Patterson, in *Slavery and Social Death*, of course disputes this). The "savage," by contrast, is the appropriate analogue for the stateless person, since both are "thrown back, in the midst of civilization, on their natural givenness, on their mere differentiation" (302). Arendt is clear that stateless people are a threat to "our political life" in much the same "way as the wild elements of nature once threatened the existence of man-made cities and countrysides" (302), noting that this savage threat now comes from Europe itself, "from within, not outside, our civilization" (302). The sudden, widespread, atavistic emergence of "savagery" within an otherwise civilized European order is Arendt's real concern with human rights deprivations (more so than the sufferings of stateless people), a civilizationalist investment that echoes her upset over the Dutch slavers' retrogression (which exceeds any concern about the enslavement and massacre of Africans) and is too often overlooked by those who would salvage this chapter for some kind of progressive politics regarding the plight of refugees.

79. Arendt, *On Revolution*, 53.

80. Arendt's account of the failings of the French Revolution consists essentially in the fact that it was a revolution in the name of "necessity"—in the name of bread—rather than freedom. Once the abject poor appeared on the political scene, bringing with them the wretched necessities of their deprived bodies, "the result was that the power of the old regime became impotent and the new republic was stillborn; freedom had to be surrendered to necessity, to the urgency of the life process itself" (50). "Their need was violence, and, as it were, prepolitical; it seemed that only violence could be strong and swift enough to help them" (81). Arendt blames not simply the failure of the Revolution but also its violent excesses on this same fact: "It was necessity, the urgent needs of the people, that unleashed the terror and sent the Revolution to its doom" (50). Strangely, Mbembe follows Arendt on this matter as well. Although he does not quote her explicitly, his analysis is unmistakably Arendtian: Marx failed to distinguish between labor and work, blurring the distinction between freedom and necessity; therefore, Marxism aims fundamentally "at the eradication of the basic human condition of plurality," which it sees "as the chief obstacle to the eventual realization of a predetermined telos of history" and which therefore justifies "terror and killing as the means of realizing" it. Mbembe, "Necropolitics," 20.

81. Arendt, *Human Condition*, 26–27; cf. 43.

82. Arendt, 32–33, 199.

83. Arendt, 43.

84. Arendt, 26–27.

85. Arendt, 43.

86. Arendt, 43.

87. Arendt, 160.

88. For example, Jimmy Casas Klausen is at pains to defend Arendt's racism by renaming it "antiprimitivism," by which he means a disdain for uncultured humanity that does not turn on skin color; hence her critique of the Dutch settlers as well as the indigenous African tribes (and "savages" in general) for being lesser, or less developed, human beings. Yet Klausen does not consider that "primitivism" is itself an artifact of racism and could not exist as a civilizational determinant without the concomitant rise and construction of biological races, an endeavor undertaken by Europeans in their encounter with the so-called New World in order to rationalize colonial domination. Thus Arendt's critique of the Boers for having "sunk back to the level of savage tribes" (Arendt, *Origins of Totalitarianism*, 207) is indeed racist even if it is a critique of white people because the "primitiveness" to which the Dutch sank was clearly non-European and "primitivity" still denotes civilizational inferiority, a category that would not exist without the racialized non-Europeanness that was a necessary function of colonial domination. See Klausen, "Hannah Arendt's Antiprimitivism." A notable exception to political theory's skittishness here is Norton, "Heart of Darkness."

89. As Gines rather generously puts it, "Hannah Arendt might be seen as a case study for the limitations of the Western philosophical tradition." Gines, *Hannah Arendt and the Negro Question*, xi.

90. Many feminist care theorists have argued as much. Challenging Arendt's views of slavery, womanhood, labor, and necessity even more radically, Angela Davis argues that the role of slave women in constituting the household and fulfilling precisely the domestic labors of which Arendt complains was not simply necessary for the reproduction of life but, as such, was an eminently political practice of resistance to slavery: "in the infinite anguish of ministering to the needs of the men and children around her (who were not necessarily members of her immediate family), she was performing the only labor of the slave community which could not be directly and immediately claimed by the oppressor." Davis, "Reflections on the Black Woman's Role in the Community of Slaves," 115–116, original emphasis. Moreover, this labor helped "lay the foundation for some degree of autonomy," development of which could take place in the only "realm which was furthermost removed from the immediate arena of domination . . . the living quarters, the area where the basic needs of physical life were met"; Davis thus describes the enslaved "black woman as the custodian of a house of resistance" (118).

91. Marx's (supposed) error—which the American founders did not replicate—was to think that poverty was a political, not natural, human condition. Arendt, *On Revolution*, 52–53. He thereby authorized necessity's entrance into political life and (improperly) made it the basis of revolution, thus facilitating modern decadence: "he finally strengthened more than anybody else the pernicious doctrine of the modern age, namely that life is the highest good, and that the life process of society is the very centre of human endeavor" (54). By contrast, the American founders did not believe poverty was political, and therefore instituted a republic that would allow "the majority of the population" to be excluded "from active participation in government—though, of course, not from being represented and from choosing their representatives" (58–59). Remarkably, Arendt asserts that poverty did not exist in North America at the time of the American Revolution, and so therefore the laboring classes "were not driven by want, and the revolution was not overwhelmed by them" (58). She ignores the existence of indigenous peoples entirely (cf. her claims in *Origins of Totalitarianism* that Canada and Australia "were almost empty and had no serious population problem" [182]) and dismisses the fact of "Negro slavery" by saying that the Founders' silence on slavery and its obvious incompatibility with the freedom they were founding "must be blamed on slavery" (61) itself rather than the Founders. This is because "the institution of slavery carries an obscurity even blacker than the obscurity of poverty" (61). In other words, the Founders overlooked slavery because of the "darkness" of its activity, which is even "darker" than the people doing it. Hence the Founders ought not be criticized but rather praised insofar as they recognized the basic constraints of the human condition.

92. Arendt, *Human Condition*, 31.

93. The valiant efforts of contributors to the volume *Agamben and Colonialism* to apply the insights of *Homo Sacer* to the colonialism Agamben consistently overlooked must, for this reason, necessarily fail, since it is impossible to extract an anticolonial commitment from Agamben's political theory (more on colonialism in the next chapter). The

same goes for Ewa Płonowska Ziarek's patient and careful attempt to "[mobilize] bare life for emancipatory struggle" (Ziarek, "Bare Life on Strike," 98) or render it "a new weapon of oppositional movements" (101).

94. See, for example, Agamben, *Homo Sacer*, 2, 131, 188.

95. Agamben, *Homo Sacer*, 131–134.

96. Agamben, 177–179. This is the belief Marx shares with "Hitler's philosophy" (151), an aside that implicitly analogizes Marx with Hitler and elliptically echoes Arendt's conflation of Communist and National Socialist regimes in the form of government she calls "totalitarianism."

97. Agamben, 176–177. Although here, at least, Agamben explicitly credits Arendt; nevertheless, this distinction, too, becomes another iteration of the *zoē/bios* divide. Canovan implausibly suggests that Arendt's earlier distinction between "the mob" and the laboring classes in *Origins* reflects her "radical populist orientation," ignoring the fact that such a distinction itself is a form of respectability politics that purchases legitimacy for the working classes at the expense of an elitist dismissal of the *lumpenproletariat* or the great unwashed. Canovan, " 'Totalitarian Elements in Marxism,' " 65. In an analysis apposite to both Arendt and Agamben on this issue, James Scott observes the "highly partisan" nature of making such distinctions in the first place: "dominant elites attempt to portray social action . . . as, metaphorically, a parade, thus denying, by omission, the possibility of autonomous social action by subordinates. Inferiors who actually assemble at their own initiative are typically described as mobs or rabble" (Scott, *Domination and the Arts of Resistance*, 45–46).

98. As Ziarek notes, Agamben simply "ignores . . . the way bare life is implicated in the gendered, sexist, colonial, and racist configurations of biopolitics." Ziarek, "Bare Life on Strike," 93. Taking inequality seriously, then (which Agamben's Arendtian commitments necessarily disallow), raises the question of for whom the crisis of modernity (Agamben, *Homo Sacer*, 175) is actually a crisis. As Scott Morgensen dryly observes, "Ongoing reaction to the U.S. Patriot Act or the war on terror by many white Europeans and white settlers suggests that their potential exposure to bare life comes as an unwelcome surprise." Morgensen, "The Biopolitics of Settler Colonialism," 72.

99. Agamben, *Homo Sacer*, 51, 60. Cf. Agamben's public statement explaining his refusal to enter the United States because he would have had to be fingerprinted in order to do so. He insists his refusal is not the "the immediate superficial reaction to a procedure that has long been imposed on criminals and political defendants," but rather a rejection of the ever-diminishing space of the political to the point that "techniques and . . . devices invented for the dangerous classes" are now being used on everyday citizens, "to the point that humanity itself . . . has become the dangerous class" (Agamben, "No to Bio-Political Tattooing"). Žižek seems to take a similar position in his sympathy with Agamben's argument: "in today's 'post-politics,' the very democratic public space is a mask concealing the fact that, ultimately, we are all Homo sacer." Žižek, *Welcome to the Desert of the Real*, 126.

100. Agamben, *Homo Sacer*, 122.

101. Agamben, 9.

102.   Agamben, 90.

103.   Agamben, 174.

104.   As Ziarek (rather generously) puts it, although Agamben's "heterogeneous examples of bare life . . . are always diversified along racial, gender, and ethnic and historical lines, his conceptual analysis does not follow the implications of such heterogeneity." Ziarek, "Bare Life on Strike," 93. Thomas Lemke has a slightly different complaint about Agamben's failures of differentiation: "Even if all subjects are *homines sacri*, they are so in different ways. . . . It remains woefully unclear to what extent and in what manner the comatose in hospitals share the fate of prisoners in concentration camps; whether the asylum seekers in the prisons are bare life to the same degree and in the same sense as the Jews in the Nazi camps. . . . He even regards people killed on motorways indirectly as *homines sacri*." Lemke, "'A Zone of Indistinction,'" 7–8.

105.   I will always use quotation marks when designating this term in English, both to underscore its artificiality as jargon and to dispel any misunderstanding of it in my usage as referring to actual Muslim people.

106.   "The Muslim," like virtually every figure, personage, and example in Agamben, is definitively and demonstrably male. As Penelope Deutscher notes, "With the exception of Karen Quinlan, women's bodies are impressively absent from Agamben's writing." Deutscher, "The Inversion of Exceptionality," 59. Indeed, women are present either not at all or, as will become clear, as figures of horror and monstrosity. The only other mention of women aside from Quinlan that I can find in the *Homo Sacer* texts comes in Agamben's (lack of) commentary on a hideous experiment undertaken by Nazi doctors that he relates in *Homo Sacer*: "Particularly grotesque was the experiment on so-called heat reanimation, in which VPs were placed in a cot between two naked women who had also been taken from among the Jews detained in the camps; the documentation tells of a VP who was able to have sexual relations, which facilitated the recuperation process" (155). Here women are present but Agamben does not recognize them as either worthy of analysis or, notably, objects of torture, not simply by the doctors in this scenario but also by the VP himself, who here makes use of rape as a survival strategy.

107.   Agamben, *Remnants of Auschwitz*, 41.

108.   Agamben, 85, 155–156.

109.   Agamben, 45.

110.   Jill Jarvis documents Agamben's lack of historicization of this term and failure to offer a sufficient etymology for it in "Remnants of Muslims": "Given his assiduous attention to every other term in his lexicon [for example, *witness*, *Holocaust*], it is striking that Agamben offers no etymological or historical information about the word 'muselman' beyond its function in the jargon of the Lagers. . . . The distinct but dubious impression fostered by *Remnants of Auschwitz* is that a limit case for absolute subjection called something like 'muslim' appeared in the modern world at Auschwitz between 1939 and 1945" (718). She notes further that "Agamben's narrow resignification of the word 'muselman' is made available to him in part by Levi's own limited understanding of the term. Though he has ample opportunity not to be parochial, Agamben amplifies Levi's opacities and omissions" (710).

111. Agamben, *Homo Sacer*, 184–185.
112. Agamben, *Remnants of Auschwitz*, 41.
113. Agamben, 42.
114. Agamben, 45.
115. Agamben, 44.
116. Agamben, 44. Sunera Thobani notes "unmistakable" character of "the Orientalist chain of signification that binds these names to the actual Muslim" (Thobani, "Empire, Bare Life and the Constitution of Whiteness," 10), and of course the association of this abjection with Islam itself reflects an obvious Islamophobia. It is also important in this context to note the use of *Weib* in the term *Muselweiber*. In German, *Weib* is the word for the female of an animal species; *Frau* is the word for "woman" and would indicate human status.
117. As Weheliye observes, "Most scholars who write about the Muselmann do not pause to reflect on the name of this figure, thereby leaving intact the bonding of an abject process/status to a racio-religious label." Weheliye, *Habeas Viscus*, 54.
118. Agamben, *Remnants of Auschwitz*, 70.
119. Jarvis, "Remnants of Muslims," 720.
120. Agamben, *Remnants of Auschwitz*, 111.
121. Jarvis, "Remnants of Muslims," 720.
122. Agamben, *Remnants of Auschwitz*, 52.
123. Agamben, 47–48, 55, 59.
124. Agamben, 53.
125. Agamben, 55.
126. Agamben, 69.
127. Agamben, 63. This metaphor is not simply misogynist; more importantly, it is outrageously trivializing of the traumas of Auschwitz. Indeed, in this outlandish reading, the hideous experiences that produce "Muslim"-like behavior in death camp inhabitants are analogized to a mythological experience of looking at an ugly or frightening woman.
128. See also Agamben's bizarre discussion of the passive subjectivity of "the Muslim" as the "purely receptive pole" within "the homosexual relation." Agamben, *Remnants of Auschwitz*, 110–111. For relevant commentary situating these imperialist rationalizations and habits of thought, see Mirzoeff, "Invisible Empire"; Puar, *Terrorist Assemblages*; Puar and Rai, "Monster, Terrorist, Fag"; Said, *Orientalism*.
129. Thobani observes, "both 'man' and 'non-man' remain stubbornly 'Western' in Agamben's analysis, the actual, embodied Muslim in his/her onto-epistemological specificity, is barred from the analytic field. In an act of epistemic erasure, Agamben too turns away from the Muselmann in his ready acceptance of the seemingly innocent explanation that the limit figure of the 'Muselmann' reminded the survivors of Muslims in prayer. Treating the Muselmann as simply concept metaphor, Agamben re-inscribes the historical Muslim as non-human absence, a nonentity in-and-for him/herself." Thobani, "Empire, Bare Life and Whiteness," 12.
130. Agamben, *State of Exception*, 3–4, emphases added.

131.   As is also evident from his public statement defending his refusal enter the United
       States, wherein he compares the cataloguing of fingerprints and retinal measurements
       of foreigners to the tattooing of Auschwitz inmates with prisoner numbers. Agamben,
       "No to Bio-political Tattooing." Not only does Agamben fail to recognize any excep-
       tionalized population other than the Jews of Europe in the 1940s, but he also tends to
       assimilate every form of political injustice to that of the camp that is the result of sov-
       ereign exceptionalism. As contributors to *Agamben and Colonialism* make clear, how-
       ever, not every outrage is a form of exceptionalism, not every space of marginality is a
       camp, and not every marginalized population exists as bare life (and I am grateful to
       Daniel Finn for making these fine distinctions to me years ago). As Marcelo Svirsky
       puts it, "there is something about the idea of exceptionality, and specifically in the way
       Agamben uses it, which makes us search for exceptionalism everywhere a wrong is
       committed." Svirsky, "The Cultural Politics of Exception," 54.
132.   LaCapra, "Approaching Limit Events," 134. LaCapra's essay offers a useful compendium
       of the hidden moralisms, conceits, and self-congratulatory pieties in Agamben's writ-
       ing vis-à-vis the Holocaust, Primo Levi, and representation.
133.   There is now a substantial literature examining this conflation of Muslim and Arab, or
       the Muslim/Arab/"terrorist" figure, as both a new and specific form of racialization
       and a particular ideological plank of US empire; for a useful index of some of this lit-
       erature, see Jamal and Naber, *Race and Arab Americans Before and After 9/11.*
134.   Žižek comments: "Incidentally, the traces of anti-Arab racism in this designation ['the
       Muslim'] are more than evident: the designation 'muslim,' of course, emerged because
       the prisoners identified the behavior of the 'living dead' as close to the standard West-
       ern image of a 'Muslim,' a person who is totally resigned to his fate, passively enduring
       all calamities as grounded in God's will. Today, however, in view of the Israeli-Arab
       conflict, this designation regains its actuality: the 'Muslim' is the extimate kernel, the
       zero-level, of the 'Jew' himself." Žižek, *Did Somebody Say Totalitarianism?*, 73. Despite
       this astute observation (and his welcome suspicion of Arendt's category "totalitarian-
       ism"), Žižek himself nevertheless fails to muster any further critique of Agamben or
       his use of the term *Muslim*, and uncritically adopts both in this text. In *Welcome to the
       Desert of the Real*, Žižek endorses Agamben's analysis of homo sacer to the extent that
       he claims, rather inadequately, that "Palestinians in the occupied territories are
       reduced to the status of Homo sacer, the object of disciplinary measures and/or even
       humanitarian help, but not full citizens" (147–148) and refers perennially in this text
       to "the Jews" as exemplary victims of, variously, racism, oppression, empty ideological
       interpellation, and political scapegoating. At one point, Žižek reduces the Israeli/
       Palestinian conflict to a generalized Jewish/Arab "question," itself a (poor) substitute
       for the fundamental antagonism of capital, the only true resolution of which is social-
       ism (170–171).
135.   Agamben, *Homo Sacer*, 176. De la Durantaye, "The Paradigm of Colonialism."
136.   Agamben, *Homo Sacer*, 22.
137.   Agamben, 166.

138. Agamben, 179.
139. Agamben, 188.
140. Agamben, *Remnants of Auschwitz*, 13.
141. Agamben, 30–31. To be fair, Agamben does not see himself as doing this. Indeed, he positions *Remnants* at least in part as a refutation of the views of Elie Wiesel and others who would consign the Holocaust to that which can be neither adequately comprehended nor spoken of. For Agamben, such a view elevates the Holocaust, "contributes to its glory" (33), and is complicit with Nazism (57). However, it is difficult to understand what the claim of Auschwitz's historical uniqueness could possibly mean other than to demarcate its exceptionalism; otherwise, such a statement is banal. Coupled with Agamben's copious references to the various superlative catastrophes represented and incurred by the Holocaust (see, for example, 62, 65, 69, 80–82, 99, 101, 128, 148), it is clear that, whatever his intentions may be, "Auschwitz" stands for an exceptional catastrophic event. (Cf. Žižek's conclusion to *Welcome to the Desert of the Real*, 173–198.) As LaCapra puts it, "Agamben attributes uniqueness to Auschwitz that goes beyond any notion of specificity or distinctiveness and is related to the world-historical, even apocalyptic significance he attributes to it, both in placing in question and even eliminating the relevance of all preexisting or conventional ethics (whose nature he does not really investigate) and in posing the problem of rethinking ethics from the ground up, indeed from an indistinct point of virtuality that undercuts any conceivable ground." LaCapra, "Approaching Limit Events," 135–136.
142. See Morton, "Reading Kenya's Colonial State of Emergency After Agamben," and Shenhav, "Imperialism, Exceptionalism, and the Contemporary World," both in Svirsky and Bignall, *Agamben and Colonialism*.
143. Mbembe, "Necropolitics," 23.
144. Thobani, "Empire, Bare Life and the Constitution of Whiteness," 7.
145. Weheliye, *Habeas Viscus*, 11. Weheliye argues that such omission "only highlights just how routine the brutalization of black flesh continues to be in the world of Man," and asks, "How would Foucault's and Agamben's theories of modern violence differ if they took the Middle Passage as their point of departure rather than remaining entrapped within the historiographical cum philosophical precincts of fortress Europe?" (38); cf. Sexton, "People-of-Color-Blindness."
146. Agamben, *Homo Sacer*, 55; cf. Benjamin, "Theses on the Philosophy of History," 257.
147. See Césaire, *Discourse on Colonialism*.
148. This is the latent moralism at work in Agamben's reprimand of Foucault, whose alleged silence about the most significant political phenomenon of the twentieth century renders him potentially complicit with the very biopolitical machinations he should have been documenting (and, it seems, condemning). As Agamben observes, "The inquiry that began with a reconstruction of the grand enfermement in hospitals and prisons did not end with an analysis of the concentration camp." Agamben, *Homo Sacer*, 119. On Agamben's moralizing rebuke of Foucault, see Schotten, "Against Totalitarianism."
149. Holocaust Exceptionalism explains why Hitler is such a frequent recourse in philosophy classes when an example of insupportable wrongdoing is required to adjudicate

hypothetical ethical scenarios, a phenomenon not limited to the undergraduate classroom; see, for example, Butler, *Undoing Gender*, 224; Nehamas, "Nietzsche and 'Hitler'"; Žižek, *Welcome to the Desert of the Real*, 86.

150. As Mamdani observes, "The Holocaust was born at the meeting point of two traditions that marked modern Western civilization: 'the anti-Semitic tradition and the tradition of genocide of colonized peoples.' The difference in the fate of the Jewish people was that they were to be exterminated as a whole. In that, they were unique—but only in Europe." Mamdani, *Good Muslim, Bad Muslim*, 7, original emphasis.

151. Weheliye, *Habeas Viscus*, 36.

152. Part of the reason for this oversight may be, as Atkinson notes, the "willful amnesia that works to forget the Italian colonial period" in Italy; another part, however, may be Agamben's commitment to a Holocaust Exceptionalism that presents itself as antioppression while simultaneously disregarding other injustices (since they are, by definition, less significant, meaningful, or historically decisive). Atkinson, "Encountering Bare Life in Italian Libya," 156.

153. Jarvis, "Remnants of Muslims," 709, original emphasis. Jewish exceptionalism and Muslim abjection seem on display even here, in this nineteenth-century colonial policy; Jarvis records that "indigènes israélites" were extended full citizenship in French Algeria by 1865, but "indigènes musulmans" not until 1946, just prior to the Algerian Revolution.

154. Jarvis, "Remnants of Muslims," 710.

155. Jarvis, 711.

156. I take no position as to whether or not the Jews constitute a people. My insertion of "(the)" is meant to emphasize that one could certainly derive such a view from Agamben, who hypostasizes the Jews of 1940s Europe in ways that at times suggest an individual archetype—"the Jew"—and at others suggests a distinctive, archetypal people/population—"the Jews."

157. Agamben, *Homo Sacer*, 114.

158. It should be noted that Agamben refuses to use the word *Holocaust*, because of both its etymological entanglement with sanctity and its historical entanglement with antiSemitism. Agamben, *Remnants of Auschwitz*, 29–31). Strikingly, he does not uphold the same antiracist principles with regard to "der Muselmann."

159. Agamben, *Homo Sacer*, 174.

160. Agamben, 175.

161. Agamben, 180.

162. On this, see Schotten, "Reading Nietzsche in the Wake of the 2008–09 War on Gaza." Alyson Cole argues that the Holocaust has become the premier narrative of legitimate victimization in the United States, and ironically notes its appropriation as a metaphor for US suffering in the wake of 9/11 in *The Cult of Pure Victimhood*.

2. THE BIOPOLITICS OF SETTLEMENT

1. Edelman, *No Future*, 9.

2. Hobbes, *Leviathan*, 54.

3. Byrd, *Transit of Empire*, 206.

4. Bayoumi, *This Muslim American Life*, 10.

5. Gregory, *The Colonial Present*.

6. Byrd, *Transit of Empire*, xiii.

7. Anderson, *American Foreign Policy and Its Thinkers*, 3.

8. Jung, "Constituting the U.S. Empire-State and White Supremacy," 3, 5.

9. See, among others, Byrd, *Transit of Empire*; Morgensen, "The Biopolitics of Settler Colonialism"; Smith, "American Studies Without America"; Tadiar, "Decolonization, 'Race,' and Remaindered Life Under Empire." See also Goldstein, *Formations of United States Colonialism*, which aims "to place U.S. overseas empire and settler colonialism into the same analytic frame . . . [in order to] argue that addressing the multiple histories and present-day formations of colonialism in North America, the Caribbean, and the Pacific are essential for coming to terms with how and why the United States is what it is today" (4).

10. Foucault, *"Society Must Be Defended,"* 254.

11. Foucault, 254.

12. Foucault, 255.

13. Foucault, 256.

14. Rifkin, "Making Peoples Into Populations," 178.

15. Ann Stoler broke the ground on this critique with her *Race and the Education of Desire*.

16. Bruyneel, *Third Space of Sovereignty*, ix.

17. See, among others, Foucault, *"Society Must Be Defended"*; Foucault, *History of Sexuality*, vol. 1; Foucault, *Security, Territory, Population*.

18. Joanne Barker ("For Whom Sovereignty Matters") notes the differences between racial minorities, who may seek inclusion within US frames of rights and privileges, and indigenous peoples, who either do not recognize US sovereignty or view themselves as already sovereign peoples. In the US context, Robert Nichols ("Contract and Usurpation") argues that understanding the oppression of indigenous peoples as a problem of racial inclusion can actually further settler colonialism. For a compelling critique of racialization as a recolonizing "logic of genocide" when applied to native peoples, see Kauanui, *Hawaiian Blood*. Meanwhile, from the other side, Jared Sexton rejects Achille Mbembe's "subsumption" of racial slavery under the larger rubric of colonial necropolitics, while Afro-pessimism more generally insists on the importance of distinguishing between, as Frank Wilderson puts it, "red, white, and black" political and ontological positions. See Sexton, "People-of-Color-Blindness," 37; Wilderson, *Red, White and Black*.

19. As Tom Roach explains, "If biopolitical disciplinarity functions through lived behavioral norms which aid in reproducing the status quo, it likewise benefits from a normative conception of death. Taking into account Lee Edelman's claim in *No Future* that queerness plays the fantasmatic role of the death drive in reproductive futurism, we can see that the 'death' so important to biopower is not only physiological but also imbued with a sexual, relational and communal essence." Roach, "Sense and Sexuality," 168.

20. Collins, *Global Palestine*.

21. Parts of this section have been adapted from Schotten, "Homonationalist Futurism."

22. Many have criticized *No Future* for its neglect of any facet of subjectivity and social life other than sexuality (for example, race, class, gender, nation, and (dis)ability, among others). The most famous of these, which functions as a kind of précis of these criticisms, is José Esteban Muñoz's claim, in reference to *No Future*, that "It has been clear to many of us, for quite a while now, that the antirelational in queer studies was the gay white man's last stand." Muñoz, "Thinking Beyond Antirelationality and Antiutopianism in Queer Critique," 825). I engage these criticisms substantively and at length in chapter 4.

23. With the exception of John Brenkman, who extensively engaged the ideas that led to *No Future* in a public exchange with Edelman in the journal *Narrative* in 2002, which I return to later. Regarding feminism, I remain grateful to Carolyn Terranova's close study of Edelman's references to abortion in her memorable undergraduate thesis, which used Edelman to analyze the queerness of clitoral sexual pleasure and, therefore, female sexuality. Terranova's argument is distinctly at odds with J. Halberstam's claim that "Edelman always runs the risk of linking heteronormativity in some essential way to women, and, perhaps unwittingly, woman becomes the site of the unqueer." Halberstam, *The Queer Art of Failure*, 118.

24. Edelman, *No Future*, 2.

25. Edelman, 3.

26. Edelman, 1.

27. Edelman, 2.

28. Edelman, 2.

29. Edelman, "Post-Partum," 182.

30. Edelman, *No Future*, 13, first emphasis added.

31. Brenkman, "Queer Post-Politics," 176.

32. In chapter 1's now-famous footnote 19, Edelman preemptively critiques the call to historicize his work as oblivious to its own reproduction of the futurist logic he is seeking to dismantle. Edelman, *No Future*, 157–158. I take up a broader version of this criticism in chapter 4; for now, I would simply say that I agree with Kevin Floyd that while Edelman's own textual references to politics and history are limited, "this doesn't mean one cannot productively read as historically specific a claim he tries to make absolute, that politics are by definition oriented toward the future." Floyd, "The Importance of Being Childish," 328. On the importance of situating Edelman's work more concretely within history, see Duggan, "Atlas Shrugging"; Reddy, *Freedom with Violence*; Winnubst, "Review Essay." I am grateful to Shannon Winnubst for pressing me on this point.

33. Edelman, "Against Survival," 148. In this sentence Edelman is making the claim that *Hamlet* remains an important text because it "anticipates" this modern ideology of survival.

34. Edelman, "Antagonism, Negativity, and the Subject of Queer Theory," 822. Floyd would likely reject Edelman's analogizing of futurism to capitalism, however, insofar as he reads Edelman's overall ahistoricism as "symptomatic of a moment in which capital's

colonization of the future appears both unassailable—in, for example, the narrative of 'no alternative' Edelman would critique with such forceful abstraction that he seems to reinscribe it—and concretely violent in a way that suggests the opposite: accumulation's radical fragility." Floyd, "The Importance of Being Childish," 336.

35.   Edelman, "Ever After," 470.

36.   Edelman, 470.

37.   Edelman, 471.

38.   He also describes the queering of those noncooperative unbelievers in survival as a "calamity," noting that "reproductive futurism is one of the forms this calamity takes." Edelman, 471, emphasis added. In *No Future*, he observes that "The Child, in the historical epoch of our current epistemological regime, is the figure for this compulsory investment in the misrecognition of figure" (18, emphasis added). Futurism itself, however, he calls "the substrate of politics" (60).

39.   Edelman, *No Future*, 11.

40.   Nyong'o, "Do You Want Queer Theory (or Do You Want the Truth)?"

41.   Edelman, *No Future*, 17. Indeed, it is not even wedded to terms of the human: "As my insistent refusal of identity politics should be taken to suggest, the sinthomosexual has no privileged relation to any sex or sexuality—or even, indeed, to any species, as chapter 4 [on Alfred Hitchcock's film *The Birds*] makes clear" (165n10).

42.   Edelman, 17. And indeed, the seduction of futurism's lure for gay folks is painfully apparent in the mainstream LGB movement's near-obsession with "marriage equality"; on this, see Schotten, "Homonationalist Futurism."

43.   Edelman, *No Future*, 3.

44.   Edelman, 27, original emphasis.

45.   Edelman, 24–25.

46.   Edelman, 28.

47.   Edelman, 17, original emphases.

48.   Edelman, 6.

49.   Schmitt, *Political Theology*, 5.

50.   Nichols, "Realizing the Social Contract."

51.   Hobbes, *Leviathan*, 88.

52.   Hobbes, 89.

53.   Hobbes, 89.

54.   When I have taught Hobbes in classes, student veterans have attested to how well he describes this enduring present that characterizes combat. Waiting, poised, unsure what will happen next—one student declared that, in such situations, he never knew if a few minutes had passed or several hours.

55.   Hobbes, *Leviathan*, 88–89, original emphasis. Foucault reads this passage as indicating that there is not, in fact, any actual war in the state of nature, but rather "a sort of unending diplomacy between rivals who are naturally equal." The "tract of time" Hobbes uses to define war "designates, then, the state and not the battle, and what is at stake is not the forces themselves, but the will, a will that is sufficiently known, or in other words a system of representations and manifestations that is effective within

this field of primal diplomacy." Foucault, *"Society Must Be Defended,"* 92–93. A brilliant reading, it nevertheless does not foreclose the possibility, much less the inevitability, of "blood" or "corpses" whatsoever, which Foucault is at pains to declare absent in the Hobbesian state of nature. On Foucault's erasure of war from Hobbes's account of sovereignty, see Bargu, "Sovereignty as Erasure."

56.   Although they certainly did in the case of the confessed shooting deaths of twenty-three-year-old Deah Barakat, his twenty-one-year-old wife, Yusor Mohammad, and her sister, nineteen-year-old Razan Mohammad Abu-Salha, by neighbor Craig Hicks on February 11, 2015, in Chapel Hill, NC, in a seemingly clear-cut case of Islamophobic violence. Ironically, a Hobbesian reading of the biopolitics of US empire might have made their deaths more predictable, if not necessarily more preventable. More on this later on and also in chapter 5.

57.   And Hobbes likens the sovereign to the sun elsewhere in *Leviathan*, when he enumerates the various prerogatives of sovereignty in chapter 18.

58.   As Hobbes says, we join the Commonwealth from the "foresight" of our own preservation. Hobbes, *Leviathan*, 117. Thanks to Carolyn Terranova, who first drew my attention to this significant word in this important sentence.

59.   Hobbes, *Leviathan*, 9.

60.   Hobbes, 87.

61.   Hobbes, 90.

62.   Hobbes, 87.

63.   Hobbes, 90.

64.   Hobbes, 41, original emphasis. Despair is the aversive motion Hobbes contrasts with the appetitive motion of hope. He defines hope as "Appetite with an opinion of attaining" and despair as "the same, without such opinion" (41).

65.   Hobbes defines fear as "aversion with opinion of hurt from the object," and contrasts it not with hope, as we might expect, but rather with courage, that is, fear plus the "hope of avoyding that Hurt by resistance." Hobbes, 41.

66.   Hobbes, 88–89.

67.   Asma Abbas affirms "the centrality of time" (Abbas, "In Terror," 504) to the formation of modern postcolonial subjects, calling time itself "a conceit folded into the concept of sovereignty" and arguing that if we are to extricate ourselves from these formations, "desire itself needs to be rethought" (523).

68.   Hobbes, *Leviathan*, 88, emphases added.

69.   Hobbes, 89, emphases added.

70.   Hobbes, 89, emphases added.

71.   Hobbes, 89, original emphasis.

72.   Hobbes, 89.

73.   William Connolly poetically notes how this sentence performs the bereftness of life in the state of nature, with clauses and words falling out of the locution until eventually we are left simply with a series of adjectives. This "grammatical structure combines with other rhetorical elements to elicit in the reader something of the loss of continuity, the emptiness, the fear that would govern life were there no common power to

bring order to it." Connolly, *Political Theory and Modernity*, 30. Nichols observes that this sentence is "rarely read in relation to its practical implications for the people living in his time: or, if it is, the circle of influence is limited to those western European nations in which Hobbes' works were widely read. However, there is another group of peoples who are directly implicated in this Hobbesian depiction—the Amerindians." Nichols, "Realizing the Social Contract," 47.

74.   Nichols, "Realizing the Social Contract," 47. This differs from critical race accounts that explain such hierarchies via focus on the determination of the *human* rather than *life*. For example, Alexander Weheliye describes racialization "as a conglomerate of sociopolitical relations that discipline humanity into full humans, not-quite-humans, and nonhumans" (Weheliye, *Habeas Viscus*, 3), while Charles Mills defines the social contract as a racial contract, or a set of agreements among white people to constitute nonwhite people as "of a different and inferior moral status, subpersons" (Mills, *The Racial Contract*, 11). The project of Afro-pessimism takes this claim further, arguing that blackness is the ontological void upon which the human itself is constituted, thereby rendering all humanisms forms of antiblackness (see, for example, Warren, "Onticide"). *Queer Terror* offers a rethinking of biopolitics in terms of "life" rather than "the human"; in this, I diverge not only from the biologisms at stake in racism and antiracist inquiry but also from the centralization of race "itself" to the biopolitical project (although Warren makes room for contesting not simply "the human" but also the values of "life" and "survival" for biopolitics in his "Black Nihilism and the Politics of Hope"). This is not to dispute that race and racism are biopolitical endeavors, that biopolitical racism is definitive of European modernity, or that settler colonialism can also operate according to biologically racialized logics. Rather, it is an effort to zero in on and specify the particular version of settler colonial biopolitics that does not operate primarily in terms of either biology or racism, but rather the presence or absence of "civilization." I touch very briefly on if and how the kind of sovereign biopolitics I examine in this book might function within the United States as a form of racialization in chapter 4; however, fuller engagement with this issue remains a task for future work.

75.   Hobbes, *Leviathan*, 90, emphases added.

76.   Hobbes does suggest that we can conclude the state of nature is real via inference by noting what happens when states are rent by civil war, confirming the view that *Leviathan* is, among other things, a critique of the English civil war. In this sense, Mills rightly notes that Hobbes is exceptional among the social contract theorists insofar as he allows for the possibility that Europeans themselves are capable of savagery. Mills, *Racial Contract*, 65–67. However, one wonders if this allowance is of the Arendtian variety, namely, one that traffics in a racialized civilizationalism wherein "savagery" belongs, naturally, to non-Europeans, and thus European "savagery" becomes the outrageous, anomalous scandal that is worse than the colonization that founds and perpetuates it.

77.   Veracini, "Introducing *Settler Colonial Studies*," 3.

78.   Wolfe, "Settler Colonialism and the Elimination of the Native."

79.   Veracini, "Introducing *Settler Colonial Studies*," 3.

80.   Coulthard, *Red Skins, White Masks*. Nichols argues that "North American settler states have moved from openly coercive and violent relations with indigenous communities towards a more flexible, docile, politics of recognition and assimilation—a move away from the 'hard infrastructure' of military operations and residential schools to the 'soft infrastructure' of public apologies and cultural accommodation." Nichols, "The Colonialism of Incarceration," 448. See also Simpson, *Mohawk Interruptus*.

81.   Jean O'Brien, for example (in *Firsting and Lasting*), examines the "ideological process" by which New England settlers constituted their own modernity: through various narratives of the "first"-ness of Anglo culture, by replacing native people and places with settler names, monuments, and histories, and by narrating Indians as already extinct.

82.   Veracini, *Settler Colonial Present*, 51.

83.   Byrd, *Transit of Empire*; Morgensen, "Biopolitics of Settler Colonialism"; Wolfe, "Settler Colonialism and the Elimination of the Native"; O'Brien, *Firsting and Lasting*; Simpson, *Mohawk Interruptus* and "The State Is a Man."

84.   Veracini, *Settler Colonial Present*, 52.

85.   Veracini, *Settler Colonialism*, 33–52.

86.   Nichols, "Realizing the Social Contract," and Nichols, "Theft Is Property!"

87.   Hobbes, *Leviathan*, 38.

88.   Hobbes, 38.

89.   Edelman, *No Future*, 9.

90.   Edelman, 9.

91.   Edelman, 2–3, original emphases.

92.   Edelman, 13.

93.   Hobbes, *Leviathan*, 123–124.

94.   Goldstein, "Introduction," 3.

95.   Hobbes, *Leviathan*, 70, emphases added.

96.   Hobbes, 70.

97.   Hobbes, 46, original emphasis.

98.   Hobbes, 46.

99.   Hobbes, 54.

100.   Hobbes, 70.

101.   Hobbes, 70.

102.   For Nichols, incarceration serves this purpose, a practice of empire that is also importantly distinct from it: "the contemporary carceral system colonizes and re-colonizes in a classical sense: by providing a solution to that which exceeds and destabilizes sovereignty via a spatial reorganization of populations and a depoliticization of that process. While this apparatus is currently situated within empire and manifests itself in fully racialized terms of articulation today, it cannot be reduced to these other formations." Nichols, "The Colonialism of Incarceration," 454.

103.   Byrd, *Transit of Empire*, xiii.

104. Indeed, Iyko Day suggests that American exceptionalism, coupled with a "history of empire building," is "possibly the most exemplary expressions of settler colonialism." Day, "Being or Nothingness," 104.

105. Silliman, "The 'Old West' in the Middle East," 242.

106. Silliman, 241.

107. Lubin, "'We Are All Israelis,'" 684.

108. Byrd, *Transit of Empire*, xxi.

109. Byrd, 227.

110. As is the case with any origin story and every variation on the state of nature. As Andrea Smith aptly notes, "When we critique a contemporary context through an appeal to a prior state 'before the fall,' we are necessarily masking power relations through evoking lost origins." Smith, "Queer Theory and Native Studies," 46. I would add that this is true regardless of whether the story told is one of progress or decline—in either case, the prerequisites for the desired outcome are projected onto a mythical past that serves to anchor, naturalize, and legitimate the predetermined outcome the sto-ryteller is invested in perpetuating. "Thus," says Marx, "the theologian explains the origin of evil by the fall of Man—that is, he assumes as a fact, in historical form, what has to be explained." Marx, "Estranged Labor," 71.

111. To quote Smith once more: "Normative futurity depends on an 'origin story.'" Smith, "Queer Theory and Native Studies," 47. That origin story is the state of nature in the social contractarian account, which in Edelman is cast as the narrativization of desire. In either case, however, that founding fiction is, in the case of sovereignty, a civilizationalist one that abjects or "queers" all those who fail to abide by its tempo-ral mandates.

112. For Hobbes's impact on modern conservatism, see chapter 2 of Robin, *The Reaction-ary Mind*.

113. Hobbes, *Leviathan*, 11.

114. Roach, "Sense and Sexuality," 168.

115. See, for example, Hobbes, *Leviathan*, 120, wherein Hobbes declares "terror" to be the means by which the Sovereign shall secure peace.

116. Donald Trump swiftly followed suit by having al-Awlaki's eight-year-old daughter killed in a US raid in Yemen, the first military operation of his administration. Unlike her brother Abdulrahman, Nawar was not a US citizen; however, this act was perhaps a fulfillment of Trump's campaign promise not simply to go after "terrorists," but also "to take out their families." www.cnn.com/2015/12/02/politics/donald-trump-terrorists -families/.

117. Sima Shakhsari argues, in parallel fashion, that the "people of Iran" is a population constituted as rightfully killable, both in the name of human rights and in order to protect human rights: "Standing between biopolitics and necropolitics, the politics of rightful killing explains the contemporary political situation in the 'war on terror' where those whose rights and protection are presented as the raison d'être of war, are sanctioned to death and therefore live a pending death exactly because of those rights." Shakhsari, "Killing Me Softly with Your Rights," 103.

3. FOUCAULT AND QUEER THEORY

1. Foucault, "Interview with Michel Foucault," 294–295.
2. Edelman, *No Future*, 24, original emphasis.
3. This unlikely project is not without precedent; see, for example, Drucilla Cornell and
    Stephen D. Seely's claim ("There's Nothing Revolutionary About a Blowjob") that Fou-
    cault was a thinker who never stopped worrying about revolution and whose work can
    be marshaled to think through a radical queer politics. As will become clear, while I
    support Cornell and Seely's ambitions to restore queer's radicalism, in particular by
    returning to Foucault to reread his revolutionary commitments, I disagree fundamen-
    tally with their reading of Edelman, who I see as continuing this emancipatory impulse
    rather than stifling it.
4. Different versions of these critiques were especially prevalent within US academic
    feminism; emblematic was Nancy Hartsock's essay "Foucault on Power: A Theory for
    Women?" The second problem, the question of normative foundations, continues to
    plague poststructuralist critics as it has since their ascendancy in the 1990s; particu-
    larly within philosophy-based Foucault studies, it has come to simply be called "the
    normative question," one to which Dianna Taylor offers a deft and, one hopes, finally
    conclusive response in "Normativity and Normalization."
5. A recent and pointed articulation of this argument is James Penney's *After Queer
    Theory*, but see also Rosemary Hennessey's classic statement to this effect in her
    Profit and Pleasure and "Queer Theory, Left Politics." While queer theory experi-
    enced a fleeting resurgence of interest in Marx and Marxism, this revival focused
    much more on rethinking totality (see, for example, Kevin Floyd, *Reification of
    Desire*) or dialecticizing neoliberalism so as to further attune it to historical contra-
    dictions (see, for example, the special issue of *GLQ*, Rosenberg and Villarejo, "Queer
    Studies and the Crises of Capitalism") than on the question of specifically revolution-
    ary or liberatory politics. Margot Weiss's work might be considered as examining
    this particular theoretico-political juncture, although she, too, ultimately rejects (or
    at least is worried enough not to wholeheartedly endorse) queer theory as a sufficient
    basis for radical political resistance to capitalism (see Weiss, *Techniques of Pleasure*
    and "Queer Economic Justice"). In this sense, the early Marxist and Marxian-inspired
    accounts of homosexuality and gay liberation are more in line with the kind of libera-
    tory politics I am imagining in this book; see, for example, the work of John D'Emilio
    but in particular his iconic essay "Capitalism and Gay Identity," and that of Jonathan
    Ned Katz, particularly *The Invention of Heterosexuality*.
6. This section is adapted from Schotten, "Against Totalitarianism."
7. Foucault, *"Society Must Be Defended,"* 39.
8. Foucault, 39–40.
9. Foucault, *History of Sexuality*, 1:159.
10. A suggestion that has been much mined by feminists and queer theorists for thinking
    through various practices of resistance; see, most prominently, McWhorter, *Bodies and
    Pleasures*; Sawicki, *Disciplining Foucault*. Judith Butler has suggested that "sexuality

and power" is a better pairing for this task than "bodies and pleasures." Butler, "Revisiting Bodies and Pleasures," 19.

11. Foucault, "The End of the Monarchy of Sex," 217. Here Foucault is explicit that the question of politics is, quite simply, the question as to "whether or not the revolution is desirable" (223). As Tom Roach puts it, Foucault is "certainly critical, although never disparaging, of a liberationist politics that links truth and sexuality." What "his work demands, however, [is] that we continually question the strategies and objectives of such a politics." Roach, "Sense and Sexuality, 164.

12. Foucault, *History of Sexuality*, 1:88–89.

13. Foucault, *"Society Must Be Defended,"* 34.

14. Colin Koopman ("Two Uses of Michel Foucault in Political Theory") has paid close attention to and defended Foucault's methodology, albeit without attending to the politics of Foucault's methodological approach or the political stakes of choosing Foucauldian methodology over any other kind.

15. Foucault, *Security, Territory, Population*, 119–120n.

16. Foucault, 116.

17. Foucault, 247.

18. Foucault, *"Society Must Be Defended,"* 30.

19. Foucault, *History of Sexuality*, 1:94, emphasis added.

20. Foucault, *"Society Must Be Defended,"* 30.

21. Foucault, *Security, Territory, Population*, 119; cf. Foucault, *Birth of Biopolitics*, 186.

22. Foucault, *"Society Must Be Defended,"* 4.

23. Foucault, 4.

24. Foucault, 5.

25. Foucault, 5, emphasis added.

26. Foucault, 5.

27. Foucault, "Interview with Michel Foucault," 283.

28. Foucault, *"Society Must Be Defended,"* 7.

29. Foucault, 7.

30. Foucault, 7.

31. Foucault, 8.

32. Foucault, 8.

33. Foucault, 8. I can't help but hear echoes of Foucault's methodology in the work of James Scott, who has spent a lifetime researching the "infinitesimal" modes of resistance that, precisely because of their slightness as well as the vulnerable and precarious position of those "from below" who practice them, tend to be excluded from the historical record. The difference between Scott and Foucault may simply be one of focus; whereas Scott focuses on the minute resistances of those subject to "elaborate and systematic forms of social subordination: the worker to the boss, the tenant or sharecropper to the landlord, the serf to the lord, the slave to the master, the untouchable to the Brahmin, a member of a subject race to one of the dominant race," the existence of which Foucault does not deny, Foucault by contrast is rather more interested in "mobile and transitory points of resistance" that produce "cleavages in a society that shift about,

fracturing unities and effecting regroupings." Foucault, *History of Sexuality*, 1:96. See Scott, *Domination and the Arts of Resistance*, 2, and Scott, *Weapons of the Weak*.

34. I see no reason to exclude Foucault's first book, *History of Madness*, from this characterization, and Lynne Huffer's recent rereading of this text suggests as much to me, particularly in her emphasis throughout on a passage from an unpublished interview wherein Foucault says that for twenty years he has been worrying about "my little mad ones, my little excluded ones, my little abnormals." Huffer argues that, in this gesture, "Foucault declares his solidarity with those who belong to 'society's shadow,' those he calls the 'excluded ones.'" Huffer, *Mad for Foucault*, 23. Nevertheless, this is not a reading (of *Madness* or, perhaps, of Foucault's oeuvre) that Huffer would accept, insofar as she does not see madness as coincident with "resistance" in Foucault and places great emphasis on his prefatory warning that to articulate the voices and experiences of the mad is already to fold them into the domain of reason and erase their existence *as* mad.

35. Foucault, *"Society Must Be Defended,"* 32.

36. Foucault, 31.

37. Foucault, 9.

38. Foucault, 9.

39. Foucault, 10.

40. See, for example, in addition to *History of Sexuality*, "The Ethics of the Concern for Self as a Practice of Freedom," wherein Foucault stresses his emphasis on "practices of freedom" rather than liberation as such, not because the latter does not exist, but because "Liberation paves the way for new power relationships, which must be controlled by practices of freedom" (282–284). Michael Dillon argues that Foucault's "insurrection of subjugated knowledges" in this lecture series "may be a powerful politicising manoevre," suggesting that Foucault may be seeking to incite the resistance he is documenting methodologically. Dillon, "Cared to Death," 38*n*4. Brady Heiner attributes Foucault's shift to genealogy, focus on prisons, and centering of race in the discussion of biopolitics (among many other definitive aspects of this period of his writing, including the insurrection of subjugated knowledges) to the influence of the Black Panther Party, and particularly the writings of Angela Davis and George Jackson, on Foucault's thinking. Heiner, "Foucault and the Black Panthers."

41. Foucault, *"Society Must Be Defended,"* 6.

42. I am grateful to Lynne Huffer for raising these objections.

43. Foucault, *"Society Must Be Defended,"* 7–8.

44. Foucault, *Discipline and Punish*, 236.

45. Foucault, 192–193.

46. Foucault, *"Society Must Be Defended,"* 45–46.

47. Foucault, "Intellectuals and Power," 79. While the language of lack here may seem to allude to the commoditized view of power he otherwise rejects or to somehow suggest that power is something one does or does not have, in *"Society Must Be Defended,"* Foucault states, "My goal was not to analyze power at the level of intentions or decisions, not to try to approach it from inside, and not to ask the question (which leads us, I think, into a labyrinth from which there is no way out): So who has power? What is

going on in his head? And what is he trying to do, this man who has power? The goal was, on the contrary, to study power . . . by looking, as it were, at its external face, at the point where it relates directly and immediately to what we might, very provisionally, call its object, its target, its field of application, or, in other words, the places where it implants itself and produces its real effects." Foucault, *"Society Must Be Defended,"* 28.

48. Foucault, *"Society Must Be Defended,"* 9, emphasis added.

49. Foucault, 28.

50. Foucault, "Questions of Method," 235–236.

51. Foucault, 236. For an examination of the ways in which Foucault's political activism influenced and informed his theorizations about power, see Hoffman, *Foucault and Power.*

52. Foucault, "Intellectuals and Power," 75. This is in direct contrast with Noam Chomsky's position that "the responsibility of intellectuals [is] to speak the truth and to expose lies" (Chomsky, "The Responsibility of Intellectuals") and somewhat at odds with Gayatri Spivak's critique of Foucault in this interview as unaware of his embeddedness within European institutional modes of knowledge and complicity with global capitalism (Spivak, "Can the Subaltern Speak?").

53. As Barbara Cruikshank astutely notes in her capable Foucauldian study of the modes of subjection at work in modern citizenship technologies, "It is impossible to speak in the voice of the voiceless without first constituting their inability to speak for themselves." Cruikshank, *The Will to Empower*, 34.

54. Foucault, "Intellectuals and Power," 75, emphasis added.

55. Foucault, "Practicing Criticism," 155.

56. Foucault, 155.

57. Foucault, "Questions of Method," 236.

58. I am grateful to Aaron Lecklider for his insight on this matter and the many conversations we have had about queer theory, survival, and AIDS activism.

59. Warner, "Introduction," xxvi.

60. Warner, xxvi.

61. Berlant and Warner, "Sex in Public," 548n2.

62. Foucault, *History of Sexuality*, 1:95.

63. For different versions of this view, see David Halperin, "The Normalization of Queer Theory," and Annamarie Jagose, *Queer Theory.*

64. Warner, "Introduction," xxvi.

65. Warner, xxvi.

66. De Lauretis, "Queer Theory," v.

67. Warner notes, "When Teresa de Lauretis and her colleagues at the University of California at Santa Cruz organized a conference called 'Queer Theory' in 1990, it was manifestly provocative. The term 'queer' in those days was not yet a cable-TV synonym for gay; it carried a high-voltage charge of insult and stigma. The term caught on because it seemed to catalyze many of the key insights of previous years and connect them to a range of politics and constituencies that were already developing outside academe, in

a way that looked unpredictable from the start." Nevertheless, "By 1994, de Lauretis was already complaining that the term had 'very quickly become a conceptually vacuous creature of the publishing industry'" ("Queer and Then"). In 1999, de Lauretis complained that the "Queer Theory" bookshelf at A Different Light bookstore in San Francisco reflects "the banality and shallow trendiness that has characterized the mobilization of queer in North American academic studies and so-called alternative media." De Lauretis "Gender Symptoms," 258.

68. Butler, "Imitation and Gender Subordination," 13.

69. Sedgwick, *Tendencies*, 8.

70. Warner, "Introduction," xxvi.

71. Warner, xxvi.

72. Foucault, *"Society Must Be Defended,"* 28. As Sedgwick muses, "A hypothesis worth making explicit: that there are important senses in which 'queer' can signify only when attached to the first person. One possible corollary: that what it takes—all it takes—to make the description 'queer' a true one is the impulsion to use it in the first person." Sedgwick, *Tendencies*, 9, original emphases.

73. Warner, "Introduction," xxvi.

74. Berlant and Warner, "What Does Queer Theory Teach Us About X?," 345. Cf. Sedgwick's similar cautions against assuming, with culture, that gender of object choice demarcates the most primary, significant, or meaningful axis of sexuality, sexual identity, or "queerness" (see her famous list of all sorts of possible sexual "differences" in *Epistemology of the Closet*, 25–26, and *Tendencies*, 7–8; on this matter, see Kate Bornstein as well, who provides a lengthy list of the many other factors "which could be more important than gender" upon which "we could base sexual orientation" in her classic *Gender Outlaw*, 33–38). Sedgwick also calls into question the assumption that members of a category—for example, homosexuals, men, women—are basically and significantly different from those in the "other" or "opposite" categories. Sedgwick, *Epistemology of the Closet*, 24–25; cf. Sedgwick, *Tendencies*, 7n6 and Bornstein, *Gender Outlaw*.

75. Warner, "Introduction," xi.

76. Warner, xxiv.

77. Warner, xxiv–xxv. Hennessey cites the sentence fragment "class is conspicuously useless" clearly out of context in order to criticize Warner unfairly for his "dismissive separation of class analysis from sexuality," a separation that she argues characterizes "much of queer theory." Hennessey, *Profit and Pleasure*, 54.

78. This fact is sidestepped entirely in the largely apolitical consideration of "Queer Theory Without Antinormativity," a special issue of *differences* compiled to address what its editors call "the prevailing supposition that a critique of normativity marks the spot where queer and theory meet." Wiegman and Wilson, "Introduction," 1. While the words *politics* and *political* do surface in the introduction and various of the essays, the discussion of "norms" in this issue strangely devolves into a consideration of the functioning of mathematical averages within statistical analysis that somehow manages to blame *queer theory* for stabilizing norms in order to position itself as properly

resistant to them. I think this misses the fundamentally political force and content of queer theory's "antinormativity," which certainly can be read reductively as "opposition to norms," but can also be more carefully understood as resistance to what Foucault calls "normalization," and which Warner justly characterizes as, among other things, regimes of violence. It is *these regimes*, not queer theory, that are responsible for the institutionalization of norms into normativity. If, then, as Annamarie Jagose contends, "antinormativity stands as queer theory's privileged figure for the political" (Jagose, "The Trouble with Antinormativity," 27), the task of queer theory is not to jettison antinormativity but rather to specify more precisely queer theory's specific contribution to and understanding of the political—a task largely deflected by this issue's contributors, who prefer to position themselves as searching for queer theory "without" antinormativity, a search that has the ironic effect of presenting itself and its contributors as more cutting-edge than queer theory and yet somehow also more consistently queer in seeking "a politics of motility and relationality" rather than "a politics of insubordination." Wiegman and Wilson, "Introduction," 14.

79. Warner, "Introduction," vii.

80. The special issue of *differences*, "Queer Theory Without Antinormativity," is emblematic of this; see also Kadji Amin's insightful essay, "Haunted by the 1990s," on the historicity of "queer," its political inheritances, and potential futures.

81. Puar, *Terrorist Assemblages*, 21–23.

82. Huffer, *Mad for Foucault*, 97.

83. See also, in this regard, Tom Roach's *Friendship as a Way of Life*, a shift from his earlier "Sense and Sexuality," which suggests a more politicized interest in Foucauldian desubjectivation. In this essay, Roach uses David Wojnarowicz's memoirs to theorize queer forms of sexual intimacy that go beyond identity politics and institutional acceptance, not to mention a political movement wherein "queers might invent relational worlds less amenable to the 'morality' of the market and less in step with neoliberalism's march" (165) and "an activism that puts death to work in the service of a biopolitics 'from below'" (170).

84. Ross, "Beyond the Closet as a Raceless Paradigm."

85. Cohen's primary examples of this single-axis analysis are the antics and activism of Queer Nation, whose manifesto, "Queers Read This: I Hate Straights," was distributed anonymously in 1990 at NYC Pride. Yet Erin Rand has noted the outsized role Queer Nation has played in academic texts on queer theory and, therefore, in the founding of the field itself, despite its negligible membership and duration in the real world. She writes: "if Queer Nation has, in fact, effected a resignification of 'queer' and made that label available as an identity category, it is, at least to some extent, a consequence of queer theorists' documenting and taxonomizing the shift in terms." Citing important founding queer theory essays such as Cohen's "Punks," Lisa Duggan's "Making It Perfectly Queer," and Lauren Berlant and Elizabeth Freeman's "Queer Nationality" (in *Fear of a Queer Planet*), Rand notes that "if Queer Nation illustrates some of the pitfalls of identity politics by attempting to reconfigure the basis of identity itself, it is in no small part because queer scholars put the group's practices in conversation with the

contemporary interventions of poststructuralism and postmodernism. In other words, had Queer Nation not been taken up as the poster child of queer activism within the whirlwind proliferation of queer theory in the early 1990s, it is doubtful that now, nearly twenty years since the demise of the last chapter, it would be so sturdily archived in queer history." Rand, *Reclaiming Queer*, 5.

86. Cohen, "Punks, Bulldaggers, and Welfare Queens," 36.

87. Cohen, 26.

88. Cohen, 25.

89. Amin observes that queer theory "remains haunted by the political and transgressive charge of the early 1990s moment and that this haunting orients it toward particular political and intellectual projects in the present." Amin, "Haunted by the 1990s," 182.

90. Puar, *Terrorist Assemblages*, 23, 221–222.

91. Puar, "'I Would Rather Be a Cyborg Than a Goddess,'" 60.

92. Puar, *Terrorist Assemblages*, 212.

93. Puar, "'I Would Rather Be a Cyborg Than a Goddess,'" 62.

94. Puar, 167.

95. Puar, "Prognosis Time," 162.

96. Puar, "'I Would Rather Be a Cyborg Than a Goddess,'" 63.

97. Puar, *Terrorist Assemblages*, 215.

98. As Amin observes, "scholarship on homonationalism and homonormativity seems still to be animated by the now injured aspiration that queer sexuality ought to attach to radical politics and to an antiassimilationist stance toward the institutions of the state. That is, it seems to me that what drives the prominence of critiques of homonormativity and homonationalism in contemporary queer studies is a historical disappointment of those political and antiassimilationist energies that continue to reverberate in *queer*, even as some versions of queer sexuality have become absorbable into a neoliberal politics of lifestyle choice and anodyne diversity." Amin, "Haunted by the 1990s," 183, original emphasis.

99. Huffer, *Mad for Foucault*, 63.

100. Huffer, 65–66. Although a seemingly familiar argument and critical target, I'm not sure anyone in queer theory actually claims this. In even the most evasive instances of *queer*'s definition as dissidence, *queer* still means something specific, even if that specificity is its corrosive, undermining, or excessive character. Queerness may be underspecified definitionally, then—it names a generic content or indicates a type of movement, rather than a specific person, practice, or political position—but that is different from claiming that queerness is undecidable or stands in for undecidability. I have similar questions regarding Cohen's emphasis on queerness as entailing gender or sexual "fluidity," a claim she makes throughout "Punks"—while certainly familiar, does anyone actually claim that queerness means gender or sexual fluidity? These notions of queerness as "undecidability" or "fluidity" may have more to do with the popularization or activist usage of queer than with field-defining terminologies in queer theory, an issue I return to in chapter 5.

101. Huffer, *Mad for Foucault*, 67. Cf. Marcus, "Queer Theory for Everyone."

102.   Huffer, *Mad for Foucault*, 86.

103.   Huffer, 67.

104.   Huffer, 68. Even worse, in its explicit focus on the specificities and vicissitudes of queer experience and sexuality, Huffer argues that queer theory reiterates the very sexual subjectivation Foucault cautioned us to reject. As queer scholars take delight in the improprietous academic rehearsal of sex acts and perversions (the example she uses in this chapter is fist-fucking), Huffer makes the Foucauldian point that not only is such academic speech not per se transgressive, but also it is in fact an object lesson in the repressive hypothesis Foucault cautioned us to be wary of duplicating. Huffer calls this dilemma queer theory's "foundational contradiction" (Huffer, 74) and links it directly to queer theory's inability or refusal to relinquish subjectivity in its theorization of sexual ethics.

105.   As Warner observes of *Terrorist Assemblages*, "while Puar wants to associate queer theory with a liberal imperial imagination, she does so in terms that she takes from queer theory itself. Despite its criticisms of (some) queer theory, then, Puar's book is itself an example of vital work queer theory enables, with or without the rubric." Warner, "Queer and Then."

106.   Nealon, *Foucault Beyond Foucault*, 80.

107.   Nealon, 109.

108.   Nealon, 111, original emphasis.

109.   Nealon, 111, original emphases.

110.   Amin's "Haunted by the 1990s" is extremely useful and important in this regard, and makes the persuasive case that if queer theory is to be put to work in other political and geographical contexts, its US inheritance from the 1990s needs to be explicitly owned and acknowledged. That said, Amin neglects to specify the political radicalism or dissidence of queer theory in the 1990s as a specifically left commitment and characterizes this political residue in terms of affect rather than argument or political commitment.

111.   "They alone who are willing to risk their lives to bring it about can answer the question" of "whether the revolution is worth it and what kind." Foucault, "The End of the Monarchy of Sex," 225.

4. SOCIETY MUST BE DESTROYED

1.   Lyon, *Manifestoes*, 10.

2.   Foucault, *"Society Must Be Defended,"* 79.

3.   Cohen, "Punks, Bulldaggers, and Welfare Queens," 445.

4.   Edelman, "Antagonism, Negativity, and the Subject of Queer Theory," 822.

5.   Bersani, *Homos*, 8.

6.   As Dean Spade and Craig Willse write, in a critique not of Edelman but of any so-called "progressive" queer politics, "It is unethical for movements to prioritize those with the most access. We should prioritize those vulnerable to the most severe

manifestations of homophobia and transphobia." Spade and Willse, "Marriage Will Never Set Us Free."

7. Such a move is not without precedent; Grace Kyungwon Hong, for example, argues that post–World War II liberatory social movements were not at all based on a limited "recognition and preservation of life" agenda, but rather have been remembered as such by a neoliberal project that itself only recognizes and protects valuable life at the expense of expendable and targeted populations. Thus, she says, "death can and indeed must be the basis of a politics in the contemporary moment, impossibly alongside the antagonistic pursuit of a politics based on the preservation of life." Hong, *Death Beyond Disavowal*, 8. Hong's argument is at least in part a quarrel with Afro-pessimist thinkers such as Frank Wilderson, who also, however, argues that the accession to the social and ontological death that is blackness is the only possible meaning and form of black emancipation; see Wilderson, *Red, White, and Black*.

8. In this sense, *No Future* can be read as a rejoinder to Wendy Brown's lament at the loss of revolution as left aspiration, which she deems "historically outmoded, exhausted as an ambition, ruptured as political ontology," and "discredited by contemporary political epistemology." Brown, "Feminism Unbound," 112. Brown's suggestion in response to this loss is that we "recuperate a utopian imaginary absent a revolutionary mechanism for its realization" (114). My interest is rather the opposite, however; namely, to preserve the revolutionary "mechanism"—that is, desire—and do without the utopianism. I began to explore this problematic near the end of Schotten, *Nietzsche's Revolution*, 199–206.

9. Calvin Warren, for example ("Black Nihilism and the Politics of Hope"), complains about the disciplinary demand that blacks invest in hope, futurity, "the political process," and the American Dream or else be cast off and rejected as insane, self-destructive, or morally and socially bankrupt, that is, as nihilist.

10. *No Future*—as well as my appropriation of it—bears significant resemblance to what Warren calls "black nihilism." Indeed, Warren's critique of antiblackness and Edelman's critique of reproductive futurism run virtually parallel to each other, with both arguing that the temporality of hope abjects blacks and queers (respectively) from the social order and requires this abjection in order to function *as* a social order for everyone else. In addition, both argue against the possibility of political recuperation or liberation from this abjection, with Warren arguing that "Black emancipation is world destructive. . . . it is impossible to emancipate blacks without literally destroying the world" (Warren, "Black Nihilism and the Politics of Hope," 239) and Edelman arguing that any real accession to queerness would destroy both the subjectivity and the social order that require its void to function. As is perhaps clear, I am extremely sympathetic with both of these political projects, although I differ from them not only in my focus on moralism but also in my claim that nihilism or negativity is politically thinkable and practicable, an attempt both would resoundingly reject. Despite the parallels in their arguments, however, Warren would reject Edelman's version of queerness as a refusal to recognize the importance of the transatlantic slave trade, which transformed "humans" into "things" and thus constituted "the human" as and upon

antiblackness. Edelman, in turn, would argue that Warren's "black" occupies the same structural position as the "queer" of his analysis of reproductive futurism, an interchangeability that Warren would not accept; see, for example, Warren, "Onticide".

11.   It is Lauren Berlant and Edelman who refer to this panel "as the most concentrated venue" of the "performance" of the debates over the antisocial thesis in their preface to *Sex, or the Unbearable*, xii. This performance may have been eclipsed, however, by their more recent, acerbic exchange with Tim Dean in the pages of *American Literary History*: Dean, "No Sex Please, We're American," Berlant and Edelman, "Reading, Sex, and the Unbearable," and Dean, "Clear and Sonorous."

12.   Caserio, "Conference Debates."

13.   Berlant and Edelman, "Reading, Sex, and the Unbearable," 627.

14.   Dean makes this case in his contribution to "The Antisocial Thesis in Queer Theory" panel: Dean, "The Antisocial Homosexual," 827. For a critique of Edelman's failure to incorporate Hocquenghem, despite being "deeply indebted" to his work, see the anonymous, collective, anarchist essay "Queers Gone Wild" in *bædan: journal of queer nihilism*. I am grateful to Carolyn Terranova for bringing this exquisite publication to my attention.

15.   See, for example, Caserio: "Bersani's formulation and others like it" ("Conference Debates"); José Esteban Muñoz, who discusses "The prime examples of queer antirelationality in Bersani's *Homos*, Edelman's *No Future*, and all the other proponents of this turn in queer criticism" (Muñoz, *Cruising Utopia*, 14); and J. Halberstam, who says "the antisocial turn in queer theory" is "exemplified by the work of Bersani, Edelman, and others" (Halberstam, *Queer Art of Failure*, 109) or, more dramatically, by "Bersani, Edelman, and countless others" (Halberstam, "Anti-Social Turn in Queer Studies," 151).

16.   Roach, *Friendship as a Way of Life*, 14.

17.   Claiming that the work of antisocial thesis thinkers "resists the increasing hetero- and homonormativity of queer culture," Roach argues that these projects are "antiassimilationist to the core" (Roach, 14).

18.   Halberstam, "Anti-Social Turn in Queer Studies."

19.   See, for example, Halberstam, *Queer Art of Failure*.

20.   Edelman, *No Future*, 143.

21.   Dean, "Antisocial Homosexual," and Dean, "An Impossible Embrace."

22.   Halberstam, "Politics of Negativity in Recent Queer Theory," and Halberstam, "Anti-Social Turn in Queer Studies."

23.   Love, *Feeling Backward*, 163.

24.   Indeed, in *Homos*, Bersani cites Edelman's earlier work in *Homographesis* as participating in queer theory's "de-gaying" of gay people (69).

25.   Bersani, "Shame on You," 107.

26.   I owe my understanding of the performative character of the manifesto to Puchner, *Poetry of the Revolution*, chaps. 1–3; see also Laura Winkiel, "The 'Sweet Assassin' and the Performative Politics of SCUM Manifesto." I'm not the first to see *No Future* as a manifesto; in 2011, Teresa de Lauretis wrote: "I still see *No Future* as a manifesto

written to impact the twenty-first century as some of its predecessors did the twentieth century, a manifesto . . . with the passion and risk-taking intelligence of the best examples of the genre." De Lauretis, "Queer Texts, Bad Habits, and the Issue of a Future," 257.

27.   Dean, "Impossible Embrace." Drucilla Cornell and Stephen D. Seely also criticize Edelman for failing to read Lacan in a properly psychoanalytic way ("There's Nothing Revolutionary About a Blowjob," 4 and 20n6). While I take no position on the relative astuteness of Edelman's reading of Lacan, as will become clear, I do take issue with Cornell and Seely's conclusion that *No Future* engages in a "relentless struggle to keep us safe from the emancipatory desire" (6).

28.   Lyon, *Manifestoes*, 14; cf. Puchner, *Poetry of the Revolution*, chap. 3.

29.   Dean, "Impossible Embrace," 126.

30.   Dean, 125, 138; cf. 130 and 130n24.

31.   Halberstam, "Anti-Social Turn in Queer Studies," 142.

32.   These latter three descriptors are taken from Snediker, "Queer Optimism."

33.   Dean, "Impossible Embrace," 127; cf. Brenkman, "Politics, Mortal and Natal," and Winnubst, "Review Essay."

34.   Dean, "Impossible Embrace," 126.

35.   Dean's frustration with Edelman's embrace of right-wing/homophobic logic is long-standing; see also Dean, "The Antisocial Homosexual."

36.   Dean, "Impossible Embrace," 125, 131, 138.

37.   Dean, 125.

38.   Dean, *Unlimited Intimacy*.

39.   Dean, "Impossible Embrace," 138.

40.   Dean, 125.

41.   Dean writes, "the appeal of *No Future* lies less in its thesis or conceptualization than in its rhetorical style and the irrational passion that style conveys." Dean, "Impossible Embrace," 126. By contrast, although he shares Dean's wariness, John Brenkman cites the overwhelming cogency of *No Future* as grounds for suspicion: "When I originally heard Lee Edelman give his lecture 'The Future is Kid Stuff,' I found it so compelling in its passion and coherence and so disturbing in its conclusions that I had to look back at its argument and ask whether perhaps what was wrong with the argument was its very coherence." Brenkman, "Queer Post-Politics," 174.

42.   I take "political voice" from Puchner (*Poetry of the Revolution*, chap. 2); more on this later. Elided here, of course, is the fact that it is difficult to claim *No Future* as simply one thing or another—as either a work of psychoanalytic theory or a manifesto, either queer theory scholarship or a piece of political writing. Indeed, what both Dean's and my interpretations of Edelman discount is the fact that rhetorical excesses are not nearly as ubiquitous in *No Future* as either of us might wish.

43.   Dean, "Impossible Embrace," 127.

44.   Similar criticisms object to the hardened, ahistorical inevitability of the Lacanian Symbolic in Edelman's text (Winnubst, "Review Essay") or "(hetero)normative conceptions of temporality" (Cornell and Seely, "There's Nothing Revolutionary About a

Blowjob"), the seemingly inescapable, all-determining, hegemonic power of repro-ductive futurism (Dean, "Impossible Embrace"; Snediker, "Queer Optimism"), or the subsumption of all homosexuality to nonreproductivity (and all heterosexuality to reproduction) (Puar, *Terrorist Assemblages*, 210–211). In the special issue of *differ-ences*, "Queer Theory without Antinormativity," Robyn Wiegman dismisses entirely an even broader project she calls "the antinormative thesis" due to its limiting, "dualistic account of the political." Wiegman, "Eve's Triangles," 66.

45. Lyon, *Manifestoes*, 2–3.

46. Edelman, *No Future*, 31, original emphasis.

47. Edelman, 31, original emphasis. In an a similar us-vs.-them vein, Edelman writes: "We, the *sinthom*osexuals who figure the death drive of the social, must accept that we will be vilified as the agents of that threat. But 'they,' the defenders of futurity, buzzed by negating our negativity, are themselves, however unknowingly, its secret agents too, reacting, in the name of the future, in the name of humanity, in the name of life, to the threat of the death drive we figure with the violent rush of a jouissance, which only returns them, ironically, to the death drive in spite of themselves" (153).

48. Lyon, *Manifestoes*, 9. As Winkiel writes of Valerie Solanas's *SCUM Manifesto*, "The emo-tive rhetoric of the polemical tract works to create a highly charged atmosphere of com-plicity between the speaker and her audience. The high-pitched polemic leaves no room for debate or qualified assent. The seeming spontaneity of the polemical utterance unabashedly asserts the correctness of its political position and assumes the pre-existence of SCUM females." Winkiel, "The 'Sweet Assassin' and the Performative Politics of *SCUM Manifesto*," 63.

49. It is, however, the fitting title of Carla Freccero's review of *No Future* in *GLQ*. The most relevant, oft-cited passage in this regard is the following:

> Queers must respond to the violent force of such constant provocations not only by insisting on our equal right to the social order's prerogatives, not only by avowing our capacity to promote that order's coherence and integrity, but also by saying explicitly what [Cardinal Bernard] Law and the Pope and the whole of the Symbolic order for which they stand hear anyway in each and every expression or manifestation of queer sexuality: Fuck the social order and the Child in whose name we're collectively terrorized; fuck Annie; fuck the waif from *Les Mis*; fuck the poor, innocent kid on the Net; fuck Laws with both capi-tal *l*s and small; fuck the whole network of Symbolic relations and the future that serves as its prop. (Edelman, *No Future*, 29)

50. Lyon, *Manifestoes*, 12.

51. Edelman, *No Future*, 3; cf. 5. For an insightful consideration of polemic as a rhetorical form and its relationship both with queer theory and with a new notion of "queer agency," see Erin Rand's discussion of Larry Kramer in *Reclaiming Queer*, chap. 2.

52. This is not to say, however, that manifestos are not or cannot be contributions to knowledge. *The Communist Manifesto*, which both inaugurated the genre and set the precedent for all future manifestos, is frequently considered to offer one of the clearest expositions of Marx's and Engels's dialectical materialism.

53. It seems clear enough both in this article and elsewhere that ethics is Dean's more primary concern; as he says, for example, "The issue of whether any particular cultural practice or text is radical or reactionary, transgressive or conservative, has never struck me as very interesting." Dean, "Bareback Time," 94n2.

54. Dean, "Impossible Embrace," 129.

55. Edelman, *No Future*, 28. I address the question of revolutionary persuasion in more detail in chapter 3 of Schotten, *Nietzsche's Revolution*.

56. Puchner, *Poetry of the Revolution*, 12.

57. Puchner, 26.

58. Puchner, 22. Cf. Winkiel on the *SCUM Manifesto*: "The performative aspect of the manifesto brings something into being that did not exist before: it constitutes a new political community through its enunciation of an imaginary group of women, SCUM. It, in effect, creates the political actors by calling them into being." Winkiel, "The 'Sweet Assassin' and the Performative Politics of *SCUM Manifesto*," 63.

59. Puchner, *Poetry of the Revolution*, 22, 31–32.

60. Edelman, *No Future*, 14–15.

61. Edelman, 14–5, 157–158n19.

62. For example, Scrooge from Charles Dickens's *A Christmas Carol* (*No Future*, 41–50) and the title character of George Eliot's *Silas Marner* (53–59). Because this is Edelman, and not just any English professor, performative figuration also happens via reference to characters in Alfred Hitchcock's films, specifically, Leonard in *North by Northwest* (chapter 3) and the birds in Hitchcock's film *The Birds* (chapter 4).

63. This is where the polemic as Rand defines it and the manifesto occupy shared ground – in the articulation of a truth that is personal to the speaker. The difference is that, according to Rand, polemical articulation of this truth becomes a moralizing universalization of the first-person experience and results in an "alienating" expression of emotion that does not "satisfy or motivate" the audience. Rand, *Reclaiming Queer*, 73. By contrast, the manifesto's declaration of truth is offered as a mode of consciousness raising and motivation to political action. It seeks to persuade and empower, not lecture or shame.

64. Puchner, *Poetry of the Revolution*, 5.

65. Puchner, 22.

66. Puchner, 22.

67. Puchner, 43.

68. I take this evocative expression from Yack, *The Longing for Total Revolution*.

69. Heather Love puts this point differently still, in a warning about revolutionary desire: "A central paradox of any transformative criticism is that its dreams for the future are founded on a history of suffering, stigma, and violence. Oppositional criticism opposes not only existing structures of power but also the very history that gives it meaning." Love, *Feeling Backward*, 1.

70. Edelman, *No Future*, 5.

71. Edelman, 4. This response is an echo of Foucault's insistence, discussed in the previous chapter, that the critic ignore the complaint that she offers no "solution" to address the problem she is critiquing. Perhaps similarly, Warren notes its disciplinary function

in continuously returning blacks to a sociopolitical order based entirely on their fungibility and annihilation, thereby reiteratively enlisting blacks in ensuring and perpetuating their own social death. Warren, "Black Nihilism and the Politics of Hope."

72. He makes clear he is aware of this structuring paradox in his follow-up text with Berlant, *Sex, or the Unbearable*; see chapter 1, esp. 18–19.

73. De Lauretis, "Queer Texts, Bad Habits, and the Issue of a Future," 258.

74. Dean, "Antisocial Homosexual," 827.

75. Dean, 31.

76. I think this is something of what Chandan Reddy is getting at in his complaint that Edelman's "methodological formalism . . . neither seeks to enunciate the limits of that formalism nor attempts to offer an account (however inaccurate and inadequate) of its historical determination," which therefore "produces an epistemology that has no need to ask about those social and cultural formations that exist as the limit of its critique." Reddy, *Freedom with Violence*, 176.

77. This is no less true of European political thought, which Dipesh Chakrabarty seeks to "provincialize," and precisely in the domains of history and politics (in *Provincializing Europe*). On the one hand, the European legacy is everyone's legacy, since "Europe's acquisition of the adjective 'modern' for itself is an integral part of the story of European imperialism within global history" (43). On the other hand, it cannot expel the other histories, other modernities, which leave traces even in its own texts and logics; see Chakrabarty's reading of history in Marx and his proposal of History2 as that which cannot be assimilated or reduced to the history of capital (chapter 2).

78. Simpson, "The State Is a Man."

79. Edelman, *No Future*, 30.

80. Edelman, "Ever After," 473.

81. Edelman, *No Future*, 76.

82. Muñoz, "Thinking Beyond Antirelationality and Antiutopianism in Queer Critique"; Winnubst, "Review Essay," 183. Similar arguments critique Edelman's and the antisocial thesis's narcissistic celebration of white gay male sexuality and sexual culture (Muñoz, *Cruising Utopia*, 14, 17; Rodríguez, "Queer Sociality and Other Sexual Fantasies") or their deliberate turn away from intersectionality in queer critique (Eng, *The Feeling of Kinship*, 34).

83. Winnubst, "Review Essay," 183.

84. Muñoz, *Cruising Utopia*, 94.

85. Muñoz, 95.

86. Muñoz, 94–95.

87. Kafer, *Feminist, Queer, Crip*, 31, original emphasis.

88. Kafer, 34.

89. Kafer, 33.

90. Muñoz, *Cruising Utopia*, 112, emphasis added.

91. Davis, "Reflections on the Black Woman's Role in the Community of Slaves," 116.

92. I am grateful to Jason Lydon for discussing these issues with me; the example of the struggle against chattel slavery is his.

93. Berlant and Warner, "What Does Queer Theory Teach Us About X?," 348.

94. The thesis of chapter 2, which demands that we read homosexuality as the concrete "cultural Figure" that symptomatizes futurism's disavowed and destructive jouissance (*No Future*, 39), makes this clear. Later, Edelman weakly defends his privileging of *male* homosexuality by saying he wants to avoid "the introduction of taxonomic distinctions" that might "dissipate the force of my larger argument against reproductive futurism" (166*n*10).

95. Reddy, *Freedom with Violence*, 175–176.

96. Cohen, "Punks, Bulldaggers, and Welfare Queens," 458. Cf. Aliyyah Abdur-Rahman, *Against the Closet*, chap. 1, and Dorothy Roberts's rehearsal of the stigmatizing taxonomy of futureless black womanhood: "A popular mythology promoted over centuries portrays Black women as unfit to bear and raise children. The sexually licentious Jezebel, the family-demolishing matriarch, the devious welfare queen, the depraved pregnant crack addict, accompanied by her equally monstrous crack baby—all paint a picture of a dangerous motherhood that must be regulated and punished. An unmarried Black woman represents the ultimate irresponsible mother—a woman who raises her children without the supervision of a man." Roberts, "Feminism, Race, and Adoption Policy," 45.

97. The manufactured anti-immigration election year discourse around so-called anchor babies comes readily to mind here; cf. Reddy, *Freedom with Violence*, 175–176 and, in particular, Andrea Ritchie's devastating documentation of police violence against black pregnant women and pregnant women of color in chapter 8 of *Invisible No More*, "Policing Motherhood."

98. Smith, "Queer Theory and Native Studies," 48.

99. Warren clearly rejects this version of queerness insofar as it obscures not only the anti-blackness constitutive of subjectivity and the social order, but also its own complicity with the humanist project premised upon the "onticide" of blacks. Although he cites Edelman as exemplary of this particular version of queerness in the earlier, online version of his argument, the reference disappears in the later, published version; see Warren, "Onticide: Afropessimism, Queer Theory, and Ethics," www.scribd.com/doc/252308869/calvin-warren-onticide-afropessimism-queer-theory-ethics-pdf (2015); and Warren, "Onticide: Afro-Pessimism, Gay Nigger #1, and Surplus Violence" (2017). Jared Sexton would reject my comparing blackness and indigeneity as somehow analogous or parallel axes of social oppression; see Sexton, "The *Vel* of Slavery." Meanwhile, Justin Leroy has recently argued ("Black History in Occupied Territory") against the "exceptionalism" that defines both Afro-pessimistic black studies and settler colonial studies, which he says obscures the historical fact that "Settler colonialism is a logic of indigenous erasure that has developed and sustained itself through anti-blackness. Anti-black racism, in turn, has overcome the setbacks of emancipation and the black freedom struggle by calling upon discourses of securitization and militarized occupation with roots in colonialism."

100. Halberstam, "The Anti-Social Turn in Queer Studies," 151; Halberstam, "Politics of Negativity in Recent Queer Theory," 824; Halberstam, *Queer Art of Failure*, 109.

101. Halberstam, *Queer Art of Failure*; and Halberstam, *In a Queer Time and Place*, esp. chap. 7.

102. Halberstam, *Queer Art of Failure*, 2–3.

103. Halberstam, 88.

104. Halberstam, 120–121.

105. It is difficult to know, however, what or which kind of failure is queer or worthy of praise in Halberstam's schema, especially given his repeated criticisms of Edelman's own work as a failure—as failing to be sufficiently political, failing to include women and lesbians in the analysis, and failing to be sufficiently open to critique (and all of these criticisms appear in virtually identical terms each in *Queer Art of Failure*, "Anti-Social Turn in Queer Studies," and "Politics of Negativity in Recent Queer Theory"). If Edelman's work is a failure in these ways, however, it is clearly not a good kind of failure or a queer failure. What kind of failure, then, might it be? As Nishant Shahani inquires, "Do failures always fail 'well' or fail successfully" for Halberstam? And, if not, "what causes some failures to be 'happy' and others to fail in their unhappiness (and unstylishness)?" Shahani, "The Future is Queer Stuff," 553.

106. Halberstam, *Queer Art of Failure*, 110; Halberstam, "Anti-Social Turn in Queer Studies," 154; Halberstam, "Politics of Negativity in Recent Queer Theory," 824.

107. Edelman, "Antagonism, Negativity, and the Subject," 822. In a different exchange, in response to Halberstam's caution against making a "new orthodoxy" out of negativity, Edelman replies wryly: "I am struck by the fact that nothing could be more orthodox than this warning against a new orthodoxy." Edelman, "Theorizing Queer Temporalities," 194.

108. Winnubst, *Queering Freedom*, 185. Winnubst's own call for a politics of no future predates *No Future* and so does not discuss or directly critique Edelman, although it is clear from this and subsequent writings that she rejects Edelman's position. Meanwhile, Brown seems almost to anticipate this critique in her eulogy for revolution, where she also describes the temporality of no future as "perverse": "If regimes of truth are inevitably totalitarian, what remains of emancipatory claims about the best way to order and govern human beings? How even to endeavor to transform the present, whatever totalitarian elements it might harbor, without tapping this danger? Perversely, this sensitivity to fundamentalism would seem to consign us to the present." Brown, "Feminism Unbound," 101.

109. Edelman, "Antagonism, Negativity, and the Subject," 822.

110. Berlant and Edelman, *Sex, or the Unbearable*, 29.

111. Nietzsche, *On the Genealogy of Morals*, 3:23, original emphasis.

112. I defend the controversial claim that Nietzsche can be seen as an intellectual forebear of queer theory in *Nietzsche's Revolution*; Rubin's iconic essay "Thinking Sex" is well established as having inaugurated the field.

113. The continuing relevance and usefulness of these charts as both a map of reigning social-sexual hierarchies and a pedagogical tool for political education are

demonstrated in Spade and Willse's reproduction of them in their article "Marriage Will Never Set Us Free" (2013).

114. Rubin, "Thinking Sex," 279.

115. Rubin, 283.

116. Rubin, 280.

117. Rubin, 282.

118. Rubin's broader argument in "Thinking Sex" is related to moral panics—she argues that at times of great political turmoil, social and political energies get redirected toward sex/uality in diversions from the actual issues at stake. A big part of the controversy of this essay was its suggestion that feminism was responsible for an emerging moral panic in the 1980s around, in particular, pornography and sadomasochism. Rubin suggested that antipornography and anti-SM feminism constituted "a very conservative sexual morality" (302) and, in a particularly memorable passage, criticized lesbian feminism by suggesting its alignment with the Catholic Church: "Sounding like the lesbian feminist Julia Penelope, His Holiness explained that 'considering anyone in a lustful way makes that person a sexual object rather than a human being worthy of dignity'" (298). This particular and important episode of the feminist sex wars suggests that queer theory emerges at least in part as a response to and rejection of a specifically left movement that, in and because of its moralism, became a conservative, even reactionary and oppressive force in women's lives. In this vein, see also Califia, "A Secret Side of Lesbian Sexuality"; Moraga and Hollibaugh, "What We're Rollin' Around in Bed With."

119. Butler, "Contingent Foundations," 39.

120. Butler, 41.

121. Rubin, "Thinking Sex," 293.

122. Rubin, 267.

123. Edelman, "Ever After," 469.

124. Edelman is explicit in his celebration of queer sexuality and/as deviance; Rubin, by contrast, purposefully uses the word *pervert* and simply divorces it from any negative connotation, thereby performing queer subversion in a subtler and only seemingly more neutral fashion: "I use the term 'pervert' as a shorthand for all the stigmatized sexual orientations. It used to cover male and female homosexuality as well but as these become less disreputable, the term has increasingly referred to other 'deviations.' Terms such as 'pervert' and 'deviant' have, in general use, a connotation of disapproval, disgust, and dislike. I am using these terms in a denotative fashion, and do not intend them to convey any disapproval on my part." Rubin, "Thinking Sex," 312. It is perhaps worth noting that *Deviations* is the title of the volume collecting Rubin's influential body of work and, as with "Thinking Sex," potentially suggests that rather more than merely denotative content may be found therein.

125. Edelman, *No Future*, 17.

126. Muñoz, *Cruising Utopia*, 27.

5. QUEER TERROR

1.   Netanyahu, *Fighting Terrorism*, xii (text of remarks delivered to the US Congress, September 20, 2001).

2.   Edelman, *No Future*, 3.

3.   Terminologically, homonationalism has developed beyond the original parameters set forth in *Terrorist Assemblages*, such that Puar now suggests it functions more broadly as a demarcator of modernity, neoliberalism, and the sovereign nation-state. On these developments, see Schotten, "Homonationalism." For an important qualification of homonationalism as specific to US Christian nationalist formations, one that cannot be generalized to European or other imperial projects, see Nichols, "Empire and the Dispositif of Queerness," 49–53. For an argument regarding the precarity of homonationalism even for those gays and lesbians "at the pinnacle of their inclusion" in the United States, see Chávez, "The Precariousness of Homonationalism," 34.

4.   Foucault, *History of Sexuality*, 1:144–145.

5.   Junaid Rana has argued that the racialization of Muslims is distinct within US projects of "racial becoming" insofar as Muslims are a race that is not one, a race of intractably identifiable and subordinate beings who nevertheless cannot be a race because they are a religion comprising people of variable phenotypes and national and ethnic origins, a race that "incorporates the portability of a number of race concepts, such as blackness, indigeneity, colonialism, genocide, immigration, and religion, in a system that appears contradictory and nonsensical." Rana, "The Racial Infrastructure of the Terror-Industrial Complex," 120. For two very different accounts of the US racialization of Islam after 9/11, see Bayoumi, *This Muslim American Life*, chap. 3 ("Racing Religion"), and Naber, "'Look, Mohammed the Terrorist is Coming!'" On the racialization of "the terrorist" as a conglomeration of "persons who appear 'Middle Eastern, Arab, or Muslim,'" see Volpp, "The Citizen and the Terrorist."

6.   As Rana makes clear, it is not necessary to say "Muslim" when one says "terrorist"; the equivalence is both implicit and presumed. Rana, "The Racial Infrastructure of the Terror-Industrial Complex," 111–112.

7.   Lisa Stampnitzky convincingly argues that "evil" is the defining contemporary mark of "terrorism" in her important study *Disciplining Terror*.

8.   In this sense, it is a premier example of what Silvia Posocco calls "wounded whiteness," an identificatory phenomenon through which subjects "make whiteness suddenly appear wounded," thereby "displacing the object and subject of racist aggression." Posocco, "(Decolonizing) the Ear of the Other," 259.

9.   See part 1 of the three-part investigative series by Alleen Brown, Will Parrish, and Alice Speri at *The Intercept*, "Leaked Documents Reveal Counterterrorism Tactics Used at Standing Rock to 'Defeat Pipeline Insurgencies,'" https://theintercept.com/2017/05/27/leaked-documents-reveal-security-firms-counterterrorism-tactics-at-standing-rock-to-defeat-pipeline-insurgencies/.

10. Abbas, "In Terror, in Love, out of Time," 505.

11. Naber, "Diasporas of Empire."

12. Naber, "'Look, Mohammed the Terrorist is Coming!,'" 278.

13. Abbas, "In Terror," 507.

14. See Stampnitzky, *Disciplining Terror*, upon which much of this section relies, as well as Kapitan, "The Terrorism of 'Terrorism'"; Jackson, "Knowledge, Power and Politics in the Study of Political Terrorism"; Brulin, "Compartmentalization, Context of Speech, and the Israeli Origins of the American Discourse on 'Terrorism'"; and Brulin, "Defining 'Terrorism.'" In addition to this definitional failure, Stampnitzky observes that "terrorism" expertise lacks both rigor and coherence: "terrorism experts have never consolidated control over the production of either experts or knowledge. New 'self-proclaimed' experts constantly emerge, no licensing body exists to certify 'proper' expertise, and there is no agreement among terrorism experts about what constitutes useful knowledge. In sociological terms, the boundaries of the field are weak and permeable. There is little regulation of who may become an expert, and the key audience for terrorism expertise is not an ideal-typical scientific community of other terrorism experts but, rather, the public and the state." Stampnitzky, *Disciplining Terror*, 12–13.

15. Naber, *Arab America*, 61; as Naber elsewhere observes, "the attacks of September 11, 2001 [were] a turning point, as opposed to the starting point, of histories of anti-Arab racism in the United States." Naber, "Introduction," 4. See also Mamdani, *Good Muslim, Bad Muslim*.

16. As with Holocaust Exceptionalism of the Agambian variety, however, it is just important to ask in the case of 9/11 for whom this event "changed everything"; the answer is indicative of the settler civilizationalism that values some forms of life as "life itself" and disregards others as not really lives at all or, when it does regard them, views them only as threats and annihilation. For more on the connection between 9/11 and the Holocaust in American cultural discourses of victimization, see Cole, *The Cult of Pure Victimhood*.

17. Stampnitzky, *Disciplining Terror*, 9.

18. See Gleason, *Totalitarianism*. This is, in rough outline, Hannah Arendt's argument in *The Origins of Totalitarianism*, and raises important if unexplored questions regarding the connections between Arendt's work and the postwar emergence of US neoconservatism and its battles with the New Left over communism, anticolonialism, Third-Worldism, and antiblack racism (on the latter, see also her *On Violence*, an explicit response to Sartre, Fanon, and black student protest in the United States). In his study of *Commentary* magazine, for example, Benjamin Balint argues that Hannah Arendt was crucial to providing the "theoretical foundation for hard anti-Communism" among neoconservatives, in particular via her theorization of totalitarianism. Balint, *Running Commentary*, 66–67. I would add that both Arendt's and the neoconservatives' focus on "terror" is a purposeful invocation of the French Revolution and part of their efforts to link left regimes and movements with dogmatism and murder.

19. Brulin, "Compartmentalization, Contexts of Speech, and the Israeli Origins of the American Discourse on 'Terrorism'"; Brulin, "Defining 'Terrorism'"; Collins, *Global Palestine*.

20. Brulin, "Compartmentalization, Contexts of Speech, and the Israeli Origins of the American Discourse on 'Terrorism'"; Said, "The Essential Terrorist."
21. Netanyahu, "Foreword."
22. Netanyahu, Preface to Opening Session on "The Face of Terrorism," 1.
23. Netanyahu, 1.
24. Netanyahu, 1.
25. Netanyahu, 1.
26. Netanyahu, "Chairman's Opening Remarks," 5.
27. Netanyahu, "Preface," 1.
28. Johnson, "Seven Deadly Sins of Terrorism," 15. The broader context of Johnson's remark is this: "When I say that terrorism is war against civilization, I may be met by the objection that terrorists are often idealists pursuing worthy aims—national or regional independence, and so forth. I do not accept this argument. I cannot agree that a terrorist can ever be an idealist, or that the objects sought can ever justify terrorism. The impact of terrorism, not simply on individual nations, but on humanity as a whole, is intrinsically evil, necessarily evil and wholly evil, and it is so for a number of demonstrable reasons." Those reasons are, as Johnson's title indicates, the "Seven Deadly Sins" of "terrorism."
29. Netanyahu, "Terrorism," 204.
30. Referencing not Netanyahu but the rhetoric of Donald Rumsfeld in justifying indefinite detention at Guantánamo Bay, Judith Butler writes: "When Secretary Rumsfeld was asked why these prisoners were being forcibly restrained and held without trial, he explained that if they were not restrained, they would kill again. He implied that the restraint is the only thing that keeps them from killing, that they are beings whose very propensity is to kill: that is what they would do as a matter of course. Are they pure killing machines? If they are pure killing machines, then they are not humans with cognitive function entitled to trials, to due process, to knowing and understanding a charge against them. They are something less than human, and yet—somehow—they assume a human form." Butler, *Precarious Life*, 73–74. Cf. Darryl Li's description of the "secular demonology" otherwise known as the literature on "jihadism": a "discourse on monsters who are actually human but whose monstrousness must nevertheless be reasserted." Li, "A Jihadism Anti-Primer."
31. Netanyahu, "Terrorists and Freedom Fighters," 29–30.
32. Brulin, "Compartmentalization, Contexts of Speech, and the Israeli Origins of the American Discourse on 'Terrorism.'" 93–98, 103–104; Stampnitzky, *Disciplining Terror*, 112–116.
33. The positive review of the book by John Gross in the *New York Times* makes clear its timeliness and persuasiveness, particularly in the wake of the United States' then-recent bombing of Libya.
34. Netanyahu, "Defining Terrorism," 14.
35. Netanyahu, 14.
36. Netanyahu, "Terrorism," 225.

37. See Derek Gregory's discussion of "America's Israel," formed through shared experiences of divinely inspired colonial settlement and influxes of Jewish refugees, and consolidated by the Islamification of "terrorism" and its elevation into a top foreign policy priority during the Reagan administration. Gregory, *Colonial Present*, 76–88.

38. Netanyahu, "Terrorism and the Islamic World," 61–62.

39. Netanyahu, "Terrorism and Totalitarianism," 39.

40. Kirkpatrick, "The Totalitarian Confusion," 56.

41. Netanyahu, "The International Network," 86.

42. Shultz, "The Challenge to the Democracies," 20.

43. Moynihan, "Terrorists, Totalitarians, and the Rule of Law," 41.

44. Netanyahu, "Defining Terrorism," 11–12.

45. Netanyahu, "Defining Terrorism," 12. The strong emergence of a neoconservative position in this analysis—anticommunism, antitotalitarianism, rejection of the New Left, moralized American exceptionalism, and prioritization of Israel in US foreign policy—much less the presence of the earlier generation of neocons at these conferences (for example, Moynihan, Kirkpatrick) suggests that the relationship of US neoconservatism with the formation of "terrorism" discourse is an area worthy of further study; see, for example, Haşimi, "Neoconservative Narrative as Globalising Islamophobia." On the rise (and fall) of the neoconservatives in relation to the George W. Bush administration and what has become known as the Bush Doctrine, see Heilbrunn, *They Knew They Were Right*, and Mann, *Rise of the Vulcans*. On the historical relationship of neoconservative intellectuals with US foreign policy more generally, see Ehrman, *The Rise of Neoconservatism*.

46. For a compelling read of the split introduced into the American Jewish Left by the state of Israel, the challenges leveled by black liberation's critique of Israel as a colonial project, and the subsequent emergence of neoconservatism's specifically racialized worldview, see Feldman, *A Shadow Over Palestine*; see also Heilbrunn, *They Knew They Were Right*, and Ehrman, *The Rise of Neoconservatism*. For an insider's account of the emergence of neoconservatism from the formerly Marxist and Jewish left, see Balint, *Running Commentary*.

47. www.washingtonpost.com/wp-srv/nation/specials/attacked/transcripts/bushaddress_092001.html. Note again the allusion to Nietzsche here in the invocation of "the will to power." The implication is that, like Nietzsche, "terrorists" are antimorality or somehow "beyond good and evil," a nihilism that the civilized world must necessarily reject.

48. Arendt recognized this weakness in her text and attempted to rectify it; the result was *The Human Condition*, which, along with her other lectures and writing on Marx, was originally planned to reveal what she called "Totalitarian Elements in Marxism." Not succeeding in this endeavor either, however, the result was that "her analysis of what it was about Marxism that contributed to totalitarianism was never explained in print." Canovan, *Hannah Arendt*, 64; see also Gleason, *Totalitarianism*, 112–113. Arendt also presents anti-Semitism as a premier element of totalitarian governments, yet this was

largely absent from Bolshevism. Wolin, "The Hannah Arendt Situation," 97–98. As even Balint concedes regarding "Islamo-fascism," "Needless to say, Islamism did not create concentration camps, nor did al-Qaeda—despite its yearnings for a caliphate—control a state apparatus. Nevertheless, Hannah Arendt had predicted that totalitarian tendencies would survive the death of totalitarian states. Certain members of the family now looked through the lens Arendt had fashioned to see more clearly how the new jihadism bore the marks of the totalitarian impulse." Balint, *Running Commentary*, 188.

49.   Midge Decter, "The Theory of Grievances." Along with Gertrude Himmelfarb (wife of Irving Kristol), Heilbrunn calls Decter (wife of Norman Podhoretz) one of the "matriarchs" of neoconservatism. Heilbrunn, *They Knew They Were Right*, 59, 75.

50.   Netanyahu, "Terrorism and the Islamic World," 63.

51.   Netanyahu, 62–63, original emphasis.

52.   Brulin, "Compartmentalization, Contexts of Speech, and the Israeli Origins of the American Discourse on 'Terrorism.' "

53.   Said, *Question of Palestine*, 37.

54.   Said, 37, original emphasis.

55.   Said, 29.

56.   On this cycle of rehabilitation and annihilation, see Zertal, *Israel's Holocaust and the Politics of Nationhood*, and Schotten, "Reading Nietzsche in the Wake of the 2008–09 War on Gaza."

57.   Haritaworn, Taquir, and Erdem, "Gay Imperialism," 81.

58.   See Nietzsche, *On the Genealogy of Morals*, and Schotten, "Reading Nietzsche in the Wake of the 2008–09 War on Gaza."

59.   Puar, *Terrorist Assemblages*, xxii.

60.   Puar, xiii.

61.   Foucault, *"Society Must Be Defended,"* 254.

62.   Puar, *Terrorist Assemblages*, xxv.

63.   Puar, 22.

64.   I am grateful to Lee Edelman for talking through the politics of queer exceptionalism with me.

65.   Puar, *Terrorist Assemblages*, 22, emphasis added.

66.   That these sorts of questions and confusions endure is, I think, part of the unresolved legacy of Judith Butler's *Gender Trouble*. In proposing a (frequently misconstrued) performative understanding of gender and suggesting that identity is not the precursor to politics but rather its site, *Gender Trouble* has often been taken as suggesting that political struggle can and should be waged at the *level* of identity—by cultivating transgressive desires or appearance, for example, or doing drag. But *Gender Trouble* does not offer any specific proposals regarding political action or the best way to think about political movements in the wake of its critique of identity and importantly ends by posing precisely this question. Hence, although it is technically correct that one takeaway of *Gender Trouble* is that "everything is political"—from sex to gender to hairstyle to sexual partner—this is very different from claiming that any particular sex or gender

or hairstyle or sexual partner is a form of political praxis, a claim that Butler does not make and that, I think Puar is rightly suggesting, is both theoretically incorrect and politically insufficient.

67. Ben-Moshe, Gossett, Mitchell, and Stanley, "Critical Theory, Queer Resistance, and the Ends of Capture," 267, original emphasis.

68. I am thinking of antics like Boston's Fag Rag Collective's banner in early Pride marches that declared, in black letters on pink taffeta, "PORNOGRAPHY, PROSTITUTION, PROMISCUITY, PEDERASTY!" (Hoffman, *An Army of Ex-Lovers*, 5) or Harvey Milk and the Lesbian Avengers' repeated public avowals that they "recruit." Or, as Deborah Gould relates, of the following ACT-UP protest in Atlanta:

> Five hundred activists from ACT UP chapters across the country demonstrated at the Georgia state capitol on the opening day of the legislature in 1990. Holding signs that read "Sodomy: the law is the perversion" and chanting "Suck my dick, lick my clit, sodomy laws are full of shit," demonstrators simulated sex acts as they blocked traffic. In response to the governor's description of the action as "repulsive," one demonstrator stated, "it was an audacious affirmation of lesbian and gay *sex*." (Gould, *Moving Politics*, 263, original emphasis)

All of these examples share (at least) two things: first, a commitment to the undoing of the social order in some deep and profound sense, itself named as the source of the queerness of queers; and, second, the suggestion that it is precisely through embodying and even typifying the very loathsomeness of queer life and practice that the social will be undone. Both the strategy and the message are the same: "Fuck you." And they are proffered in the name of nothing but that very loathsomeness itself, an embodiment of that which threatens to dismantle sociality as "we" know it.

69. Ben-Moshe, Gossett, Mitchell, and Stanley, "Critical Theory, Queer Resistance, and the Ends of Capture," 267. Stanley's remarks are a concise and fitting response to the recent special issue of *differences* "Queer Theory Without Antinormativity," the antipolitics of which I discuss in chapter 3, note 78.

70. Johnson, "Seven Deadly Sins of Terrorism," 12–13. In these same pages, Johnson notes that "It is almost impossible to exaggerate the threat which terrorism holds for our civilization."

71. Parts of this section have been adapted from Schotten, "Homonationalist Futurism."

72. Ali, Clifton, Duss, Fang, Keyes, and Shakir, *Fear, Inc.*

73. Five of the seven funders of the Islamophobia Network—the Scaife, Bradley, Becker, Berrie, and Fairbrook Foundations—are also significant funders of what the International Jewish Anti-Zionist Network (IJAN) calls "backlash," the coordinated and even more amply funded movement to silence or suppress criticism of Israel and Palestine solidarity activism on college campuses and communities across the United States. International Jewish Anti-Zionist Network, *The Business of Backlash*. CAP refuses to make any connection between these donors' simultaneous funding of the Islamophobia and backlash networks, even though, as this chapter has demonstrated, Islamophobia and Zionism are intimately and historically intertwined (Hatem Bazian notes that, despite the general

increase in academic study of Islamophobia, "one critical blind spot in research is the explicit link between pro-Israeli groups and organizations and the effort at demonization and otherization of Islam and Muslims in the United States and Europe with a focus on maintaining and consolidating support for Israel." Bazian, "The Islamophobia Industry and the Demonization of Palestine," 1057). IJAN does not shy away from this connection, however, much less its triangulation with US empire, laying bare the main harm of the backlash and Islamophobia Networks, which is not, as CAP puts it in their later report, "discrimination against American Muslims in the forms of racial profiling and occasionally even violence" (Duss, Taeb, Gude, and Sofer, *Fear, Inc. 2.0*, 54), but rather the crushing of peoples' movements: "The elite funders whom we identify in this paper have ideological and financial investments that benefit from support for Israel, and the promotion of anti-Arab and anti-Muslim racism. But it is not a surprise that they also fund a whole host of other reactionary causes such as climate change denialism, war, and the destruction of public services. Many of their investments benefit from all these great harms and injustices that social movements in the United States and internationally are working to stop. Thus, they have a shared interest in stopping such movements." International Jewish Anti-Zionist Network, *Business of Backlash*, 16.

74. Bayoumi, *This Muslim American Life*, 161.
75. Said, *Covering Islam*, 5.
76. Sayyid, "Out of the Devil's Dictionary," 15–16.
77. www.youtube.com/watch?v=8fSvyvourTE.
78. CAP cites Horowitz and his well-funded David Horowitz Freedom Center, which hosts a slew of websites and online magazines (for example, *FrontPage Magazine, Jihad Watch*) as Islamophobia "popularizers" and "the primary movers of anti-Muslim messages and myths" along with Pamela Geller and her blog, *Atlas Shrugs*. Geller was largely responsible for the virulent protest movement against Park51, an Islamic community center that was never built in downtown New York City, which she successfully dubbed the "Ground Zero Mosque." Ali, Clifton, Duss, Fang, Keyes, and Shakir, *Fear, Inc.*, 85–89. In 2012, Geller attracted renewed attention for her poster campaign in public transportation systems in Washington, DC, San Francisco, New York City, and Portland, OR, that said, "In any war between the civilized man and the savage, support the civilized man. Support Israel. Defeat Jihad."
79. This claim is one of Horowitz's pet theses; he regularly claims that US Muslim organizations—campus MSAs in particular—are founded, if not funded, by the Muslim Brotherhood. It is a more specific version of the larger, vaguer claim made by other members of the Islamophobia Network that the Muslim Brotherhood (or, more simply, Muslim Americans) are infiltrating the government and attempting to impose Sharia law—frequently described as "totalitarian"—on the United States. The student's question of evidence is a good one, then, since there effectively is none to back Horowitz's claim here, although this has not stopped him from repeating it across the country, both in person and in print.

80. Similarly, in "The Forgotten '-ism,'" Nadine Naber, Eman Desouky, and Lina Baroudi point out that merely identifying oneself as Palestinian is taken to be a political act by US audiences. The complex reasons for this are made explicit in this video. As Said notes, "Until today [that is, 1979], it is a striking fact that merely to mention the Palestinians or Palestine in Israel, or to a convinced Zionist, is to name the unnameable, so powerfully does our bare existence serve to accuse Israel of what it did to us." Said, *Question of Palestine*, xliii.

81. This is another hobbyhorse of both the Islamophobia Network and many right-wing Zionists, although the evidence for it is mixed. Not only is it unclear if Hassan Nasrallah said this but, if he did, it's unclear what he meant by it. Omar Baddar thinks the quotation is real, but lacking proper contextualization. He writes, "The speech in question doesn't seem to be available through Hezbollah's official media site (www .almanar.com.lb/), or any reliable outlet. After a fairly extensive search, I also couldn't find video of the speech anywhere (not even YouTube). All of this introduces a sliver of doubt into any conclusions that could be drawn about the quote. Nonetheless, I'm pretty familiar with Nasrallah's voice, and the audio clip used by Tablet Magazine's Yair Rosenberg (www.youtube.com/watch?v=oTFAnCPUpjU) sounds authentic. I also cross-checked that audio clip against an Arabic transcript of the speech that was posted on a random blog in 2002 (http://bahrainonline.org/showthread.php?t=44416), so my judgment is that the quote is real." Baddar then supplies what he calls the "missing context" of the quotation: "In this speech, Nasrallah was discussing end-of-times prophecies in different religious traditions. He starts with how religious Jews see the end of times and how they're preparing for the battle of Armageddon. After that he moves to Christian Zionism and discusses their apocalyptic vision for Israel and end times. Then he moves on to the Muslim version of the end of days with the now infamous quote (my translation): 'Among the signs . . . [stops to add a disclaimer]. But when I say this is one of the signs it doesn't mean we should gather the Jews and let them rule Palestine. But one of the signs that guide us and point us [to the end of times] says yes: It is in Islamic prophecies and not just Jewish prophecies for that country [Israel] to be established, and for the Jews to gather from all over the world in occupied Palestine; but not so that their false messiah would rule the world, but because God wants to spare you having to go to them all over the world, so they'll gather in one place, and that's when the final, conclusive battle will happen.'" Not only does the context Baddar supplies here seem relevant, but so, too, does the fact that, in his questioning, Horowitz has moved from asking about Albahri about Hamas to asking about Hezbollah, perhaps on the assumption that, since both are "terrorist" groups (or both Arab, or both Muslim), both must advocate and believe the same things. Finally, regarding Nasrallah himself, Baddar adds, "Nasrallah is inconsistent: Sometimes talks about 'the Jews,' and other times he makes an explicit distinction between Jews and Zionists." Omar Baddar, personal communication.

82. https://fortruthforjustice.wordpress.com/2010/05/16/ucsd-muslim-student-responds -to-david-horowitz-event/.

83. www.youtube.com/watch?v=PgeeXlLyKvM.

84. CAP identifies Jasser as one of "a select group of individuals who claim inside knowledge about the realities of radical Islam" who "has emerged as the Muslim validator for Islamophobia propaganda" and notes that he "lacks any policy or academic expertise." Ali, Clifton, Duss, Fang, Keyes, and Shakir, *Fear, Inc.*, 56. His organization, AIFD, appears to have no members aside from himself, its founder. Jasser narrated the Clarion Fund film *The Third Jihad*, which argues that Islam is threatening and infiltrating the United States and was shown as a training video to almost fifteen hundred New York City police officers.

85. CAP ranks Fox News and particular of its anchors, including Hannity and, previously, Bill O'Reilly and Glenn Beck, with the David Horowitz Freedom Center as equivalent media purveyors of Islamophobia and popularizers of Islamophobic "expert" misinformation. Ali, Clifton, Duss, Fang, Keyes, and Shakir, *Fear, Inc.*, 97–98.

86. Some scholars attempt to normalize "terrorism" by subjecting it to rational choice methodology, thereby rendering "terrorist" activity no different from, say, saving for retirement or deciding whom to vote for in an election. This more liberal approach nevertheless obscures—and thus perpetuates—the futurist fundaments of settler sovereignty by assimilating even "terrorists" to the rationality of its "civilization." It is marginally less racist insofar as it attempts to include Muslims and "terrorists" within the domain of rationality, an inclusive gesture that attributes signature Enlightenment values to otherwise "savage" figures. As with Hobbes, however, it is not that Islamophobes or political scientists have somehow failed to grasp the rational character of "terrorism." It is rather that "rationality" is another term for "civilized" and thus applies only to those behaviors comprehensible to a similarly "civilized" adjudicator. Were "terrorism" to become successfully definable or explicable within the terms of European rationality, the "savage" would become civilized, the "terrorist" delinked from nihilism and evil, and Muslims newly thinkable as lives worthy of protection. This would effectively admit "terrorism" into the domain of the political as a possible position within the futurist, biopolitical order, an admission that would either neutralize the meaning of "terrorism" (via assimilation) or destroy that very social order as such (via revolution) (my preference is clearly for the latter). Notably, despite acknowledging the ways that necropolitics "reconfigure[s] the relations among resistance, sacrifice, and terror," Achille Mbembe nevertheless accommodates the "terrorist" to this rational choice version of futurism, declaring that the suicide bomber as martyr evidences "the desire for eternity" and "can be seen as laboring under the sign of the future": "The besieged body becomes a piece of metal whose function is, through sacrifice, to bring eternal life into being." Mbembe, "Necropolitics," 39, 37.

87. Human Rights Watch, *Illusion of Justice*, 13.

88. Human Rights Watch, 1.

89. Hage, "'Comes a Time We Are All Enthusiasm,'" 72.

90. Bayoumi, *This Muslim American Life*; Center for Human Rights and Global Justice, Asian American Legal Defense and Education Fund, *Under the Radar*; Cincotta, *Manufacturing the Muslim Menace*.

91. Palestine Legal and the Center for Constitutional Rights, *The Palestine Exception to Free Speech*.

92. Apuzzo and Goldman, *Enemies Within*.

93. Ali, Clifton, Duss, Fang, Keyes, and Shakir, *Fear, Inc.*, 8.

94. Ali, Clifton, Duss, Fang, Keyes, and Shakir, 125.

95. Ali, Clifton, Duss, Fang, Keyes, and Shakir, 8. CAP is apparently in favor of the FBI's notoriously failed program of enlisting Muslims as informants, a program that has ruined the lives of both those who comply with and those who refuse its demands to serve the US government and entrap "terrorist" "suspects." See Human Rights Watch, *Illusion of Justice*.

96. Duss, Taeb, Gude, and Sofer, *Fear, Inc. 2.0*, 25.

97. Ali, Clifton, Duss, Fang, Keyes, and Shakir, *Fear, Inc.*, 126.

98. Duss, Taeb, Gude, and Sofer, *Fear, Inc. 2.0*, 18.

99. Duss, Taeb, Gude, and Sofer, 3.

100. Duss, Taeb, Gude, and Sofer, 2.

101. Bayoumi, *This Muslim American Life*, 136.

102. This occurs throughout the text but see, for example, Bayoumi, *This Muslim American Life*, 127.

103. Bayoumi, *This Muslim American Life*, 146.

104. Bayoumi, 122.

105. Bayoumi, 10.

106. Ali, Clifton, Duss, Fang, Keyes, and Shakir, *Fear, Inc.*, 125.

107. Duss, Taeb, Gude, and Sofer, *Fear, Inc. 2.0*, 53.

108. For example, the importance of distinguishing between "radical" or "fundamentalist" Islam and "moderate" or regular Islam in order to more accurately isolate the enemy is thematic in the work of Daniel Pipes, founder of the Middle East Forum, one of the key organizations of the Islamophobia Network. For a concise statement of this thesis, see, for example, Pipes, "Who Is the Enemy?" For a more recent suggestion from Pipes that "moderate" Muslims must be an internal counter or "reformation" in Islamism, see Pipes, "Can Islam Be Reformed?" (all of Pipes's writings are available for free online at the Middle East Forum, www.danielpipes.org).

109. Bayoumi, *This Muslim American Life*, 13.

110. Bayoumi, 13.

111. Ali, Clifton, Duss, Fang, Keyes, and Shakir, *Fear, Inc.*, 6.

112. Arun Kundnani critiques the uptake of this discourse by left (not liberal) commentators, who he argues advance Islamophobia by critiquing "Islamism": "The distinction between Islam and Islamism is important, for it insulates this discourse from straightforward charges of Islamophobia. . . . Whereas the neoconservatives see Muslims en masse as inherently anti-modern, the new liberals see individual Muslims as choosing the wrong kind of modern politics. Whereas the former talk of a clash of civilisations, the latter talk of a clash within civilisations between extremists and moderates, enlisting Muslims or ex-Muslims, such as Ed Husain and Ayaan Hirsi Ali, in support of their agenda." Kundnani, "Islamism and the Roots of Liberal Rage," 42. Kundnani focuses

on British writers Martin Amis, Andrew Anthony, Nick Cohen, Michael Gove, and Christopher Hitchens; for an American version of this pseudo-left discourse, see Michael Walzer's concerns about "Islamic zealotry" in his "Islamism and the Left."

113. www.youtube.com/watch?v=jqPbM7WGSIQ.
114. Bayoumi, *This Muslim American Life*, 101.
115. Pappé, "Genocide in Gaza." Operation Protective Edge served only to confirm this thesis, as Pappé wrote in a follow-up article, "Israel's Incremental Genocide in the Gaza Ghetto."
116. Breaking the Silence, *This is How We Fought in Gaza*.
117. Breaking the Silence.
118. Salaita (@stevesalaita), "You may be too refined to say it, but I'm not: I wish all the fucking West Bank settlers would go missing," Twitter, June 19, 2014, 6:59 PM, https://twitter.com/stevesalaita/status/479805591401922561?lang=en.
119. www.youtube.com/watch?v=EHXCq8thQJo.
120. See also Salaita, *Inter/Nationalism*.
121. Hage, "'Comes a Time We Are All Enthusiasm,'" 72n16.
122. Salaita, *Uncivil Rites*, 18.
123. A Google image search will yield multiple photos of this mural; one is here: www.flickr.com/photos/14490658@N08/1470254026/.
124. Abunimah, *One Country*, 50; cf. Shehadeh, *The Third Way*.
125. Morgensen, "Settler Homonationalism," 117.
126. See, for example, White, *Palestinians in Israel*, chap. 3.
127. Abunimah, Keynote Address. As Israeli then-parliamentarian and now-Minister of Justice Ayelet Shaked wrote on her Facebook page during Israel's war on Gaza in 2014, "it's best to eliminate the Palestinians entirely," including the "mothers of the martyrs, who send [their children] to hell with flowers and kisses" because, if they are not killed, these women will give birth to more "little snakes" (original Facebook post is archived here: https://archive.is/zWrrG; translation is provided in Ben Norton, "Netanyahu Appoints Ayelet Shaked—Who Called for Genocide of Palestinians—as Justice Minister in new government," Mondoweiss, May 6, 2015, http://mondoweiss.net/2015/05/netanyahu-palestinians-government/.
128. Edelman, *No Future*, 31, emphasis added.

BIBLIOGRAPHY

Abbas, Asma. "In Terror, in Love, Out of Time." In *At the Limits of Justice: Women of Color on Terror*, edited by Suvendrini Perera and Sherene Razack. Toronto: University of Toronto Press, 2014.

Abdur-Rahman, Aliyyah. *Against the Closet: Black Political Longing and the Erotics of Race*. Durham: Duke University Press, 2012.

Abunimah, Ali. Keynote Address, Penn BDS Conference, University of Pennsylvania (February 4, 2012).

——. *One Country: A Bold Proposal to End the Israeli-Palestinian Impasse*. New York: Metropolitan, 2006.

Agamben, Giorgio. *Homo Sacer: Sovereign Power and Bare Life*. Translated by Daniel Heller-Roazen. Stanford: Stanford University Press, 1998.

——. *Means Without End: Notes on Politics*. Translated by Vincenzo Binette and Cesare Casarino. Minneapolis: University of Minnesota Press, 2000.

——. "No to Bio-Political Tattooing." *Le Monde Diplomatique*, January 10, 2004.

——. *Remnants of Auschwitz: The Witness and the Archive*. Translated by Daniel Heller-Roazen. New York: Zone, 2002.

——. "Security and Terror." Translated by Caroline Emcke. *Theory and Event* 5, no. 4 (2002).

——. *State of Exception*. Translated by Kevin Attell. Chicago: University of Chicago Press, 2005.

——. "The Work of Man." Translated by Kevin Attell. In *Giorgio Agamben: Sovereignty and Life*, edited by Matthew Calarco and Steven DeCaroli. Stanford: Stanford University Press, 2007.

Ali, Wahajat, and Eli Clifton, Matthew Duss, Lee Fang, Scott Keyes, and Faiz Shakir. *Fear, Inc.: The Roots of the Islamophobia Network in America*. Washington, DC: Center for American Progress, 2011.

Amin, Kadji. "Haunted by the 1990s: Queer Theory's Affective Histories." *WSQ: Women's Studies Quarterly* 44, nos. 3–4 (Fall/Winter 2016): 173–189.

Anderson, Perry. *American Foreign Policy and Its Thinkers*. New York: Verso, 2015.

Anonymous. "Queers Gone Wild." *bædan: journal of queer nihilism* 1 (2012): 57–93.

Apuzzo, Matt, and Adam Goldman. *Enemies Within: Inside the NYPD's Secret Spying Unit and bin Laden's Final Plot Against America*. New York: Touchstone, 2013.

Arendt, Hannah. *The Human Condition*. Chicago: University of Chicago Press, 1958.

——. *On Revolution*. 1963; New York: Penguin, 2006.

——. *On Violence*. Orlando: Harcourt, 1970.

——. *The Origins of Totalitarianism*. New York: Harcourt Brace, 1973.

Aristotle. *Politics*. Translated by C. D. C. Reeve. Indianapolis: Hackett, 1998.

Atkinson, David. "Encountering Bare Life in Italian Libya and Colonial Amnesia in Agamben." In *Agamben and Colonialism*, edited by Marcelo Svirsky and Simone Bignall. Edinburgh: Edinburgh University Press, 2012.

Austin, J. L. *How to Do Things with Words*. Cambridge: Harvard University Press, 1975.

Azoulay, Ariella, and Adi Ophir. "Abandoning Gaza." In *Agamben and Colonialism*, edited by Marcelo Svirsky and Simone Bignall. Edinburgh: Edinburgh University Press, 2012.

Balint, Benjamin. *Running Commentary: The Contentious Magazine That Transformed the Jewish Left Into the Neoconservative Right*. New York: Public Affairs, 2010.

Bargu, Banu. "Sovereignty as Erasure: Rethinking Enforced Disappearances." *Qui Parle* 23, no. 1 (Fall/Winter 2014): 35–75.

Barker, Joanne. "For Whom Sovereignty Matters." In *Sovereignty Matters: Locations of Contestation and Possibility in Indigenous Struggles for Self-Determination*, edited by Joanne Barker. Lincoln: University of Nebraska Press, 2005.

Bayoumi, Moustafa. *This Muslim American Life: Dispatches from the War on Terror*. New York: New York University Press, 2015.

Bazian, Hatem. "The Islamophobia Industry and the Demonization of Palestine: Implications for American Studies." *American Quarterly* 67, no. 4 (December 2015): 1057–1066.

Benjamin, Walter. "Theses on the Philosophy of History." In *Illuminations*, edited by Hannah Arendt, translated by Harry Zohn. New York: Schocken, 1968.

Ben-Moshe, Liat, Che Gossett, Nick Mitchell, and Eric A. Stanley. "Critical Theory, Queer Resistance, and the Ends of Capture." In *Death and Other Penalties*, edited by Geoffrey Adelsberg, Lisa Guenther, and Scott Zeman. New York: Fordham University Press, 2015.

Berlant, Lauren. *Cruel Optimism*. Durham: Duke University Press, 2011.

Berlant, Lauren, and Lee Edelman. "Reading, Sex, and the Unbearable: A Response to Tim Dean." *American Literary History* 27, no. 3 (2015): 625–629.

——. *Sex, or the Unbearable*. Durham: Duke University Press, 2014.

Berlant, Lauren, and Michael Warner. "Sex in Public." *Critical Inquiry* 24, no. 2 (Winter 1988): 547–566.

——. "What Does Queer Theory Teach Us About X?" *PMLA* 110, no. 3 (May 1995): 343–349.

Bersani, Leo. *Homos*. Cambridge: Harvard University Press, 1995.

——. "Is the Rectum a Grave?" In *AIDS: Cultural Analysis, Cultural Activism*, edited by Douglas Crimp. Cambridge: MIT Press, 1988.

——. "Shame on You." In *After Sex? On Writing Since Queer Theory*, edited by Janet Halley and Andrew Parker. Durham: Duke University Press, 2011.

Bignall, Simone. "Potential Postcoloniality: Sacred Life, Profanation and the Coming Community." In *Agamben and Colonialism*, edited by Marcelo Svirsky and Simone Bignall. Edinburgh: Edinburgh University Press, 2012.

Bignall, Simone, and Marcelo Svirsky. "Introduction: Agamben and Colonialism." In *Agamben and Colonialism*, edited by Marcelo Svirsky and Simone Bignall. Edinburgh: Edinburgh University Press, 2012.

Bordo, Susan. *Unbearable Weight: Feminism, Western Culture, and the Body*. Berkeley: University of California Press, 1993.

Bornstein, Kate. *Gender Outlaw: On Men, Women, and the Rest of Us*. New York: Vintage, 1994.

Braun, Kathrin. "Biopolitics and Temporality in Arendt and Foucault." *Time and Society* 16, no. 1 (2007): 5–23.

Breaking the Silence. *This Is How We Fought in Gaza: Soldiers' Testimonies and Photographs from Operation "Protective Edge."* Jerusalem: Breaking the Silence, 2014.

Brenkman, John. "Politics, Mortal and Natal: An Arendtian Rejoinder." *Narrative* 10, no. 2 (May 2002): 186–192.

——."Queer Post-Politics." *Narrative* 10, no. 2 (May 2002): 174–180.

Brown, Alleen, Will Parrish, and Alice Speri. "Leaked Documents Reveal Counterterrorism Tactics Used at Standing Rock to 'Defeat Pipeline Insurgencies.'" *Intercept* (May 27, 2017). https://theintercept.com/2017/05/27/leaked-documents-reveal-security-firms-counter terrorism-tactics-at-standing-rock-to-defeat-pipeline-insurgencies/.

Brown, Wendy. "Feminism Unbound: Revolution, Mourning, Politics." In *Edgework: Critical Essays on Knowledge and Politics*. Princeton: Princeton University Press, 2005.

——. *Manhood and Politics: A Feminist Reading in Political Theory*. Totowa, NJ: Rowman and Littlefield, 1988.

Brulin, Rémi. "Compartmentalization, Contexts of Speech, and the Israeli Origins of the American Discourse on 'Terrorism.'" *Dialectical Anthropology* 39, no. 1 (2015): 69–119.

——. "Defining 'Terrorism': The 1972 General Assembly Debates on 'International Terrorism' and Their Coverage by the *New York Times*." In *If It Was Not for Terrorism: Crisis, Compromise, and Elite Discourse in the Age of War on Terror*, edited by Banu Baybars-Hawks and Lemi Baruh. Newcastle upon Tyne: Cambridge Scholars, 2011.

Bruyneel, Kevin. *The Third Space of Sovereignty: The Postcolonial Politics of U.S.-Indigenous Relations*. Minneapolis: University of Minnesota Press, 2007.

Butler, Judith. "Contingent Foundations." In *Feminist Contentions: A Philosophical Exchange*, edited by Linda Nicholson. New York: Routledge, 1995.

——. *Frames of War*. London: Verso, 2010.

——. *Gender Trouble: Feminism and the Subversion of Identity*. New York: Routledge, 1990.

——. "Imitation and Gender Subordination." In *Inside/Out: Lesbian Theories, Gay Theories*, edited by Diana Fuss. New York: Routledge, 1991.

——. *Precarious Life: The Powers of Mourning and Violence*. London: Verso, 2006.

——. "Revisiting Bodies and Pleasures." *Theory, Culture, and Society* 16, no. 11 (April 1999).

——. *Undoing Gender*. New York: Routledge, 2004.

Byrd, Jodi. *The Transit of Empire: Indigenous Critiques of Colonialism*. Minneapolis: University of Minnesota Press, 2011.

Califia, P. "A Secret Side of Lesbian Sexuality." In *Public Sex: The Culture of Radical Sex*, 2nd ed. 1979; San Francisco: Cleis, 2000.

Canovan, Margaret. *Hannah Arendt: A Reinterpretation of Her Political Thought*. Cambridge: Cambridge University Press, 1994.

——. "Hannah Arendt as a Conservative Thinker." In *Hannah Arendt: Twenty Years Later*, edited by Larry May and Jerome Kohn. Cambridge: MIT Press, 1997.

Caserio, Robert. "The Antisocial Thesis in Queer Theory," In "Conference Debates: The Antisocial Thesis in Queer Theory," special issue, *PMLA* 121, no. 3 (2006).

Center for Human Rights and Global Justice, Asian American Legal Defense and Education Fund. *Under the Radar: Muslims Deported, Detained, and Denied on Unsubstantiated Terrorism Allegations*. New York: New York University School of Law, 2011.

Césaire, Aimé. *Discourse on Colonialism*. Translated by Joan Pinkham. 1955; New York: Monthly Review Press, 2000.

Chakrabarty, Dipesh. *Provincializing Europe: Postcolonial Thought and Historical Difference*. Princeton: Princeton University Press, 2000.

Chávez, Karma. "The Precariousness of Homonationalism: The Queer Agency of Terrorism in Post-9/11 Rhetoric." *QED: A Journal in GLBTQ Worldmaking* 2, no. 3 (Fall 2015): 32–58.

Chomsky, Noam. "The Responsibility of Intellectuals." *New York Review of Books*, February 23, 1967.

Chomsky, Noam, and Michael Foucault. *The Chomsky-Foucault Debate on Human Nature*. 1971; New York: New Press, 2006.

Cincotta, Thomas. *Manufacturing the Muslim Menace: Private Firms, Public Servants, and the Threat to Rights and Security*. Somerville, MA: Political Research Associates, 2011.

Cohen, Cathy. "Punks, Bulldaggers, and Welfare Queens: The Radical Potential of Queer Politics?" *GLQ: A Journal of Lesbian and Gay Studies* 3 (1997): 437–465.

Cole, Alyson. *The Cult of Pure Victimhood: From the War on Welfare to the War on Terror*. Stanford: Stanford University Press, 2007.

Collins, John. *Global Palestine*. London: Hurst, 2011.

Connolly, William. "A Critique of Pure Politics." *Philosophy and Social Criticism* 23, no. 5 (September 1997).

——. *Political Theory and Modernity*. New York: Basil Blackwell, 1988.

Cornell, Drucilla, and Stephen D. Seely. "There's Nothing Revolutionary About a Blowjob." *Social Text* 32, no. 2 (Summer 2014): 1–24.

Coulthard, Glen. *Red Skins, White Masks: Rejecting the Colonial Politics of Recognition*. Minneapolis: University of Minnesota Press, 2014.

Crimp, Douglas. "How to Have Promiscuity in an Epidemic." In *AIDS: Cultural Analysis, Cultural Activism*, edited by Douglas Crimp. Cambridge: MIT Press, 1988.

Cruikshank, Barbara. *The Will to Empower: Democratic Citizenship and Other Subjects*. Ithaca: Cornell University Press, 1999.

Darkmatter: In the Ruins of Imperial Culture. Issue 3, "Racism in the Closet: Interrogating Postcolonial Sexuality." 2008. www.darkmatter101.org/site/category/issues/3-post-colonial-sexuality/.

Davis, Angela. "Reflections on the Black Woman's Role in the Community of Slaves." In *The Angela Y. Davis Reader*, edited by Joy James. 1972; Malden, MA: Blackwell, 1998.

Day, Iyko. "Being or Nothingness: Indigeneity, Antiblackness, and Settler Colonial Critique." *CES: Journal of the Critical Ethnic Studies Association* 1, no. 2 (Fall 2015): 102–121.

Dean, Tim. "The Antisocial Homosexual." In "Conference Debates: The Antisocial Thesis in Queer Theory," special issue, *PMLA* 121, no. 3 (2006).

——. "Bareback Time." In *Queer Times, Queer Becomings*, edited by E. L. McCallum and Mikko Tuhkanen. Albany: State University of New York Press, 2001.

——. "Clear and Sonorous: A Reply to Lauren Berlant and Lee Edelman." *American Literary History* 27, no. 3 (2015): 630–633.

——. "An Impossible Embrace: Queerness, Futurity, and the Death Drive." In *A Time for the Humanities: Futurity and the Limits of Autonomy*, edited by James J. Bono, Tim Dean, and Ewa Płonowska Ziarek. New York: Fordham University Press, 2008.

——. "No Sex Please, We're American." *American Literary History* 27, no. 3 (2015): 614–624.

——. *Unlimited Intimacy: Reflections on the Subculture of Barebacking.* Chicago: University of Chicago Press, 2009.

Decter, Midge. "The Theory of Grievances." In *Terrorism: How the West Can Win*, edited by Benjamin Netanyahu. New York: Avon, 1986.

de la Durantaye, Leland. "The Paradigm of Colonialism." In *Agamben and Colonialism*, edited by Marcelo Svirsky and Simone Bignall. Edinburgh: Edinburgh University Press, 2012.

de Lauretis, Teresa. "Gender Symptoms, or, Peeing Like a Man." *Social Semiotics* 9, no. 3 (1999): 257–270.

——. "Queer Texts, Bad Habits, and the Issue of a Future." *GLQ: A Journal of Lesbian and Gay Studies* 17, nos. 2–3 (2011).

——. "Queer Theory: Lesbian and Gay Sexualities, An Introduction." *GLQ: A Journal of Lesbian and Gay Studies* 3, no. 2 (1991): iiv–xviii.

D'Emilio, John. "Capitalism and Gay Identity." In *Powers of Desire: The Politics of Sexuality*, edited by Ann Snitow, Christine Stansell, and Sharan Thompson. New York: Monthly Review Press, 1983.

Deutscher, Penelope. "The Inversion of Exceptionality: Foucault, Agamben, and 'Reproductive Rights.'" *South Atlantic Quarterly* 107, no. 1 (Winter 2008).

Dietz, Mary. "Feminist Receptions of Arendt." In *Feminist Interpretations of Hannah Arendt*, edited by Bonnie Honig. University Park: Pennsylvania State University Press, 1995.

Dillon, Michael. "Cared to Death: The Biopoliticised Time of Your Life." *Foucault Studies* 2 (May 2005): 37–46.

Dinshaw, Carolyn, Lee Edelman, Roderick A. Ferguson, Carla Freccero, Elizabeth Freeman, Judith Halberstam, Annamarie Jagose, Christopher S. Nealon, and Tan Hoang Nguyen. "Theorizing Queer Temporalities: A Roundtable Discussion." *GLQ: A Journal of Lesbian and Gay Studies* 13, no. 2 (2007): 177–195.

Dubreuil, Laurent. "Leaving Politics: *Bios, Zoē*, Life." *diacritics* 36, no. 2 (Summer 2006): 83–98.

Duggan, Lisa. "Atlas Shrugging: The Impossible Queer Desire of Ayn Rand." Keynote Address, 2nd Annual International Feminist Journal of Politics Conference, "(Im)possibly Queer International Feminisms," University of Sussex, May 17, 2013.

——. "Making It Perfectly Queer." *Socialist Review* 22, no. 1 (January–March 1992): 11–31.

Duss, Matthew, and Yasmine Taeb, Ken Gude, and Ken Sofer. *Fear, Inc. 2.0: The Islamophobia Network's Efforts to Manufacture Hate in America.* Washington, DC: Center for American Progress, 2015.

Edelman, Lee. "Against Survival: Queerness in a Time That's Out of Joint." *Shakespeare Quarterly* 62, no. 2 (Summer 2011): 148–169.

——. "Antagonism, Negativity, and the Subject of Queer Theory." In "Conference Debates: The Antisocial Thesis in Queer Theory," special issue, *PMLA* 121, no. 3 (2006): 821–823.

——. "Ever After: History, Negativity, and the Social." *South Atlantic Quarterly* 106, no. 3 (Summer 2007): 469–476.

——. *Homographesis: Essays in Gay Literary and Cultural Theory.* New York: Routledge, 1994.

——. *No Future: Queer Theory and the Death Drive.* Durham: Duke University Press, 2004.

——. "Post-Partum." *Narrative* 10, no. 2 (May 2002).

——. "Theorizing Queer Temporalities: A Roundtable Discussion." *GLQ: A Journal of Lesbian and Gay Studies* 13 (2007): 2–3.

Ehrman, John. *The Rise of Neoconservatism: Intellectuals and Foreign Affairs, 1945–1994.* New Haven: Yale University Press, 1995.

Eng, David. *The Feeling of Kinship: Queer Liberalism and the Racialization of Intimacy.* Durham: Duke University Press, 2010.

Eng, David, J. Halberstam, and José Esteban Muñoz, eds. "What's Queer About Queer Studies Now?" Special issue, *Social Text* 23, nos. 3–4 (Winter 2005).

Fanon, Frantz. *Black Skin, White Masks.* Translated by Charles Lam Markmann. New York: Grove, 1967.

Feldman, Keith. *A Shadow Over Palestine: The Imperial Life of Race in America.* Minneapolis: University of Minnesota Press, 2015.

Finlayson, James Gordon. "'Bare Life' and Politics in Agamben's Reading of Aristotle." *Review of Politics* 72 (2010): 97–126.

Floyd, Kevin. "The Importance of Being Childish: Queer Utopians and Historical Contradiction." *Works and Days* 30, nos. 1–2 (2012): 323–338.

——. *The Reification of Desire: Toward a Queer Marxism.* Minneapolis: University of Minnesota Press, 2009.

Foucault, Michel. *The Birth of Biopolitics: Lectures at the Collège de France, 1978–1979.* Translated by Graham Burchell. New York: Palgrave, 2008.

——. *Discipline and Punish: The Birth of the Prison.* Translated by Alan Sheridan. New York: Vintage, 1977.

——. "The End of the Monarchy of Sex." In *Foucault Live: Collected Interviews, 1961–1984,* edited by Sylvère Lotringer. New York: Semiotext(e), 1989.

——. "The Ethics of the Concern for Self as a Practice of Freedom." In *Ethics: Subjectivity and Truth,* edited by Paul Rabinow. New York: New Press, 1997.

——. *The History of Sexuality,* vol. 1, *An Introduction.* Translated by Robert Hurley. New York: Vintage, 1978.

——. "Intellectuals and Power." In *Foucault Live: Collected Interviews, 1961–1984,* edited by Sylvère Lotringer. New York: Semiotext(e), 1989.

——. "Interview with Michel Foucault." In *Power: Essential Works of Foucault, 1954–1984*, edited by Paul Rabinow. New York: Norton, 2000.

——. "Nietzsche, Genealogy, History." In *Aesthetics, Method, and Epistemology: Essential Works of Foucault, 1954–1984*, edited by James Faubion. New York: New Press, 1998.

——. "Practicing Criticism." Translated by Alan Sheridan. In *Politics, Philosophy, Culture: Interviews and Other Writings, 1977–1984*, edited by Lawrence Kritzman. New York: Routledge, 1988.

——. "Questions of Method." In *Power: Essential Works of Foucault, 1954–1984*, edited by Paul Rabinow. New York: Norton, 2000.

——. *Security, Territory, Population: Lectures at the Collège de France, 1977–1978*. Translated by Graham Burchell. New York: Palgrave, 2007.

——. *"Society Must Be Defended": Lectures at the Collège de France, 1975–1976*. Translated by David Macey. New York: Picador, 2003.

——. "The Subject and Power." In *Power: Essential Works of Michel Foucault, 1954–1984*, edited by James Faubion. New York: New Press, 1994.

Freccero, Carla. "Fuck the Future." *GLQ: A Journal of Lesbian and Gay Studies* 12, no. 2 (2006): 332–334.

Gatens, Moira. *Imaginary Bodies: Ethics, Power and Corporeality*. New York: Routledge, 1995.

Gilman, Sander. "Black Bodies, White Bodies: Toward an Iconography of Female Sexuality in Late Nineteenth-Century Art, Medicine, and Literature." *Critical Inquiry* 12 (Autumn 1985).

Gines, Kathryn. *Hannah Arendt and the Negro Question*. Bloomington: University of Indiana Press, 2014.

Gleason, Abbott. *Totalitarianism: The Inner History of the Cold War*. New York: Oxford University Press, 1995.

Goldstein, Alyosha, ed. *Formations of United States Colonialism*. Durham: Duke University Press, 2014.

——. "Introduction: Toward a Genealogy of the U.S. Colonial Present." In *Formations of United States Colonialism*, edited by Alyosha Goldstein. Durham: Duke University Press, 2014.

Gould, Deborah. *Moving Politics: Emotion and ACT UP's Fight Against AIDS*. Chicago: University of Chicago Press, 2009.

Gregory, Derek. *The Colonial Present: Afghanistan, Palestine, Iraq*. Malden, MA: Blackwell, 2004.

Hage, Ghassan. "'Comes a Time We Are All Enthusiasm': Understanding Palestinian Suicide Bombers in Times of Exighophobia." *Public Culture* 15, no. 1 (2003): 65–89.

Halberstam, J. "The Anti-Social Turn in Queer Studies." *Graduate Journal of Social Science* 5, no. 2 (2008): 140–156.

——. *In a Queer Time and Place*. New York: New York University Press, 2005.

——. "The Politics of Negativity in Recent Queer Theory." In "Conference Debates: The Antisocial Thesis in Queer Theory," special issue, *PMLA* 121, no. 3 (2006): 823–824.

——. *The Queer Art of Failure*. Durham: Duke University Press, 2011.

Halperin, David. "The Normalization of Queer Theory." *Journal of Homosexuality* 45, nos. 2–4 (2013): 339–343.

Haritaworn, Jin, Adi Kuntsman, and Silvia Posocco, eds. "Introduction." In *Queer Necropolitics*, edited by Jin Haritaworn, Adi Kuntsman, and Silvia Posocco. New York: Routledge, 2014.

——. *Queer Necropolitics*. New York: Routledge, 2014.

Haritaworn, Jin, Tamsila Tauqir, and Esma Erdem. "Gay Imperialism: Gender and Sexuality Discourse in the 'War on Terror.'" In *Out of Place: Interrogating Silences in Queerness/Raciality*, edited by Adi Kuntsman and Esperanza Miyake. York, UK: Raw Nerve, 2008.

Hartsock, Nancy. "Foucault on Power: A Theory for Women?" In *Feminism/Postmodernism*, edited by Linda Nicholson. New York: Routledge, 1990.

Haşimi, Cemalettin. "Neoconservative Narrative as Globalising Islamophobia." In *Thinking Through Islamophobia: Global Perspectives*, edited by S. Sayyid and AbdoolKarim Vakil. London: Hurst, 2010.

Heilbrunn, Jacob. *They Knew They Were Right: The Rise of the Neocons*. New York: Anchor, 2008.

Heiner, Brady. "Foucault and the Black Panthers." *City* 11, no. 3 (December 2007): 313–356.

Hennessy, Rosemary. *Profit and Pleasure: Sexual Identities in Late Capitalism*. New York: Routledge, 2000.

——. "Queer Theory, Left Politics." *Rethinking Marxism* 17, no. 3 (1994): 85–111.

Hobbes, Thomas. *Leviathan*. Edited by Richard Tuck. 1651; Cambridge: Cambridge University Press, 1996.

Hoffman, Amy. *An Army of Ex-Lovers: My Life at the Gay Community News*. Amherst: University of Massachusetts Press, 2007.

Hoffman, Marcelo. *Foucault and Power: The Influence of Political Engagement on Theories of Power*. New York: Bloomsbury, 2014.

Hong, Grace Kyungwon. *Death Beyond Disavowal: The Impossible Politics of Difference*. Minneapolis: University of Minnesota Press, 2015.

Huffer, Lynne. *Mad for Foucault: Rethinking the Foundations of Queer Theory*. New York: Columbia University Press, 2010.

Human Rights Watch. *Illusion of Justice: Human Rights Abuses in US Terrorism Prosecutions*. New York: Human Rights Institute at Columbia Law School, 2014.

International Jewish Anti-Zionist Network. *The Business of Backlash: The Attack on the Palestinian Movement and Other Movements for Justice*. March 2015. www.ijan.org/resources/business-of-backlash/.

Jackson, Richard. "Knowledge, Power and Politics in the Study of Political Terrorism." In *Critical Terrorism Studies: A New Research Agenda*, edited by Richard Jackson, Marie Breen Smyth, and Jeroen Gunning. New York: Routledge, 2009.

Jagose, Annamarie. *Queer Theory: An Introduction*. New York: New York University Press, 1997.

——. "The Trouble with Antinormativity." In "Queer Theory Without Antinormativity," edited by Robyn Wiegman and Elizabeth A. Wilson, special issue, *differences: A Journal of Feminist Cultural Studies* 26, no. 1 (May 2015): 26–47.

Jamal, Amaney, and Nadine Naber, eds. *Race and Arab Americans Before and After 9/11: From Invisible Citizens to Visible Subjects*. Syracuse: Syracuse University Press, 2008.

Jarvis, Jill. "Remnants of Muslims: Reading Agamben's Silence." *New Literary History* 45, no. 5 (Autumn 2014): 707–728.

Johnson, E. Patrick, and Mae G. Henderson, eds. *Black Queer Studies: A Critical Anthology.* Durham: Duke University Press, 2005.

Johnson, Paul. "The Seven Deadly Sins of Terrorism." In *International Terrorism: Challenge and Response,* edited by Benjamin Netanyahu. New Brunswick, NJ: Transaction, 1986.

Jung, Moon-Kie. "Constituting the U.S. Empire-State and White Supremacy: The Early Years." In *State of White Supremacy: Racism, Governance, and the United States,* edited by Moon-Kie Jung, João Costa Vargas, and Eduardo Bonilla-Silva. Stanford: Stanford University Press, 2011.

Kafer, Alison. *Feminist, Queer, Crip.* Bloomington: Indiana University Press, 2013.

Kalyvas, Andreas. "The Sovereign Weaver: Beyond the Camp." In *Politics, Metaphysics, and Death: Essays on Giorgio Agamben's* Homo Sacer, edited by Andrew Norris. Durham: Duke University Press, 2005.

Kapitan, Tomis. "The Terrorism of 'Terrorism.' " In *Terrorism and International Justice,* edited by James Sterba. New York: Oxford University Press, 2003.

Katz, Jonathan Ned. *The Invention of Heterosexuality.* New York: Plume, 1995.

Kauanui, J. Kēhaulani. *Hawaiian Blood: Colonialism and the Politics of Sovereignty and Indigeneity.* Durham: Duke University Press, 2008.

Kirkpatrick, Jeane. "The Totalitarian Confusion." In *Terrorism: How the West Can Win,* edited by Benjamin Netanyahu. New York: Avon, 1986.

Klausen, Jimmy Casas. "Hannah Arendt's Antiprimitivism." *Political Theory* 38, no. 8 (June 2010): 394–423.

Koopman, Colin. "Two Uses of Michel Foucault in Political Theory: Concepts and Methods in Giorgio Agamben and Ian Hacking." *Constellations* 22, no. 4 (2015): 571–585.

Kundnani, Arun. "Islamism and the Roots of Liberal Rage." *Race and Class* 50, no. 2 (2008): 40–68.

Kuntsman, Adi. "The Soldier and the Terrorist: Sexy Nationalism, Queer Violence." *Sexualities* 11, nos. 1–2 (2008): 142–170.

Kurnaz, Murat. *Five Years of My Life: An Innocent Man in Guantanamo.* New York: St. Martin's, 2007.

LaCapra, Dominick. "Approaching Limit Events: Siting Agamben." In *Giorgio Agamben: Sovereignty and Life,* edited by Matthew Calarco and Steven DeCaroli. Stanford: Stanford University Press, 2007.

Laclau, Ernesto. "Bare Life or Social Indeterminacy?" In *Giorgio Agamben: Sovereignty and Life,* edited by Matthew Calarco and Steven DeCaroli. Stanford: Stanford University Press, 2007.

Lemke, Thomas. "Foucault, Governmentality, and Critique." *Rethinking Marxism: A Journal of Economics, Culture, and Society* 14, no. 3 (Fall 2002): 49–64.

——. " 'A Zone of Indistinction': A Critique of Giorgio Agamben's Concept of Biopolitics." *Outlines: Critical Practice Studies* 7, no. 1 (2005).

Leroy, Justin. "Black History in Occupied Territory: On the Entanglements of Slavery and Settler Colonialism." *Theory and Event* 19, no. 4 (2016).

Li, Darryl. "A Jihadism Anti-Primer." *Middle East Research and Information Project.* Fall 2015. www.merip.org/mer/mer276/jihadism-anti-primer.

Love, Heather. *Feeling Backward: Loss and the Politics of Queer History.* Cambridge: Harvard University Press, 2009.

Lubin, Alex. " 'We Are All Israelis': The Politics of Colonial Comparisons." In *Settler Colonialism,* edited by Alyosha Goldstein and Alex Lubin, special issue, *South Atlantic Quarterly* 107, no. 4 (Fall 2008): 671–690.

Lyon, Janet. *Manifestoes: Provocations of the Modern.* Ithaca: Cornell University Press, 1999.

Mamdani, Mahmoud. *Good Muslim, Bad Muslim: America, the Cold War, and the Roots of Terror.* New York: Pantheon, 2004.

Mann, James. *Rise of the Vulcans: The History of Bush's War Cabinet.* New York: Penguin, 2004.

Marcus, Sharon. "Queer Theory for Everyone: A Review Essay." *Signs* 31, no. 1 (Autumn 2005): 191–218.

Marx, Karl. "Estranged Labor." In *The Economic and Philosophic Manuscripts of 1844,* translated by Martin Milligan. 1844; Amherst, NY: Prometheus, 1988.

Mbembe, Achille. "Necropolitics." *Public Culture* 15, no. 1 (2003): 11–40.

McWhorter, Ladelle. *Bodies and Pleasures: Foucault and the Politics of Sexual Normalization.* Bloomington: Indiana University Press, 1999.

Mills, Charles. *The Racial Contract.* Ithaca: Cornell University Press, 1997.

Mirzoeff, Nicholas. "Invisible Empire: Visual Culture, Embodied Spectacle, and Abu Ghraib." *Radical History Review* 95 (Spring 2006): 21–44.

Moraga, Cherríe, and Amber Hollibaugh. "What We're Rollin' Around in Bed With: Sexual Silences in Feminism, a Conversation Toward Ending Them." In *The Persistent Desire: A Femme-Butch Reader,* edited by Joan Nestle. Boston: Alyson, 1992.

Morgensen, Scott Lauria. "The Biopolitics of Settler Colonialism: Right Here, Right Now." *Settler Colonial Studies* 1, no. 1 (2011): 52–76.

——. "Settler Homonationalism: Theorizing Settler Colonialism Within Queer Modernities." *GLQ: A Journal of Lesbian and Gay Studies* 16, nos. 1–2 (2010).

——. "Theorising Gender, Sexuality and Settler Colonialism: An Introduction." *Settler Colonial Studies* 2, no. 2 (2012): 2–22.

Morton, Stephen. "Reading Kenya's Colonial State of Emergency After Agamben." In *Agamben and Colonialism.* Edinburgh: Edinburgh University Press, 2012.

Moynihan, Daniel Patrick. "Terrorists, Totalitarians, and the Rule of Law." In *Terrorism: How the West Can Win,* edited by Benjamin Netanyahu, 41–43. New York: Avon, 1986.

Muñoz, José Esteban. *Cruising Utopia: The Then and There of Queer Futurity.* New York: New York University Press, 2009.

——. *Disidentifications: Queers of Color and the Performance of Politics.* Minneapolis: University of Minnesota Press, 1999.

——. "Thinking Beyond Antirelationality and Antiutopianism in Queer Critique." In "Conference Debates: The Antisocial Thesis in Queer Theory," special issue, *PMLA* 121, no. 3 (2006).

Mutimer, David. "Sovereign Contradictions: Maher Arar and the Indefinite Future." In *The Logics of Biopower and the War on Terror: Living, Dying, Surviving*, edited by Cristina Masters and Elizabeth Dauphinée. New York: Palgrave, 2006.

Naber, Nadine. *Arab America: Gender, Cultural Politics, and Activism*. New York: New York University Press, 2012.

——. "Diasporas of Empire: Arab Americans and the Reverberations of War." In *At the Limits of Justice: Women of Color on Terror*, edited by Suvendrini Perera and Sherene Razack. Toronto: University of Toronto Press, 2014.

——. "Introduction: Arab Americans and U.S. Racial Formations." In *Race and Arab Americans Before and After 9/11: From Invisible Citizens to Visible Subjects*, edited by Amaney Jamal and Nadine Naber. Syracuse: Syracuse University Press, 2008.

——. "'Look, Mohammed the Terrorist Is Coming!': Cultural Racism, Nation-Based Racism, and the Intersectionality of Oppressions After 9/11." In *Race and Arab Americans Before and After 9/11: From Invisible Citizens to Visible Subjects*, edited by Amaney Jamal and Nadine Naber. Syracuse: Syracuse University Press, 2008.

Naber, Nadine, and Eman Desouky and Lina Baroudi. "The Forgotten '-ism': An Arab-American Women's Perspective on Zionism, Racism, and Sexism." In *Color of Violence: the INCITE! Anthology*, edited by INCITE! Women of Color Against Violence. Cambridge: South End, 2006.

Nealon, Jeffrey T. *Foucault Beyond Foucault: Power and Its Intensifications Since 1984*. Stanford: Stanford University Press, 2008.

Nehamas, Alexander. "Nietzsche and 'Hitler.'" *Southern Journal of Philosophy* 37, no. 1 (1999).

Netanyahu, Benjamin. "Defining Terrorism." In *Terrorism: How the West Can Win*, edited by Benjamin Netanyahu, 7–15. New York: Avon, 1986.

——. *Fighting Terrorism: How Democracies Can Defeat the International Terrorist Network*. New York: Farrar, Straus and Giroux, 2001.

——. "Foreword." In *International Terrorism: Challenge and Response*, edited by Benjamin Netanyahu. New Brunswick, NJ: Transaction, 1981.

——. "The International Network." In *Terrorism: How the West Can Win*, edited by Benjamin Netanyahu, 85–86. New York: Avon, 1986.

——, ed. *International Terrorism: Challenge and Response*. New Brunswick, NJ: Transaction, 1981.

——. Preface to Opening Session on "The Face of Terrorism." In *International Terrorism: Challenge and Response*. New Brunswick, NJ: Transaction, 1981.

——, ed. *Terrorism: How the West Can Win*. New York: Avon, 1986.

——. "Terrorism: How the West Can Win." In *Terrorism: How the West Can Win*, edited by Benjamin Netanyahu, 199–206. New York: Avon, 1986.

——. "Terrorism and the Islamic World." In *Terrorism: How the West Can Win*, edited by Benjamin Netanyahu, 61–63. New York: Avon, 1986.

——. "Terrorism and Totalitarianism." In *Terrorism: How the West Can Win*, edited by Benjamin Netanyahu, 39–40. New York: Avon, 1986.

Netanyahu, Benzion. "Chairman's Opening Remarks." In *International Terrorism: Challenge and Response*, edited by Benjamin Netanyahu, 3–7. New Brunswick, NJ: Transaction, 1981.

———. "Terrorists and Freedom Fighters." In *Terrorism: How the West Can Win*, edited by Benjamin Netanyahu, 25–30. New York: Avon, 1986.

Nichols, Robert. "The Colonialism of Incarceration." *Radical Philosophy Review* 17, no. 2 (2012): 435–455.

———. "Contract and Usurpation: Enfranchisement and Racial Governance in Settler-Colonial Contexts." In *Theorizing Native Studies*, edited by Audra Simpson and Andrea Smith. Durham: Duke University Press, 2014.

———. "Empire and the Dispositif of Queerness." *Foucault Studies* 14 (September 2012): 41–60.

———. "Realizing the Social Contract: The Case of Colonialism and Indigenous Peoples." *Contemporary Political Theory* 4 (2005).

———. "Theft Is Property! The Recursive Logic of Dispossession." *Political Theory*, April 2, 2017. DOI: 10.1177/0090591717701709.

Nietzsche, Friedrich. *Beyond Good and Evil: Prelude to a Philosophy of the Future*. Translated by Walter Kaufmann. 1886; New York: Vintage, 1989.

———. *On the Genealogy of Morals: A Polemic*. Translated by Walter Kaufmann. 1887; New York: Vintage, 1967.

———. *Twilight of the Idols, or How One Philosophizes with a Hammer*. In *The Portable Nietzsche*, translated and edited by Walter Kaufmann. 1888; New York: Penguin, 1968.

Norton, Anne. "Heart of Darkness: Africa and African Americans in the Writings of Hannah Arendt." In *Feminist Interpretations of Hannah Arendt*, edited by Bonnie Honig. University Park: Pennsylvania State University Press, 1995.

Nyong'o, Tavia. "Do You Want Queer Theory (or Do You Want the Truth)? Intersections of Punk and Queer in the 1970s." *Radical History Review* 100 (Winter 2008).

O'Brien, Jean. *Firsting and Lasting: Writing Indians Out of Existence in New England*. Minneapolis: University of Minnesota Press, 2010.

Palestine Legal and the Center for Constitutional Rights. *The Palestine Exception to Free Speech: A Movement Under Attack in the US*. September 2015. http://palestinelegal.org/the-palestine-exception.

Pappé, Ilan. "Genocide in Gaza." *Electronic Intifada* (September 2, 2006). https://electronicintifada.net/content/genocide-gaza/6397.

———. "Israel's Incremental Genocide in the Gaza Ghetto." *Electronic Intifada* (July 13, 2014). https://electronicintifada.net/content/israels-incremental-genocide-gaza-ghetto/13562.

Patterson, Orlando. *Slavery and Social Death: A Comparative Study*. Cambridge: Harvard University Press, 1982.

Penney, James. *After Queer Theory: The Limits of Sexual Politics*. New York: Palgrave, 2014.

Pipes, Daniel. "Can Islam Be Reformed?" *Commentary* (July/August 2013).

———. "Who Is the Enemy?" *Commentary* (January 2002).

Pitkin, Hannah. *The Attack of the Blob: Hannah Arendt's Concept of the Social*. Chicago: University of Chicago Press, 1998.

Posocco, Silvia. "(Decolonizing) the Ear of the Other: Subjectivity, Ethics and Politics in Question." In *Decolonizing Sexualities: Transnational Perspectives, Critical Interventions*, edited by Sandeep Bakshi, Suhraiya Jivraj, and Silvia Posocco. Oxford: Counterpress, 2016.

Puar, Jasbir. "'I Would Rather Be a Cyborg Than a Goddess': Becoming-Intersectional in Assemblage Theory." *PhiloSOPHIA: A Journal of Feminist Philosophy* 2, no. 1 (2012): 49–66.

——. "Prognosis Time: Towards a Geopolitics of Affect, Debility and Capacity." *Women and Performance: A Journal of Feminist Theory* 19, no. 2 (July 2009).

——. *Terrorist Assemblages: Homonationalism in Queer Times.* Durham: Duke University Press, 2007.

Puar, Jasbir, and Amit Rai. "Monster, Terrorist, Fag: The War on Terrorism and the Production of Docile Patriots." *Social Text* 20, no. 3 (Fall 2002).

Puchner, Martin. *Poetry of the Revolution: Marx, Manifestos, and the Avant-Gardes.* Princeton: Princeton University Press, 2006.

Rana, Junaid. "The Racial Infrastructure of the Terror-Industrial Complex." *Social Text* 34, no. 4 (December 2016): 111–138.

Rand, Erin J. *Reclaiming Queer: Activist and Academic Rhetorics of Resistance.* Tuscaloosa: University of Alabama Press, 2014.

Reddy, Chandan. *Freedom with Violence: Race, Sexuality, and the U.S. State.* Durham: Duke University Press, 2011.

Rifkin, Mark. "Indigenising Agamben: Rethinking Sovereignty in Light of the 'Peculiar' Status of Native Peoples." In *Agamben and Colonialism*, edited by Marcelo Svirsky and Simone Bignall. Edinburgh: Edinburgh University Press, 2012.

——. "Making Peoples Into Populations: The Racial Limits of Tribal Sovereignty." In *Theorizing Native Studies*, edited by Audra Simpson and Andrea Smith. Durham: Duke University Press, 2014.

Ritchie, Andrea. *Invisible No More: Police Violence Against Black Women and Women of Color.* Boston: Beacon, 2017.

Roach, Tom. *Friendship as a Way of Life: Foucault, AIDS, and the Politics of Shared Estrangement.* Albany: State University of New York Press, 2012.

——. "Sense and Sexuality: Foucault, Wojnarowicz, and Biopower." *Nebula* 6, no. 3 (September 2009): 155–174.

Roberts, Dorothy. "Feminism, Race, and Adoption Policy." In *Color of Violence: The INCITE! Anthology*, edited by INCITE! Women of Color Against Violence. Cambridge: South End, 2006.

Robin, Corey. *The Reactionary Mind: Conservatism from Edmund Burke to Sarah Palin.* Oxford: Oxford University Press, 2011.

Rodríguez, Juana María. "Queer Sociality and Other Sexual Fantasies." *GLQ: A Journal of Lesbian and Gay Studies* 17, nos. 2–3 (2011).

Rosenberg, Jordy, and Amy Villarejo, eds. "Queer Studies and the Crises of Capitalism," special issue, *GLQ: A Journal of Lesbian and Gay Studies* 18, no. 1 (2012).

Ross, Alison. Introduction to special issue of *South Atlantic Quarterly: The Agamben Effect*, edited by Alison Ross, 107, no. 1 (2008).

Ross, Marlon B. "Beyond the Closet as a Raceless Paradigm." In *Black Queer Studies*, edited by E. Patrick Johnson and Mae G. Henderson, 161–189. Durham: Duke University Press, 2005.

Rubin, Gayle. *Deviations: The Gayle Rubin Reader*. Durham: Duke University Press, 2011.

——. "Thinking Sex: Notes for a Radical Theory of the Politics of Sexuality." In *Pleasure and Danger: Exploring Female Sexuality*, edited by Carole Vance, 267–319. Boston: Routledge, 1984.

Said, Edward. *Covering Islam: How the Media and the Experts Determine How We See the Rest of the World*. New York: Vintage, 1997.

——. "The Essential Terrorist." In *Blaming the Victims: Spurious Scholarship and the Palestinian Question*, edited by Edward Said and Christopher Hitchens. 1984; London: Verso, 2001.

——. *Orientalism*. New York: Vintage, 1979.

——. *The Question of Palestine*. 1979; New York: Vintage, 1992.

Salaita, Steven. *Inter/Nationalism: Decolonizing Native America and Palestine*. Minneapolis: University of Minnesota Press, 2016.

——. *Uncivil Rites: Palestine and the Limits of Academic Freedom*. Chicago: Haymarket, 2015.

Sawicki, Jana. *Disciplining Foucault: Feminism, Power, and the Body*. New York: Routledge, 1991.

Sayyid, S. "Out of the Devil's Dictionary." In *Thinking Through Islamophobia: Global Perspectives*, edited by S. Sayyid and AbdoolKarim Vakil. London: Hurst, 2010.

Schmitt, Carl. *Political Theology*. Translated by George Schwab. Chicago: University of Chicago Press, 1985.

Schotten, C. Heike. "Against Totalitarianism: Foucault, Agamben, and the Politics of Critique." *Foucault Studies* 20 (October 2015).

——. "*Ecrasez l'infâme!* Nietzsche's Revolution for All and (N)one." In *Nietzsche's* Ecce Homo, edited by Duncan Large and Nicholas Martin. Berlin: Walter de Gruyter, forthcoming.

——. "Homonationalism: From Critique to Diagnosis, or, We Are All Homonational Now." *International Feminist Journal of Politics* 18, no. 3 (2016).

——. "Homonationalist Futurism: 'Terrorism' and (Other) Queer Resistance to Empire." *New Political Science: A Journal of Politics and Culture* 37, no. 1 (March 2015).

——. *Nietzsche's Revolution: Décadence, Politics, and Sexuality*. New York: Palgrave, 2009.

——. "Reading Nietzsche in the Wake of the 2008–09 War on Gaza." In *The Digital Dionysus: Nietzsche and the Network-Centric Condition*, edited by Dan Mellamphy and Nandita Biswas Mellamphy. Brooklyn: Punctum, 2016.

Scott, James C. *Domination and the Arts of Resistance: Hidden Transcripts*. New Haven: Yale University Press, 1990.

——. *Weapons of the Weak: Everyday Forms of Peasant Resistance*. New Haven: Yale University Press, 1987.

Sedgwick, Eve Kosofsky. *Epistemology of the Closet*. Berkeley: University of California Press, 1991.

——. *Tendencies*. Durham: Duke University Press, 1993.

Sexton, Jared. *Amalgamation Schemes: Antiblackness and the Critique of Multiracialism*. Minneapolis: University of Minnesota Press, 2008.

——. "People-of-Color-Blindness: Notes on the Afterlife of Slavery." *Social Text* 8, no. 2 (Summer 2010): 31–56.

——. "The *Vel* of Slavery: Tracking the Figure of the Unsovereign." *Critical Sociology* (2014): 1–15.

Sexton, Jared, and Huey Copeland. "Raw Life: An Introduction." *Qui Parle* (Spring/Summer 2003): 53–62.

Shahani, Nishant. "The Future Is Queer Stuff: Critical Utopianism and Its Discontents." *GLQ: A Journal of Lesbian and Gay Studies* 19, no. 4 (2013): 545–558.

Shakhsari, Sima. "Killing Me Softly with Your Rights: Queer Death and the Politics of Rightful Killing." In *Queer Necropolitics*, edited by Jin Haritaworn, Adi Kuntsman, and Silvia Posocco. New York: Routledge, 2014.

Shehadeh, Raja. *The Third Way: A Journal of Life in the West Bank*. London: Quartet, 1982.

Shenhav, Yehouda. "Imperialism, Exceptionalism, and the Contemporary World." In *Agamben and Colonialism*, edited by Marcelo Svirsky and Simone Bignall. Edinburgh: Edinburgh University Press, 2012.

Shenhav, Yehouda, and Yael Berda. "The Colonial Foundations of the State of Exception: Juxtaposing the Israeli Occupation of the Palestinian Territories with Colonial Bureaucratic History." In *The Power of Inclusive Exclusion: Anatomy of Israeli Rule in the Occupied Palestinian Territories*. London: Zone, 2009.

Sheth, Falguni. *Toward a Political Philosophy of Race*. Albany: State University of New York Press, 2009.

Shultz, George. "The Challenge to the Democracies." In *Terrorism: How the West Can Win*, edited by Benjamin Netanyahu. New York: Avon, 1986.

Silliman, Stephen. "The 'Old West' in the Middle East: U.S. Military Metaphors in Real and Imagined Indian Country." *American Anthropologist* 110, no. 2 (2008): 237–247.

Simpson, Audra. *Mohawk Interruptus: Political Life Across the Borders of Settler States*. Durham: Duke University Press, 2014.

——. "The State Is a Man: Theresa Spence, Loretta Saunders and the Gender of Settler Sovereignty." *Theory and Event* 19, no. 4 (2016).

Slahi, Mohamedou Ould. *Guantánamo Diary*. Edited by Larry Siems. New York: Little, Brown, 2015.

Smith, Andrea. "American Studies Without America: Native Feminisms and the Nation-State." *American Quarterly* 60, no. 2 (June 2008): 309–315.

——. "Queer Theory and Native Studies: The Heteronormativity of Settler Colonialism." *GLQ: A Journal of Lesbian and Gay Studies* 16, nos. 1–2 (2010): 41–68.

Smith, Andrea, and J. Kēhaulani Kauanui. "Native Feminisms Engage American Studies." *American Quarterly* 60, no. 2 (June 2008): 241–249.

Snediker, Michael. "Queer Optimism." *Postmodern Culture* 16, no. 3 (2006).

Somerville, Siobhan. "Scientific Racism and the Invention of the Homosexual Body." In *Queering the Color Line: Race and the Invention of Homosexuality in American Culture*. Durham: Duke University Press, 2000.

Spade, Dean, and Craig Willse. "Marriage Will Never Set Us Free." *Organizing Upgrade: Engaging Left Organizers in Strategic Dialogue* (September 6, 2013). www.organizingupgrade.com/index.php/modules-menu/beyond-capitalism/item/1002-marriage-will-never-set-us-free.

Spivak, Gayatri Chakravorty. "Can the Subaltern Speak?" In *Marxism and the Interpretation of Culture*, edited by Cary Nelson and Lawrence Grossberg, 271–313. Urbana: University of Illinois Press, 1988.

Stampnitzky, Lisa. *Disciplining Terror: How Experts Invented "Terrorism."* Cambridge: Cambridge University Press, 2013.

Stanley, Eric. "Near Life, Queer Death: Overkill and Ontological Capture." *Social Text* 29, no. 2 (Summer 2011): 1–19.

Stepan, Nancy Leys. "Race and Gender: The Role of Analogy in Science." In *Anatomy of Racism*, edited by David Theo Goldberg. Minneapolis: University of Minnesota Press, 1990.

Stoler, Ann Laura. *Race and the Education of Desire: Foucault's* History of Sexuality *and the Colonial Order of Things*. Durham: Duke University Press, 1995.

Svirsky, Marcelo. "The Cultural Politics of Exception." In *Agamben and Colonialism*. Edinburgh: Edinburgh University Press, 2012.

Svirsky, Marcelo, and Simone Bignall, eds. *Agamben and Colonialism*. Edinburgh: Edinburgh University Press, 2012.

Tadiar, Neferti. "Decolonization, 'Race,' and Remaindered Life Under Empire." *Qui Parle* 23, no. 2 (Spring/Summer 2015): 135–160.

Taylor, Dianna. "Normativity and Normalization." *Foucault Studies* 7 (September 2009).

Thobani, Sunera. "Empire, Bare Life and the Constitution of Whiteness: Sovereignty in an Age of Terror." *borderlands* 11, no. 1 (2012): 1–30.

Veracini, Lorenzo. "Introducing *Settler Colonial Studies*." *Settler Colonial Studies* 1, no. 1 (2011): 1–12.

——. *Settler Colonialism: A Theoretical Overview*. New York: Palgrave Macmillan, 2012.

——. *The Settler Colonial Present*. New York: Palgrave Macmillan, 2015.

Volpp, Leti. "The Citizen and the Terrorist." *UCLA Law Review* (June 2002): 1575–1599.

Walzer, Michael. "Islamism and the Left." *Dissent* (Winter 2015). www.dissentmagazine.org /article/islamism-and-the-left.

Warner, Michael. "Introduction." In *Fear of a Queer Planet: Queer Politics and Social Theory*, edited by Michael Warner. Minneapolis: University of Minnesota Press, 1993.

——. "Queer and Then: The End of Queer Theory?" *Chronicle of Higher Education* (January 1, 2012). http://chronicle.com/article/QueerThen-/130161/.

Warren, Calvin. "Black Nihilism and the Politics of Hope." *CR: The New Centennial Review* 15, no. 1 (2015): 215–248.

——. "Onticide: Afro-Pessimism, ~~Gay~~ Nigger #1, and Surplus Violence." *GLQ: A Journal of Lesbian and Gay Studies* 23, no. 3 (2017): 391–418.

——. "Onticide: Afropessimism, Queer Theory, and Ethics." 2015. www.scribd.com/doc /252308869/calvin-warren-onticide-afropessimism-queer-theory-ethics-pdf.

Weheliye, Alexander. *Habeas Viscus: Racializing Assemblages, Biopolitics, and Black Feminist Theories of the Human*. Durham: Duke University Press, 2014.

Weiss, Margot. "Queer Economic Justice: Desire, Critique, and the Practice of Knowledge." In *Global Justice and Desire: Queering Economy*, edited by Nikita Dhawan, Antke Engle, Christoph F. E. Holzhey, and Volker Woltersdorff. New York: Routledge, 2015.

——. *Techniques of Pleasure: BDSM and the Circuits of Sexuality.* Durham: Duke University Press, 2011.

White, Ben. *Palestinians in Israel: Segregation, Discrimination, and Democracy.* London: Pluto, 2012.

Wiegman, Robyn. "Eve's Triangles, or Queer Studies Beside Itself." *differences: A Journal of Feminist Cultural Studies* 26, no. 1 (2015): 48–73.

Wiegman, Robyn, and Elizabeth A. Wilson. "Introduction: Antinormativity's Queer Conventions." In "Queer Theory Without Antinormativity," edited by Robyn Wiegman and Elizabeth A. Wilson, special issue, *differences: A Journal of Feminist Cultural Studies* 26, no. 1 (May 2015): 1–25.

——, eds. "Queer Theory Without Antinormativity." Special issue, *differences: A Journal of Feminist Cultural Studies* 26, no. 1 (May 2015).

Wilderson, Frank. *Incognegro: A Memoir of Exile and Apartheid.* Cambridge: South End, 2008.

——. *Red, White and Black: Cinema and the Structure of U.S. Antagonisms.* Durham: Duke University Press, 2010.

Winkiel, Laura. "The 'Sweet Assassin' and the Performative Politics of *SCUM Manifesto*." In *The Queer Sixties*, edited by Patricia Juliana Smith, 62–85. New York: Routledge, 1999.

Winnubst, Shannon. *Queering Freedom.* Bloomington: Indiana University Press, 2006.

——. "Review Essay: *No Future: Queer Theory and the Death Drive.*" *Environment and Planning D: Society and Space* 28, no. 1 (2010): 178–183.

Wolfe, Patrick. "Settler Colonialism and the Elimination of the Native." *Journal of Genocide Research* 8, no. 4 (2006): 387–409.

Wolin, Richard. "The Hannah Arendt Situation." *New England Review* 22, no. 2 (Spring 2001).

Yack, Bernard. *The Longing for Total Revolution: Philosophic Sources of Social Discontent from Rousseau to Marx and Nietzsche.* Berkeley: University of California Press, 1992.

Young-Bruehl, Elisabeth. *Hannah Arendt: For Love of the World.* New Haven: Yale University Press, 1982.

Zertal, Idith. *Israel's Holocaust and the Politics of Nationhood.* Translated by Chaya Galai. Cambridge: Cambridge University Press, 2005.

Ziarek, Ewa Płonowska. "Bare Life on Strike: Notes on the Biopolitics of Race and Gender." *South Atlantic Quarterly* 107, no. 1 (Winter 2008).

Žižek, Slavoj. *Did Somebody Say Totalitarianism? Five Interventions in the (Mis)use of a Notion.* London: Verso, 2001.

——. *Welcome to the Desert of the Real.* London: Verso, 2002.

INDEX

NEW DIRECTIONS IN CRITICAL THEORY

Amy Allen, General Editor